Republican Principles in International Law

Also by Mortimer N. S. Sellers

AMERICAN REPUBLICANISM: Roman Ideology in the United States Constitution

REPUBLICAN LEGAL THEORY: The History, Constitution and Purposes of Law in a Free State

THE SACRED FIRE OF LIBERTY: Republicanism, Liberalism and the Law

AN ETHICAL EDUCATION: Community and Morality in the Multicultural University (*editor*)

THE NEW WORLD ORDER: Sovereignty, Human Rights and the Self-determination of Peoples (*editor*)

UNIVERSAL HUMAN RIGHTS: Moral Order in a Divided World (*co-editor with David Reidy*)

Republican Principles in International Law

The Fundamental Requirements of a Just World Order

Mortimer N. S. Sellers

palgrave
macmillan

First published in 2006 by
PALGRAVE MACMILLAN
Houndmills, Basingstoke, Hampshire RG21 6XS and
175 Fifth Avenue, New York, N.Y. 10010
Companies and representatives throughout the world.

ISBN-13: 978–1–4039–9744–9 hardback
ISBN-10: 1–4039–9744–6 hardback

This book is printed on paper suitable for recycling and made from fully managed and sustained forest sources.

A catalogue record for this book is available from the British Library.

Library of Congress Cataloging-in-Publication Data

Sellers, M. N. S. (Mortimer N. S.)
Republican principles in international law : the fundamental requirements of a just world order / Mortimer N. S. Sellers.
p. cm.
Includes bibliographical references and index.
ISBN 1–4039–9744–6 (hardback)
1. International law. 2. Republicanism. I. Title.

KZ3410.S455 2006
341—dc22 2005056580

10 9 8 7 6 5 4 3 2 1
15 14 13 12 11 10 09 08 07 06

Printed and bound in Great Britain by
Antony Rowe Ltd, Chippenham and Eastbourne

This book is dedicated with love, gratitude and admiration to Evelyn Mary Stead and to the memory of John Sumner Stead

"Neque vero hoc solum natura, id est iure gentium, sed etiam legibus populorum, quibus in singulis civitatibus res publica continetur, eodem modo constitutum est, ut non liceat sui commodi causa nocere alteri."[1]

M. Tullius Cicero, *de officiis*, III.v.23

"ut iam universus hic mundus sit una civitas communis deorum atque hominum existimanda."[2]

M. Tullius Cicero, *de legibus*, I.vii.23

Contents

Preface

From time to time politicians, academics and journalists declare that some course of action is required or (more frequently) forbidden by international law. Too often, as in so many fields, credentialed experts make bold assertions in the manner of the great wizard Oz, from behind the curtain of their supposed authority, only to stand exposed and ridiculous when simple questions reveal the moral and historical emptiness behind their pretensions. These essays return to first principles to explain why anyone should obey international law, and how to find out what the law of nations requires, in the absence of any universal authority. My argument throughout this study will be that republican principles supply the ultimate foundation of international justice. The origins and development of the law of nations have followed the same republican rationale from the beginning: law should be obeyed when it is just; law is just when it serves the common good; and the common good emerges from free deliberation among equals. Laws asserted on any other basis would not be worthy of obedience by states, peoples, individuals, or anyone else.

The first principles of republican government are worthy of study in their own right, which I have done in three previous volumes on *American Republicanism* (1994), *The Sacred Fire of Liberty* (1998), and *Republican Legal Theory* (2003), so I will not revisit them here. Italian, Dutch, Swiss, German, English, American and French scholars and politicians all developed their own republican institutions concurrently with the development of international law, and took the lead in proposing new doctrines to regulate the law of nations. But international law differs from domestic legal systems in its lack of universally respected legislative, executive or judicial power. This keeps questions of justice and justification much closer to the surface in international law than they are within most states. Supposed laws that lose touch with their basis in the common good lack legitimacy, and will not be obeyed.

Applying republican principles to international law clarifies many of the most disputed questions in international relations: the republican principle of popular sovereignty is embodied in the widely recognized but often violated right to the "self-determination of peoples"; states are bound by customary international law, because custom reflects a form of republican deliberation (and customs are only binding as law to the extent that they do so); humanitarian intervention and the right of subjugated minorities to secede from states both depend upon the construction of republican communities in pursuit of the common good. Such questions become clearer when tested against the republican principles that justify international law.

Many of the ideas presented in this volume grew out of arguments made in earlier articles and lectures. I would like to thank the *Connecticut Journal of International Law, International Legal Theory*, AMINTAPHIL, the American Society of International Law and the Internationale Vereinigung für Rechts- und Sozialphilosophie for permission to incorporate material formerly presented in their publications and conferences. I am grateful to these groups, publications and editors for their thoughtful help and suggestions.

This book is dedicated to Evelyn Mary Stead and to the memory of John Sumner Stead. Both exemplify the inclusive and tolerant attitude toward other persons, peoples and nations that is the basis of international justice, but also of friendship and decency. I admire their values and am grateful for their love and kindness to me over many years. I am also grateful to Joyce Bauguess, Donna Frank and Barbara Jones for typing this manuscript; to David Bederman, Laura Picchio Forlati, Nicholas Onuf, Francesco Parisi, Philip Pettit, Linos-Alexandre Sicilianos, Fernando Tesón, Carla Zoethout and several anonymous reviewers for reading portions of it; and to the Académie de Droit International and the University of Baltimore Educational Foundation for funding my research. As always and above all, I am grateful to Frances Mary Stead Sellers and to Cora Mary Stead Sellers for their inspiration and affection.

Bel Orme
Radnor
March 1, 2005

1
Introduction

This book is a collection of 20 short reflections on republican principles in international law, which is to say on the doctrine that international law should always serve the common good or "*res publica*" of all the world's peoples and nations. My conclusions follow from the premiss that republican doctrine is both the ultimate foundation of and the best justification for modern international law. No attempt is made to engage with the vast contemporary literature on the issues addressed in these chapters. My purpose, rather, has been to apply the fundamental principles of republican doctrine directly, boldly, and without mediation to some of the most important questions in international law and international relations, so that contemporary lawyers and statesmen can modify their practices accordingly.

Modern international law developed in the seventeenth and eighteenth centuries concurrently with republican legal theory, at the hands of the same writers and nations who did the most to revive republican politics and government. The Swiss, Dutch, English, American, French, and German authors and patriots who inspired the birth of republican freedom in Europe and North America also crafted the emerging law of nations, so that both rested on the same values of equality and independence, which apply as well to persons as they do to states. International law began, in the words of Emmerich de Vattel, as "the principles of natural law, applied to the conduct of nations."[1] Just as people (he observed) find law and justice in seeking their common good, so states find international law in the necessary structure of their own collective well-being.[2]

Vattel cited Cicero for the republican principle that all government, within and between states, should serve justice,[3] and Cicero provided the literary model for viewing the society of states as a world-wide republic of nations.[4] Christian Wolff repeated Cicero's vision of a world republic or "*civitas maxima*"[5] and Immanuel Kant perpetuated the ideal of a "*Weltrepublik*" or "*civitas gentium*"[6] Henry Wheaton repeated what became the standard nineteenth-century view of international law, when he described its requirements as "those rules of conduct which reason deduces, as consonant to justice, from the nature of society existing among independent nations."[7] Thus justice and the common good have remained closer to the surface in international law than they have in most domestic legal systems. Without a world legislature, a world judiciary or any strong international executive power, public opinion has remained the final arbiter of international legality. The principles that justify international law are also the principles that identify its content. Arguments about the content of international law must appeal directly to justice and to the common good or "*res publica*" of the universal community of states.[8] Some international lawyers look to courts, judges, or state practice as if these were the final arbiters of international legality. This has never been the case and under current conditions should not become so. International law, like all law, rests ultimately on the principles that justify its binding force. This study seeks to clarify what the law is, by explaining why it ought to be obeyed.

Republican principles in international law are the doctrines that follow directly from law's origin in the common good of the people. Republican doctrines are the oldest and most important elements in international law, because they are the elements that justify the law of nations, and make it binding on states. Without its republican foundations, international law would lose its argument for obedience. In the absence of stronger enforcement mechanisms, international law influences the behavior of states only to the extent that governments and individuals perceive it to be just. Like national governments, in regulating their citizens, international law can claim and deserves obedience only to the extent that it rests on and supports popular sovereignty, national self-determination, the rule of law, universal human rights, public deliberation and the other essential attributes of the republican system of law and government.

This study will concentrate much less on the basic content and origins of republican legal doctrine, which have been described in detail elsewhere,[9] than it will on their implications for specific questions in international law. The whole edifice of the law of nations rests on the fundamental assumption that international laws and institutions bind and should influence governments only to the extent that they reflect republican procedures of politics and legislation. Governments that disregard the voices and interests of their subjects deserve no voice themselves in international affairs. Just as all *people* everywhere should be free and equal individuals, without whose participation no legitimate national legal system can exist, so too all *peoples* everywhere should constitute free and independent states, without whose consent no legitimate international legal system can exist.

This volume is intended as a plea for international law, a brief for its binding force, and a manifesto for those who would defend it. Some representatives of international institutions and supposed advocates of international law have made unsupported *ex cathedra* pronouncements about the law's pretended requirements that have had the effect of discrediting the entire enterprise. This happens so often that many morally thoughtful and practically minded people have concluded that "international law" (as interpreted by these "experts") should be rejected or actively opposed. To counter this tendency, I have tried as much as possible in these chapters to avoid the discussion of specific cases, with regard to which too many readers will already have previous commitments to one interpretation or another, depending on national or partisan interests. Discussion will take place at a high level of abstraction. Apply these principles to the cases, and if they undermine positions that you have already taken, perhaps you should change your mind. The purpose here is to move international law back from the temporary enthusiasm of advocacy to a more stable and justified consensus.

These discourses will demonstrate how republican principles permeate international law. The principles of freedom, self-determination and equality provide such obvious sources of just and stable international relations that many governments have claimed their benefits, even while denying the same principles in their own internal affairs. In claiming to provide rules for all humanity, international law must meet certain obvious standards of justice, including the protection of universal human rights. The political right to vote has been the rock on which institutional legitimacy most often founders. All governments claim to serve the common good of their subjects, but most actually do so only to the extent that the people themselves have political power. Peoples express themselves best through states that recognize and support the regional differences between nations, but states in turn must act on behalf of their peoples, or lose legitimacy under international law.

What, then, is a "republic"? Republics are states in which the government and laws serve (as much as possible) the common good (or "*res publica*") of the nation's people or citizens. The first self-consciously "republican" ideology originated in the senatorial opposition to Gaius

Julius Caesar, which fought for and tried to identify the institutional checks and balances that would keep government committed to the common good,[10] but the idea of public service as the primary purpose of government was present already in the writing of Plato[11] and Aristotle.[12] The single most influential republican author has been Marcus Tullius Cicero, particularly as he expressed himself in his discourses *de re publica ("On the Republic")* and *de legibus ("On the Laws")*. Roman republican authors such as Cicero provided the inspiration and vocabulary for subsequent republican revolutions in France and the United States,[13] and for much of the subsequent development of western constitutionalism and of international law.

Cicero and other Roman authors such as Titus Livius (through his histories of Rome), inaugurated a republican tradition of "liberty" that fortified principled resistance to demagogues, emperors and kings for the next two thousand years.[14] Republican liberty signified the rule of law and not of men, when law is made for the common good of the people it governs.[15] Niccolò Macchiavelli did the most to revive this republican tradition in Italy, with his *Discorsi sopra la prima deca di Tito Livio* (1517).[16] The resistance of the Swiss, many Italian cities, and the United Provinces of the Netherlands against imperial control added practical models for republican liberty, as did the constitutional and theoretical writings of various English authors, in their efforts to constrain their monarchs over the centuries. The baron de Montesquieu in his *Causes de la grandeur des Romains et de leur décadence* (1734) and *De l'esprit des lois* (1748), and Jean-Jacques Rousseau, in various political writings, also adopted republican vocabulary and influenced the subsequent republican tradition, particularly in France.

This is not to say that republican legal theory was unchanged or uniform from Cicero to Rousseau, but rather that certain central themes recurred over the centuries, that these attitudes shaped the development of international law, and that they should continue to do so, because they represent correct and compelling views about justice.[17] Beyond the basic central perceptions that government should serve the common good of the people, and that "liberty" and "justice" consist precisely in doing so, republican authors tried to articulate the governmental checks and balances that make justice possible, by securing the common good. These include, at an absolute minimum: popular sovereignty, the rule of law, the separation of powers, and a basic commitment to fundamental human rights. This last requirement is also the basis of "liberal" legal theory. Liberalism differs from republicanism in its weaker commitment to democracy and the common good of the people. Republicanism has a much more robust conception of what makes governments legitimate in the first place.[18]

Republican proceduralism is important as applied to international law, precisely because the constitution of international government is so radically incomplete. Republican legal theory recognizes legitimate authority in domestic governments only to the extent that their political procedures enable them to serve the common good of the people. Since there is no world government and therefore no prospect of a cosmopolitan republic, international law must derive its authority in large part from the republican procedures *within* the separate nations that create and enforce it. Commitment to the common good is not enough. There must also be republican procedures in place to make the common good real. Without popular sovereignty, governments will overlook the common good. Without the rule of law, governments will evade the common good. Without checks and balances, governments will pervert the common good. And without fundamental human rights, governments will oppress the common good. The proper ultimate purpose of any government is to make worthwhile and fulfilling lives possible for all those subject to its rule. International law will not be worthy of notice, unless it helps them to do so.

Republican doctrine offers a political technique for discovering and protecting public justice and fundamental human rights. Republicans believe that without popular sovereignty, the rule of law, checks and balances, and fundamental human rights, the people cannot know or enjoy their obligations to each other, or to the state. The logic of republican theory is already deeply embedded in international law, through its seventeenth- and eighteenth-century origins. This is fortunate because it gives international law the moral foundations necessary to evoke obedience, even from the most powerful governments and states. Were it not for its republican basis, international law would be of purely theoretical interest, because the world's great republics would simply disregard it. If international law were not republican, it would not be just or worthy of the attention or respect of serious scholars or lawyers in the world's powerful republican states.

Every state should be a republic, with all the political controls and guarantees that republican government entails. Not all states are republics, but republican states alone can verify the content of international law through ordinary republican procedures. Human beings need society, and society requires rules. The rules of international society must be inferred from the practices of self-governing peoples. International conventions, international customs and the general principles of law recognized by "civilized" (which is to say republican) nations are all evidence of underlying truths around which an international consensus has emerged. Consensus is good evidence of truth, but only so long as all members of society have a voice, as they do in republics. Popular sovereignty and the self-determination of peoples are fundamental principles of international law because they protect the accuracy of the international *opinio juris*, by giving public opinion the broadest possible basis in the views of the people themselves.

Governments are bound by custom and other supposed sources of international law only to the extent that international customs reflect the deliberate practice of fully republican states. Customary law binds persons, states, and other subjects of international law, whether they will or no, for the same reason that any law binds anywhere, which is by providing the best available measure of what the right thing to do would be, in a given set of circumstances. To the extent that proposed norms do not do this, their status as "law" is compromised, and they do not deserve to be obeyed. The widely held view that some particular rule is law, and binding, offers very good evidence that it is in fact law, and binding, if the opinion is widely enough shared and accepted, after due deliberation and debate. Determining the binding force of any custom depends on the circumstances in which consensus emerged, among whom, and why.

Governments obey international law because they consider it to be just, and do not wish to consider themselves unjust, or to be considered unjust by others. What seems just, and therefore binding as law, will depend to a large extent on the current status of public discourse. Human communities tend towards consensus. When unjust regimes predominate, international legal discourse may encourage or validate injustice, while putting liberal republics on the defensive, by allowing tyrannical governments to reinforce and justify each other's bad behavior. Justice emerges best from the widest possible discussion, with the greatest number of sincere participants. Democratic republics provide the best systems for discovering just legal norms, and federations of democratic republics constitute the most accurate systems for authorizing proposed standards of international law.

Applying the test of republican legitimacy to international acts and institutions supplies the best and simplest measure of their legality under international law. The status and relative claims of peoples, nations and states become clearer, when calibrated against their basis in the common good. This applies as a matter of history, as well as justice, to the sources of international law, to law's development through custom, law's effectiveness in practice, its mediation through peoples, enforcement by states, and interpretation by judges. The borders of states, their economic obligations, and the power to take action against violations of law all depend on republican theories of liberty and self-determination that were present at the origin of international law, and have guided its development ever since.

Each chapter in this book addresses a different element of international law from the standpoint of its basis in the common good of the people. The questions considered here include the most fundamental issues of jurisdiction, interpretation, and enforcement. Together they offer a basis for understanding the entire structure of international law, and predicting its future development. The exercise of republican deliberation through international law is the ultimate test of all international obligations, just as the exercise of republican government is the only real measure of obligation in domestic systems of law. Governments exist for the collective and individual well-being of the people who are subject to their control. When states violate this mandate, they forfeit their authority to rule.

2
Republican Principles in International Law

Two hundred years ago, in the wake of the modern world's first great republican revolutions in France and the United States of America, Immanuel Kant endorsed a federation of independent republics as the only valid basis of international law.[1] Kant's proposed republican federation echoed the new federal Constitution of the United States, which guaranteed a "republican form of government" to every state in the Union.[2] Enlightened scholars supposed that if ever some powerful people could form a republic, republican principles would become the basis of a just world order.[3] So republican ideas permeated and inspired the developing *ius gentium*,[4] and several new states emerged to embrace the republican form of government. Republicanism, liberalism, and modern international law emerged together from Europe's belated turn to reason as the basis of law and authority, and share the same enlightened premisses of liberty, equality and popular sovereignty that justified the eighteenth-century revolutions. These principles remain the actual basis and only justifiable foundation of international law today. International law depends on republican principles for its content and moral validity, and supposed international laws and institutions bind and should influence republican governments only to the extent that they reflect republican procedures of politics and legislation.[5]

1. Republicanism

Kant's famous essay on perpetual peace recognized three elements in republican legality: the equal *freedom* of all members of society, their equal *subjection* to the legal system, and their *equality* before the law.[6] Kant's conception of "freedom" implies popular sovereignty to approve all legislation, but not what he referred to as unfettered "democracy."[7]

Kantian republics employ representation[8] and the separation of powers[9] to prevent what Kant saw as pure democracy's natural descent into despotism and injustice.[10] Thus Kant's republican "freedom" and "justice" both require equal subjection to laws made and executed with the people's consent, for the common good, rather than the lawless license of "wild" and unregulated peoples.[11]

Kant's views reflect an ancient tradition of republicanism that proposes one simple test for legal and political legitimacy: service to the *res publica*, or common good of the people.[12] To support the validity of their legal regimes, most governments now claim that the laws and institutions they impose serve the common good of the people, usually also identified as (or equated with) "justice."[13] But republican doctrine, as developed over two millennia after the fall of Rome, also proposes a universal technique for finding the common good through popular sovereignty – the "*imperium populi*" of Livy, Cicero, "Publius," and John Adams.[14] Republicans maintain that the best test of the common good of the people is the public deliberation of elected representatives through institutions designed to protect justice and reason against factions, corruption, and the private self-interest of individuals or any single section of society.[15]

The republican identification of justice as the common good requires some explanation in light of recent neo-"liberal" theories that would separate the two – theories that assume an "irreducible" pluralism of "comprehensive" conceptions of moral value.[16] The problem may be largely semantic.[17] Republicanism identifies the purpose of law and society as the harmonization of diverse talents and interests so that every citizen can live a worthwhile life.[18] Some suppose that speaking of a "common good" in this context makes harmony harder to achieve.[19] The republican premiss that justice requires all laws to serve the common good rests on a conviction that human perceptions of the good will be harmonized best through deliberation, humility, and the careful collective reflection of well-intentioned citizens.[20]

This view of human nature supports the doctrine of popular sovereignty and the republican structures that depend on it. People have different talents and life plans, embracing different perceptions of justice and the common good. Private interests color human attitudes. Decent humility requires that citizens defer to a reasonable system for resolving conflicting perceptions of the truth. Republicanism proposes that every person is capable of perceiving moral truths. This makes popular sovereignty the best source of justice. If justice and the common good exist and all people have the capacity to perceive them, then the best route to a just society will be through public deliberation. To exclude any voices from the public debate would deprive society of their insights and subject some private interests to the domination of others. Deference to a balanced system of public deliberation in search of the common good helps citizens to test private perceptions of justice, which may be wrong, and to obtain public cooperation when their perceptions are correct.[21]

Kant's three basic republican constitutional principles repeat the standard desiderata of republican political liberty as listed in John Adams' *Defence of the Constitutions of Government of the United States of America*, which require subjection to "equal laws by common consent" for the "general interest, or the public good" of the people.[22] But Kant also suggests that this same republican constitution should serve as the basis of international law and world peace.[23] Similar republican principles have driven the development of the law of nations, at least since the late eighteenth century, and should continue to do so, more openly and purposefully, now that the Soviet and other empires have receded as threats to international peace and justice.

2. Self-determination

The republican principle of popular sovereignty is embodied in the widely recognized right to the "self-determination of peoples."[24] This principle gained international prominence in 1776 with the United States Declaration of Independence, asserting the right of peoples to "alter or abolish" forms of government that deny fundamental human rights. To remedy the "abuses and usurpations" of George III, the United States claimed their "separate and equal" station among nations.[25] Woodrow Wilson renewed this republican conception of popular self-determination during the First World War with his assertion that "every people has a right to choose the sovereignty under which they shall live," and that "no peace can last, or ought to last, which does not recognize and accept the principle that governments derive all their just powers from the consent of the governed."[26] Finally, the "self-determination of peoples" achieved widespread formal recognition in Articles 1 and 55 of the United Nations Charter.[27]

The concept of self-determination rested from the beginning on two related assumptions: first, that all *people* everywhere are free and equal individuals, without whose consent no legitimate national legal system can exist; and second, that all *peoples* everywhere should constitute free and independent states, without whose consent no legitimate international legal system can exist. When Emmerich de Vattel first delineated the modern law of nations in 1758, he began with these twin assumptions, which supported his assertion that nations, being composed of free and independent individuals, should likewise be free and independent from each other, until they consent to mutual restrictions.[28] International law has always drawn strength and recognition from this powerful analogy between individual liberty and the liberty of states.[29] When citizens lose their freedom, this rationale loses its force.

Because of the support that republican principles give to their freedom of action and commercial well-being, non-republican governments have accepted republican doctrine in international instruments. Kant observed that mutual self-interest eventually creates republican institutions even between tyrants, who seek political controls against their common depravity.[30] Conquest and consolidation are the two greatest enemies of international justice because they destroy the balance of power between states that controls the passion and ambition of their rulers.[31] This explains Kant's fifth preliminary article of perpetual peace – that no state should forcibly interfere in the constitution or government of another.[32] Even despots can agree to this provision, which protects them against each other, although not against republican revolution when their peoples are ripe for rebellion.[33] Kant also insisted on the universal individual rights of humanity, against the interests of their ruling elites.[34]

Most states now recognize the right to self-determination through two international covenants. The International Covenant on Economic, Social and Cultural Rights confirms the right of "all peoples" to "self-determination" and "freely" to "determine their political status."[35] The International Covenant on Civil and Political Rights begins with exactly the same words,[36] but goes on to assert individual "liberty" and "security of person."[37] Both Covenants reflect the United Nations General Assembly's earlier Universal Declaration of Human Rights, which endorses the right of every person "to take part in the government of his country" and to vote in "periodic and genuine elections" by "equal suffrage" and "free voting procedures."[38] Numerous non-republics have endorsed these republican principles, giving republics and republican scholars a powerful rhetorical advantage against tyrants and despotic elites.[39] Arbitrary regimes accept such covenants, because of the protection that they hope to draw from the United Nation's corresponding endorsement of the "sovereign equality of all its members,"[40] and their "political independence."[41] The United Nations Charter expressly refuses to authorize intervention in matters that are essentially within the sovereign "domestic" jurisdiction of any independent state.[42]

3. Sovereignty

The sovereign independence and equality of states received its most influential endorsement and elaboration from Emmerich de Vattel, who based his argument on republican principles of freedom and equality.[43] Since all men are naturally equal, with equal rights and obligations proceeding from nature, Vattel argued, so must nations comprised of men be equal also, and inherit from nature the same obligations and rights. The relative power or weakness of states makes no difference. "A dwarf is as much a man as a giant; a small republic is no less a sovereign state than the most powerful kingdom."[44] Vattel added that the natural "liberty and independence of nations" gives all peoples the right to be governed as they see fit, so that no state may legitimately interfere in another state's government. "Of all the rights that can belong to a nation, sovereignty is, doubtless, the most precious and that which other nations ought most scrupulously to respect."[45]

Vattel's national sovereignty belonged originally and essentially to the people collectively. Nations could subsequently cede sovereignty to a senate or to a single person,[46] but only to promote the common good of all citizens.[47] When the nation's chosen sovereign exceeds or abuses this authority, the nation may reclaim his power, as the Netherlands withdrew sovereignty from Philip II of Spain.[48] Other states justly support such revolutions, in which nations take up arms against their oppressors. Vattel praised William of Orange and the Dutch for intervening to support the English revolution against James II. It was "an act of justice and generosity" to defend foreign liberty.[49]

Jean Bodin had earlier made the often repeated but tendentious argument that sovereignty should be the absolute, indivisible and perpetual power of kings.[50] Monarchs have tended to promote this doctrine, which left its residue in Hugo Grotius' early defense of slavery and a nation's power to bind itself in perpetual servitude.[51] (Since some peoples are unfit to be free.)[52] Grotius limited the republican doctrine of popular sovereignty, observing that no nation in his era had ever allowed women, minors, or paupers to join in the public debate.[53] As husbands govern wives,[54] and masters rule slaves,[55] so kings may own nations, to avoid the turbulence of uncertain jurisdiction.[56] These proto-Hobbesian arguments and assumptions would not be made openly today,[57] but they survive in the modern doctrine of non-intervention in the domestic jurisdiction of "sovereign" governments,[58] as interpreted by some contemporary commentators on international law.[59] Yet even Bodin admitted the right of intervention in a state's formerly internal affairs, when the state's sovereign oppresses his subjects,[60] and Grotius fully recognized the equivalence between slavery and regal sovereignty, while nonetheless excusing both.[61]

The concept of "sovereignty" entered the lexicon of international law through the obvious analogy between free men and free states. Some nations, as Grotius observed, are subject to others: they have no freedom or sovereignty.[62] "Sovereignty," in this sense, means independence from any other human will,[63] just as "liberty," in its original republican sense, meant independence from the will of another.[64] People are not free when subject to any power but the common good. Nations are not sovereign when subject to the will of any other person or state.

Vattel's argument for strict national sovereignty and the rigorous independence of states rested on this analogy between personal and national freedom. When Vattel was writing in the mid-eighteenth century, personal freedom hardly existed outside Switzerland and the Netherlands. At that time, it made sense for enlightened and well-meaning authors to establish an absolute principle of non-intervention in the internal affairs of sovereign states. The most likely interventions of Vattel's era would have curbed emerging popular sovereignty. Similarly, even after the French and American revolutions, preponderant power remained in the hands of European despots. Relatively progressive states, such as Britain, promoted non-intervention in defense of nascent continental liberty, as in Naples and Spain, against reactionary European monarchs.[65] The United States also embraced non-intervention to protect itself and other recently liberated American republics against the reimposition of European domination in the New World.[66] But the emergence of the United States as a world power altered this equation, and the world's republics now sometimes have the strength to protect foreign liberty, without endangering their own democratic institutions or national independence.

The fundamental republican principle of popular sovereignty ("*imperium populi*") has been at the core of the developing law of nations from the beginning. Freedom and equality are the two best rules of human relations and such obvious sources of just and stable political institutions that even tyrants have recognized liberty and independence among themselves while denying both to their terrified subjects. "Sovereignty" denotes the freedom and equality of governments. Just as legitimate national governments derive their authority from the consent of the governed, so legitimate international institutions derive their validity from the consent of the governments involved. If rational debate among citizens produces just national laws, so too should rational discussion among governments produce a just global order. But this presupposes that governments speak for the nations that they rule. The very rationale that supports the sovereign equality of states implies the sovereign equality of citizens, too. Republican principles would deny despotic governments the right to speak for the peoples that they control. Every government's claim to a national voice depends on its being, in fact, the voice of the nation.

4. Federalism

Why divide the world into nations at all? Kant proposed to build international law around a "federation of free states,"[67] but he opposed creating a world republic, despite the value of size and diversity in preventing local injustice. Why not create a cosmopolitan republic and abolish the need for a separate law of nations? Kant explained that laws lose influence as governments increase in territory, producing anarchy or despotism.[68] This repeats a standard criticism of large republics. In small republics, the common good is better known and closer to each citizen.[69] Throughout the world, geographic, linguistic, and religious differences divide people into natural units. Federal institutions allow each community to control the others' excesses in the interests of all. Kant praised this balance as nature's own design for creating and protecting a just law of nations.[70]

Federal institutions replicate the benefits of free republican government on an international scale. James Madison emphasized this point for North Americans in endorsing the ancient republican technique of balancing competing factions to counteract local self-interest.[71] John Adams claimed that a well-balanced republic could exist even "among highwaymen" by setting each rogue to watch the others.[72] Kant envisioned a successful republic of devils.[73] The United States Constitution first applied this same reasoning to sovereign states, using each state to control the others, and to provide "a republican remedy for the diseases most incident to republican government."[74]

Even if it were attainable, a world republic would not be desirable, for two important reasons. First, excessively unified international institutions create the risk that one bold usurpation could tyrannize the world, as happened in imperial Rome, turning the first republic into a universal empire. Second, peoples facing varied geographical and historical circumstances create different local values from the fabric of local experience. These values enrich their own lives, but also the cultural and political capital of their republican neighbors. Each nation provides an example for the others, and each regional innovation supplies a possible new model for justice and world peace.

5. Nationalism

The obvious existence and possible benefits of national diversity have encouraged some scholars to embrace a "multinational" conception of justice, that recognizes no rights or justice beyond each particular society's inherited traditions and political discourse.[75] Somewhat less coherently, within nations, this becomes a "multicultural" conception of justice, encouraging the disaggregation of peoples into an overlapping mosaic of ethnic, religious and cultural viewpoints.[76] Some critics of nationalism consider this progression inevitable, concluding that each recognition of national community breeds new claims by smaller sub-groups, leaving no principled basis for restricting fragmentation, or eliminating the self-indulgent excesses of tiny local majorities.[77] Proponents of the nation as a viable category must offer a rationale for dividing jurisdiction, not only between nations, but between national and international law.

Some scholars have opposed the republican principle of popular sovereignty to a "liberal" principle of human rights.[78] This misreads the basis of the republican *imperium populi*, which exists to serve justice and the common good, not private inclinations. Human rights are best discovered through public deliberation – not created, but found. Republicans do not deny the existence of universal human rights. They offer a technique for finding them – through representation, the rule of law, the separation of powers, and the ultimate sovereignty of the people.[79] Republicans hold that there can be no liberty without popular sovereignty, while recognizing that popular sovereignty alone does not guarantee justice.[80]

Scholars create a dangerous confusion when they oppose republican popular sovereignty to liberal human rights. Democracy may threaten liberty, but liberty and republicanism began and must triumph together.[81] The value of popular sovereignty in republican theory arises from its efficacy in finding the common good. Liberty is the product of this search. Thus Benjamin Constant made a fatal innovation in opposing the "liberty of the ancients," which he identified with democracy, to the "liberty of the moderns" (as individual human rights).[82] Neither is possible without the other. Popular sovereignty discovers liberty. Human rights protect the search for justice.

Self-governing nations provide a locus for establishing individual human rights. But too much emphasis on universal human rights may obscure the primary value of the nation, which lies in the continuity and large common projects that nations make possible over generations in the lives of their citizens. Human rights could be protected in a world republic, but collective identity could not. Human nature thrives best in an atmosphere of common endeavor and shared purpose among neighbors. Republican nations exist to serve this basic human need, which individual human rights leave unfulfilled. Shared devotion to human rights and constitutional procedures cannot alone preserve internal peace, or maintain a stable national identity. There must be a common culture too, developed to embrace all members of society.[83]

Peoples respect each other's sovereignty and domestic jurisdiction for two important reasons, republican and prudential, both of which have contributed to the privileged position of nations in international law. The republican reason depends on popular sovereignty within nations, which requires the deference of outsiders towards a people's own determinations of its cultural and political future. The prudential reason encourages republics to assert independence and equality against non-republican states so that they may protect their own internal liberties against outside intervention. Sometimes this requires establishing a *modus vivendi* with despotic regimes in order to preserve the republic intact. Prudence may tolerate tyranny, but does not justify it. Republics properly protect the liberty and human rights of other nations when they have the power to do so.

There is a limit to the autonomy that popular sovereignty accords to self-governing republics. Each nation is a community unto itself, but only for the old republican purposes of creating a "common sense of justice" and a "partnership for the common good."[84] Other republics, or, better still, a federation of republics, may legitimately intervene when governments or majorities exceed the scope of their national authority. Total deference to the popular will would subvert the fundamental republican principle of liberty. Democracy may violate the common good as well as any other system. Thus, the United States Constitution guarantees each constituent commonwealth not only a "republican form of government,"[85] but also "liberty" (and certain named liberties) against popular oppression.[86] Public deliberation is the best test of the common good, and a nation's voice is best expressed by the vote of its people. But international laws and institutions exist in part to extend popular sovereignty and public deliberation to a broader arena, and so to prevent national governments from abusing their power.

Kant observed that history divides humanity into natural republics[87] and agreed with Montesquieu, Rousseau, and many others that republics should remain small to keep the common good within reach of all citizens.[88] As nations become smaller, their homogeneity increases. This makes it easier to build a common culture, adapted to regional history and geography, and to develop the collective social projects that enrich communal life.[89] But it also makes it easier for local majorities and factions to control the state and to oppress their fellow citizens.[90] National republics are the natural locus of positive liberty, cultural continuity, and communal solidarity. National republics enrich their citizens' lives and defend their common interests against outside attacks. But republics may not always adequately protect their people's personal liberties against the their own government and public officials.

6. Human rights

Many governments now recognize fundamental human rights as one essential basis of a just world order, as affirmed by the Charter of the United Nations,[91] whose members have agreed to promote "universal respect for, and observance of, human rights and fundamental freedoms for all without distinction as to race, sex, language, or religion."[92] The United Nations General Assembly specified some of these rights in its 1948 Universal Declaration of Human Rights,[93] and many governments have ratified the 1966 International Covenants on Economic, Social, and Cultural Rights, and on Civil and Political Rights.[94] Along with popular sovereignty and the self-determination of peoples (both endorsed in the Declaration and Covenants), non-republican governments have accepted the universality of other human rights, perhaps assuming perpetual non-enforcement and governmental impunity.[95] Tyrannies buy respectability by recognizing the obvious rights of humanity.

The international human rights covenants make a useful distinction between economic, social, and cultural rights, which states undertake to "take steps" toward "achieving progressively,"[96] and civil and political rights (including some rights from which there may be "no derogation" even if the life of the nation is at stake),[97] which states undertake to "respect and ensure" immediately.[98] Civil and political rights are the rights without which nations cannot deliberate, self-determination cannot occur, and popular sovereignty does not exist. They embrace fundamental republican guarantees, including rights to life,[99] liberty,[100] equality before the law,[101] to vote and take part in public affairs.[102] Economic, social, and cultural rights are the rights through which nations express their individuality and cultural traditions. Civil and political rights are the rights without which no such expressions will authentically take place.

The specific lists of rights established in United Nations documents lose some authority due to the participation of non-republics in their compilation, which may have compromised the content of the lists.[103] But prominent republics such as France and the United States subsequently ratified the Covenants through accredited representatives of their respective nations.[104] All the world's leading republics have composed similar lists, including the United States Bill of Rights and the French *Déclaration des droits de l'homme et du citoyen*, both of which reflected comprehensive public deliberation. Such lists mark the rational limits of governmental power, even in republican states, against a nation's own citizens. Broad public deliberation and planning in the abstract against future unknown circumstances sought to control the people and their governments in defense of individual rights, while empowering the nation to pursue its collective social and cultural goals with a minimum of foreign intervention.

International law earns whatever validity it has by protecting justice and the common good of humanity. To remain a useful concept, the law of nations must demonstrate both the value of nations as a category, and the reasons why nations should sometimes be subject to the law. Nations derive their usefulness and domestic jurisdiction first from their actual existence and second from their value in mediating the popular sovereignty of geographically distinct peoples. International law becomes useful in policing the boundaries of this authority. Thus international law has three main purposes: first, to protect each nation's sovereignty and self-determination against external and internal threats; second, to protect the human rights of all citizens against their own people's excessive social unity or democratic enthusiasm; and finally, to advance the common good of all nations, where collective action is necessary.

7. Peoples

Republican governments exist to advance the common good of the people,[105] and republican institutions rest on the *imperium populi*, or sovereignty of the people,[106] therefore, applying republican principles to international law requires identifying the relevant "peoples" and jurisdictions involved. The success of this enterprise depends upon determining which groups deserve "equal rights" and "self-determination" as peoples,[107] who may "freely determine their political status" and "freely pursue their economic social and cultural development."[108] State practice and public debates often assume that "peoples" are "nations" and that "nations" are "states."[109] Leading scholars have deplored this "confusion" of peoples with nations as improperly disregarding the heads of states in favor of their subordinate populations.[110] But republican principles, etymology, political history, and the use of the term "peoples" in the Preamble to the Charter of the United Nations[111] all imply that the relevant "peoples" in international law are the citizens of a given state[112] and that these citizens ought to constitute a nation, which should control the state (*imperium populi*). "People," "nation," and "state" will not be separated in any just and stable system of international law.

The term "people" or "*populus*" properly refers to the citizens, or subjects, of a given state. The people's state becomes a republic when citizens come together to create a common sense of justice in pursuit of the common good.[113] This also will make them a nation, when the republic persists over time. Republics, therefore, are states in which citizens have created a nation by establishing a common culture under the sovereignty of the people. But not all states are republics, and not all nations are states. In the absence of republican government and shared civil rights, individuals properly develop communal identities around contingent ethnic, racial, religious, and linguistic attributes, which determine justice and the common good among their own members. People need society, and when the state will not provide it, they find their nations where they can.

The Roman term "*natio*" originally referred to persons sharing a common "*natus*," or birth.[114] Like the *gentes* of the original "*jus gentium*" or "law of nations," "*natio*" first indicated groups not integrated into the political form of a state, yet held together to some extent by common customs and traditions.[115] When Rome conquered the Western world, these "*nationes*" offered the obvious boundaries for the new Roman provinces and remained the basis of local identity in European Christendom, where medieval universities divided students into "nations" according to their regional origins.[116] Nations conceived of in this way are prepolitical entities, but they provide the natural outlines of new states and republics when old tyrannical, multinational empires break down.[117] People who share a common language and experience offer better foundations for republican cooperation than those who do not. Longstanding political boundaries provide a better basis for future associations than newly invented divisions. The doctrine *uti possidetis juris* reflects the obvious desirability of preserving existing political boundaries whenever it is possible to do so.[118]

The vagaries of war and empire have created many peoples that embrace several different ethnic or "national" cultures. For example, in Africa, the short history of European empires united disparate groups without developing strong common identities to support their new colonies and provinces. In Europe and Asia, the British, Austro-Hungarian, and Soviet Empires often shifted large populations between regions to preserve imperial hegemony. Such circumstances make republican unity difficult to achieve in many post-imperial successor states. The very colonies that most successfully claimed the "self-determination of peoples" to advance their autonomy[119] must now maintain "national unity and territorial integrity"[120] against their own subjugated minority populations.[121] The African ("Banjul") Charter on Human and Peoples' Rights affirms that "all peoples" have the "unquestionable and inalienable right to self-determination"[122] on a continent that also absolutely affirms the inviolability of its inherited colonial boundaries.[123]

Geographic divisions form the nature and future identity of the nations and peoples governed by international law. Republics respect the self-determination of the nation through popular sovereignty, and the republican search for justice and the common good creates national identity over time, drawing on the cultural capital of all elements among each state's population, or "people." States that maintain republican institutions deserve stable borders to deepen their unity and common purpose through shared traditions and a common future. Non-republics deny their subjects self-determination; this makes the identity of the "people" much more problematic. Geographic features offer obvious boundaries, but subjugated nations may constitute several possible peoples. Without popular sovereignty to create national consciousness, the "people" lose their common identity and must define themselves around non-political institutions, such as race, religion, language, literature, and other sources of ethnicity.[124]

The republican principle of *imperium populi* requires that all peoples enjoy self-determination and the right to vote and to be elected in genuine periodic elections by universal equal suffrage.[125] Governments that deny these rights are not republican and have no legitimate claim either to the loyalty of their subjects or to recognition by other states or nations. People subject to such governments are not fully "peoples" until they can express their identity politically, but they may constitute one or more pre-political nations whose voices would enrich international law, and whose rights are violated by their usurping masters. The voices of peoples discover the law of nations, whether "peoples" are the citizens of republican states, or the suffering subjects of non-republics, crying out against their oppressors.

8. Minorities

The equivalence between the world's "peoples" and the citizens of its various states raises the issue of minority rights. History, warfare, and migrations have divided the world into cultural units that do not always directly correspond to existing political boundaries. Even the peoples of republican states, particularly young states, may find themselves internally divided into several ethnically or culturally distinct "minority" populations. Minorities are groups within a nation's people who view themselves as in some way separated from the rest of society. Republican principles of liberty and equality require such citizens to be included in the "common good" and never denied their natural human rights on the basis of distinctions such as race, religion, or any other irrelevant social division or status.[126]

Minorities may develop sub-cultures of their own, and should be allowed to enjoy them without interference by the government or majority factions of the people of their state.[127] This has led some politicians and scholars to equate "minorities" with "peoples." On this theory "nationalities," "peoples," "minorities," and "indigenous populations" are all essentially the same.[128] This equivalence would undermine the principle of self-determination. If every self-defined group in a society constituted a "people" with a separate right to self-determination, then "self-determination" would become an incoherent and ultimately an unrealizable ambition. A citizen may belong to several different cultural minorities, but only to one people. Minorities may be geographically scattered across several states, but each people should have a territorial state of its own. Minorities may exclude their fellow citizens and neighbors, but the "people" of a given state must embrace every citizen. Every people has an imprescriptible and inalienable separate right to self-determination. Minorities do not.[129]

Individual members of minority groups in republican states enjoy their right to self-determination by virtue of their membership in the larger nation and participation in its political processes. But what of minorities in non-republics? Such minorities may offer the best foundation for liberating new republican peoples out of existing tyrannies and empires. This is the only sense in which minorities may properly be seen as equivalent to nations and peoples in international law. They provide the seeds of nations and possible origins of peoples when constructing new states out of the ruins of empire. Their status hinges on the existence (or non-existence) and protection of fundamental human rights by their governments, including civil and political rights, without distinction as to race, language, or religion.[130] Minorities that are denied their civil rights by existing governments, properly move toward secession under customary international law.[131]

All subjects of a state have the right to take part in governing their country. The fundamental insight of republican proceduralism in international law recognizes that the reasoned deliberation and judgment of the people provide the only legitimate basis of governmental authority, and that the people's voice will best be expressed through universal and equal suffrage in periodic and genuine elections. These republican truths have been recognized, even by non-republics, in the Universal Declaration of Human Rights[132] and United Nations Covenants.[133] Together they imply the right of minority groups to secede from the larger political entity when their republican rights are denied.[134] The rights of minorities should generally be exercised with respect for the interests of the community as a whole. These rights cannot authorize impairing the territorial integrity or political unity of a state unless the state violates its obligations to democratic government or fails to maintain adequate respect for the human rights and fundamental freedoms of all.[135]

A manifest and continued abuse of governmental power, to the detriment of any section of the population of a state, implicitly recognizes the victim group as a separate nation.[136] As early as 1920, a Commission of Rapporteurs reporting to the League of Nations distinguished the case of Finland, which had been oppressed by Russia, from the Aaland Islands, which were not suffering persecution by the Finns.[137] The Commission denied non-oppressed minorities the right to withdraw from the wider communities to which they belonged, because to have done so would have been "incompatible with the very idea of the State as a territorial and political unity."[138] The separation of minorities from the state of which they form a part is an exceptional solution, "a last resort when the State lacks either the will or the power to enact and apply just and effective guarantees" of fundamental human rights.[139]

9. International law

International law is the law of nations, which is to say the law governing nations, and their political basis in states. It rests on the assumption that the peoples of the world's various states deserve to develop their separate nations through their own internal self-determination, rather than collectively under the distant direction of a world-wide empire. The United Nations reflects this commitment to international federalism, as confirmed by the General Assembly in its 1970 *Declaration on Principles of International Law concerning Friendly Relations and Cooperation Among States,*[140] which repeats the principle of equal rights and self-detemination of peoples enshrined in the United Nations Charter.

The Declaration endorses every state's duty to promote the "universal" observance of human rights and fundamental freedoms through "joint and separate action," and confirms all peoples' right to "seek and receive support" in pursuit of their national self-determination.[141] But the General Assembly reiterated that none of these endorsements should be construed as authorizing or encouraging "any action which would dismember or impair, totally or in part, the territorial integrity or political unity of sovereign and independent States conducting themselves in compliance with the principle of equal rights and self-determination of peoples" and "thus possessed of a government representing the whole people belonging to the territory without distinction as to race, creed, or colour."[142]

Republican principles maintain that the only morally valid laws are laws that serve the common good,[143] and that the best technique for finding the common good requires popular sovereignty and public deliberation.[144] Law's authority, therefore, depends upon its democratic foundations.[145] Several nations have recognized this as the basis of their domestic legal institutions.[146] The doctrines of sovereign equality and independence among states arise from the same republican principles that support popular sovereignty within states. External and internal self-determination recognize this fundamental republican truth. So even in the absence of republican governments, republican principles have dominated the development of international law.

International law derives whatever substance and validity it has from the democratic deliberation of sovereign nations. This means that no law should be viewed as valid or binding without republican endorsement. Republics recognize this in their own institutions. There is no authority greater than the deliberative voice of the people: "*vox populi vox dei*" ("the voice of the people is the voice of God"),[147] but only when the people speak through their democratically elected representatives, ("*magistratus est lex loquens.*")[148] Surprisingly, non-republican governments frequently recognize these principles in formal international instruments. Popular sovereignty and the self-determination of peoples not only support and determine the law of nations, but they alone legitimately can (and have long been recognized to) do so, even among non-republican states.

Republican states and republican statesmen should always apply republican principles in finding and interpreting international law, as should anyone seeking justice in international affairs. This method requires disregarding deliberative processes tainted by the excessive participation of non-republican actors. When federal institutions embrace non-republican states, as in the American Union just before the Civil War, the federation's separate component republics and nations must deliberate within themselves to determine their proper international responsibilities. This leaves peoples open to self-deception and self-interest. Broader international debate will always be desirable, but in the absence of a larger federation of republican states, republics must rely on the largest federation they can find. Even in the context of republican federations, each nation's cultural development should remain its own internal affair.

Applying republican principles to existing international treaties reveals the best interpretation and the underlying validity of asserted international standards. For example, the Charter of the United Nations properly recognizes the ultimate sovereignty of peoples, and the equal rights of persons and of peoples under the law of nations.[149] The Charter rightly emphasizes the settlement of disputes by standing rules of justice and international law,[150] with respect for human rights and fundamental freedoms,[151] including the equal rights and self-determination of peoples.[152] But the Charter also protects a private zone of "domestic jurisdiction," which the United Nations shall not reach.[153] Republican principles reveal the scope of this zone, which does not protect transgressions against the political rights of citizens or violations of the basic political rights to national self-determination and fundamental human dignity.[154]

Too often lawyers and scholars see the "legalization" of international questions as requiring a withdrawal from justice toward supposedly "objective" considerations on the model of municipal legal systems influenced by theories of legal positivism. But neither international nor domestic legal systems deserve obedience unless they serve liberty and the common good. In the absence of any legitimate international legislature, persons and peoples must often decide for themselves which standards to apply and to enforce as "international law." Republican principles supply the basic test of international validity. Lawyers seeking objective standards in international law must look first to popular sovereignty: was the proposed law endorsed by democratic deliberation? Second, in the absence of deliberation, lawyers should look to fundamental principles: does the law serve justice, common welfare, and basic universal human rights? Because they disregard popular sovereignty, the opinions of despots and non-republican governments never legitimately play a role in determining international law, and provide no valid insights into justice or the common good of humanity.

10. International institutions

International institutions deserve political legitimacy and obedience only to the extent that they conform to republican standards of popular sovereignty and pursuit of the common good. All proposed articulations of international law, from Grotius and Vattel to the United Nations Charter, have drawn on the republican principles of consent and self-determination to gain moral authority, while at the same time conceding a great deal to the interests and influence of military power. To give their systems protection, republican theorists must accommodate despotic governments. Despotic governments accommodate, or insincerely recognize, some republican principles in order to give their power a veil of moral authority. But this remains a contingent *modus vivendi*, dependent on circumstances and the balance of military power. Non-republican powers will continue their abuses when they can. Republican governments should advance the interests of liberty and popular sovereignty whenever possible. The actual legitimacy and moral force of international institutions depend upon their republican foundations. Republics may defer to non-republican international institutions, but only when they judge it to be in the best interests of justice and liberty to do so.

Applying republican principles to the United Nations Organization and some of its dependent organs will illustrate the procedure by which republicans should test international institutions and evaluate their actions. The Charter itself was approved by the United States, France, and several other republican polities through republican procedures. The Charter's approval, through international instruments, of several fundamental republican principles, also tends to give the Organization a certain legitimacy. But this legitimacy does not exceed the scope of the commitments made, or the authority of the nation's representatives. For example, ratification of the United Nations Charter in the United States followed a vote by a greater than two-thirds majority in the United States Senate,[155] pursuant to Article II, Section 2 of the United States Constitution.[156] Treaties and Laws made pursuant to the Constitution, under the authority of the United States, are the "supreme law of the land" under the Constitution's sixth Article,[157] but this does not give treaties the power to modify either constitutional guarantees or fundamental republican principles.

The principal organs of the United Nations include the General Assembly, the Security Council, an Economic and Social Council, a Trusteeship Council, the International Court of Justice, and the Organization Secretariat.[158] The General Assembly consists of all the Members of the United Nations,[159] which is to say a group including a great many non-republican states. Each state has one vote.[160] The General Assembly may make recommendations to the Members and Security Council of the United Nations,[161] approved by a simple majority vote, or by a two-thirds majority in the case of "important questions."[162] Such recommendations do not necessarily carry any weight, even under the terms of the United Nations Charter. From a republican perspective, such recommendations should have influence only to the extent that General Assembly votes reveal attitudes or provide a vehicle for deliberation among the world's republican states. The views of non-republican governments will sometimes provide useful insights into justice and the common good of humanity, but only when those views are subject to verification by the internal republican deliberative processes of balanced republican states.

The Security Council of the United Nations consists of fifteen members,[163] five of whom are "permanent members," who must concur in all substantive decisions of the Council.[164] France, Britain, and the United States all enjoy substantially republican governments and permanent seats on the Council, which give the Council's decisions considerable legitimate influence. But current distributions of power require that Council majorities must rely on non-republican support. All members of the United Nations have agreed to "accept and carry out" the decisions of the Security Council.[165] Republican members of the United Nations have made this commitment after democratic deliberation. Even so, republics that do not enjoy permanent membership on the Security Council may find their interests overruled to placate big powers, and even permanent members will sometimes face old Council resolutions which cannot be reversed or altered due to the recalcitrance of non-republican states. Explicit commitments and the Council's structure give its decisions much more authority than recommendations of the General Assembly, but even Security Council decisions remain subject to republican confirmation, in the light of the composition and circumstances of Security Council majorities.

The Economic and Social Council of the United Nations consists of members elected by the General Assembly.[166] This makes the Council subject to the General Assembly's non-republican infirmities and very unlikely to be a representative body. In any case, the Charter subordinates the Council to the General Assembly,[167] and its draft conventions enter into force only after ratification by independent states.[168] Commissions established by the Economic and Social Council suffer from the same disabilities.[169] Thus, the Economic and Social Council may become a useful locus of discussion and has been valuable in proposing conventions, including the Convention on Civil and Political Rights, but like the United Nations General Assembly, the Economic and Social Council derives whatever authority it has from the republican nature of its members. Without such authority, its proposals must stand or fall entirely upon their own merits. The same is true of the now substantially defunct Trusteeship Council, with the added complication that half the Council's members administer trust territories, creating obvious conflicts of interest.[170]

The International Court of Justice is the principal judicial organ of the United Nations[171] and each member state undertakes to comply with the Court's decisions to which it is a party.[172] The Court may also issue advisory opinions, requested by other organs or specialized agencies of the United Nations.[173] Under its own statute, the Court's jurisdiction extends to cases that the parties refer to it, or to areas in which the parties recognize the court's compulsory jurisdiction by treaty or special declaration.[174] Republican judges in republican nations have traditionally enjoyed enormous authority concerning both their own jurisdiction and the content of the law. The rule of law is a fundamental principle of republican government,[175] and has long been seen to require both judicial independence and security in office.[176] Judges on the International Court of Justice, however, only serve for nine-year terms.[177] They are elected by the members of the Security Council and General Assembly,[178] by majority vote of each body, without a permanent member veto.[179] The subordination of the International Court of Justice to the General Assembly and the home nations of the Court's various non-republican judges vitiates its independent force as an authority on international law. Whatever authority the Court retains, it derives by direct delegation from republican nations in particular cases. Republics need not defer when they disagree with the Court, particularly on issues of jurisdiction.

Finally, the United Nations Secretariat is appointed by the Secretary-General under regulations established by the General Assembly.[180] The

Secretary-General is appointed in turn by the General Assembly upon the recommendation of the Security Council.[181] Both bodies are tainted by non-republican participation. This undermines the Secretariat's moral authority. Republics properly support the United Nations Secretariat only to the extent that it maintains high standards of efficiency, competence, integrity, and its own independence from external authority.[182] The separate republican governments must themselves independently decide whether this is the case.

None of the United Nations organs or instruments rest fully on the legitimate republican basis of popular sovereignty or the checks and balances of republican government. All organs submit in part to non-republican control, to the detriment of their moral authority. The republican principles that support international law contradict certain aspects of the United Nations regime and leave room for the separate deliberation of republican nations or, better still, for final determination by a democratic federation of republican states.

11. Republican principles in international law

A short review of the history and moral basis of international law reveals its dependence from the beginning upon republican principles in developing and defending legal doctrines and shared structures of legal and political power. The task of international law, as of all law, is to serve the common good of humanity, or at least the good of the relevant political community. This implies popular sovereignty, pursued as a deliberative test of moral truth and justice. National sovereignty may obscure this, but only if one overlooks sovereignty's own roots in the liberty and equality of nations. National self-determination involves personal self-determination. Arguments for national liberty support the personal liberties of the state's own subjects.

Immanuel Kant proposed a federation of republican states as the best basis for a just law of nations, leading to perpetual peace. The dictates of cultural history, human nature, and geographical variety require a diversity of nations. International law rests on this obvious truth and has developed legal categories that reflect this social reality. "Nations" are cultural units with a shared sense of justice and the common good. "States" are political units, controlling a determinate territory. "Peoples" are the inhabitants of the different states. Every state should be a nation, and self-determining peoples help to make this so. Basic human rights are the fundamental freedoms without which no people can exercise its self-determination.

International law depends upon the self-determination of peoples. Denying citizens a voice in the state destroys the republic and divides the nation. Systematically repressed minorities deserve self-determination and the opportunity to create a new people and a separate nation in pursuit of the common good. Otherwise, international boundaries should be stable, to provide the political basis for international law and national deliberation. The republican principles of popular sovereignty and pursuit of the common good created the underlying structure of international law. All international institutions, including the United Nations and the separate sovereign states, deserve deference only to the extent that they respect the public interest. Without democracy there can be no security. Republics are the only safe and stable basis for a just law of nations. Without justice, there will be no peace.

3
The Law of Humanity and the Law of Nations

The nineteenth-century doctrines known as "international law" developed out of the eighteenth century "law of nations" which itself grew out of seventeenth-century "*ius gentium*."[1] Each semantic shift reflected slight changes in scholarly attitudes towards the supranational legal order. Proponents (for example) of the term "international law" sought to promote a positivist doctrine, which would minimize the natural law elements of the old law of nations to privilege the views of governments and states.[2] "*Jus gentium*" implied a common set of fundamental legal principles shared by all peoples.[3] Recently, some publicists have started to speak of the "law of humanity" in order to challenge the role of nations and states in determining the world's legal order.[4] While this new usage captures the necessary universalism of supranational justice, it also threatens the premisses that support just institutions, by confusing the nature and purposes of law, nations, peoples and the state.

1. The law of nature

Early scholars of the law of nations, such as Hugo Grotius[5], Samuel von Pufendorf[6] and Emmerich de Vattel[7] applied the law of nature to nations to discover public obligations and rights among peoples. They began with the assumption that all persons are naturally free and equal. Free and equal persons properly relinquish certain rights and powers to states, nations and peoples in the interests of justice and the common good of all citizens. But states, nations, and peoples remain, on this theory, in a state of nature with regard to each other. Without a legislature to define common justice they must look directly to natural law. So the best evidence of international law is the general agreement of humanity, as reflected in the opinions and practices of all nations.[8]

This made the law of nations in a sense a "law of humanity" from the beginning. Early proponents of the *ius gentium* considered the best evidence of the law of nature and of nations to be human consensus, as reflected primarily through the laws and governments of states, acting on the international stage. But this reasoning contained two central fallacies. First, not all nations are states, at least in the original sense of the term. "Nation" implies common birth and first referred to prepolitical divisions within and around the (international) Roman empire. Nations can exist without political autonomy. Second, not all states speak for nations. Nearly all governments in Vattel's time were self-interested tyrannies. Grotius and Pufendorf suffered pointless persecution at the hands of what were by then the most enlightened governments of Europe. The voice or consensus of humanity is not always best or most clearly expressed by the governments of the states.

This observation has been the basis of the claims for "civil society"[9] advanced by proponents of the "law of humanity."[10] Governments will not always seek justice and the common good. Governmental interests may diverge from those of the people. Governments often oppress the people, or disagree amongst themselves. "Civil society" offers an alternative source of authority. To accept with Grotius and Vattel that the best expression of international law is the deliberate voice of humanity still leaves the very difficult problem of where that voice may be heard.

2. Interstate law

Critics of the existing world order stigmatize international law as mere "interstate law" among consenting tyrants.[11] They have a point. During the nineteenth century positivist followers of Jeremy Bentham and John Austin denied the very idea of a "natural law," discernible in the law of nations, as "nonsense upon stilts."[12] Positivists coined the phrase "international law" to reflect their view that law among nations exists (to the extent that it exists at all) only *between* nations, when nations agree upon firm laws through treaties or other positive acts. This view gained legitimacy from Vattel's old conception of states as free and equal actors, able to proceed without external restraint in their own internal affairs, just as free individuals or citizens properly act without restraint in their own personal ("private") affairs. Nineteenth-century liberals embraced this theory, because it protected each "nation" against outside interference by the rest.

Here again, as in the old "law of nations," the positivists' new "international law" lost moral force to the extent that it relied on self-serving, tyrannical governments. Some positivists freely admitted the moral vacuity of law as they conceived it. John Austin, for example,[13] and later H.L.A. Hart claimed to gain in clarity what they lost in justice.[14] To make law clear by limiting its sources means that there will be less law – perhaps no international law at all, according to Austin.[15] There is a certain intuitive appeal to the claim that each "nation" should pursue self-determination without reference to any external order. The Charter of the United Nations reflects the mixed origins of international law (and the analogy between states and free persons) when it echoes the United States Declaration of Independence in declaring that "We the Peoples of the United Nations" propose to (1) maintain international peace and security; (2) respect the equal rights and self-determination of peoples; (3) encourage respect for human rights; and (4) harmonize the actions of nations to achieve these common ends.[16] The actors here are "nations," but also self-determining states, committed to universal human rights. This commitment to rights (and its basis in nations) was reaffirmed in 1948 by the United Nations General Assembly's Universal Declaration of Human Rights.[17]

3. Human rights

Proponents of the "law of humanity" attribute its origins and early history to the international law of human rights.[18] Certainly, human rights have always put limits on the sovereignty of states. Even so great an advocate of absolute government as Jean Bodin admitted in his chapters on sovereignty that foreign states may intervene to protect oppressed peoples against despots.[19] So it was nothing new, after the Second World War, when the United States imposed the concept of individual human rights onto the post-war international settlement and the legal instruments that embodied it. But this widespread and necessary recognition of human rights tended to undermine the more extreme state-centered theories of international law. Why defer to unelected governments in determining the content of the rights of humanity?

The concept of rights grew up and flourished in tandem with the doctrine of popular sovereignty.[20] The earliest rights claimed in the modern world were political rights. First, peoples sought national self-determination against German or Spanish overlords, as in Switzerland and the Netherlands; then citizens sought internal self-determination against local monarchs, as in the English Commonwealth and Britain's Glorious Revolution of 1688; finally, eighteenth-century revolutionaries developed the full and self-conscious union of popular sovereignty with determinate limits on government, as in the United States Constitution.

Political rights and protections guaranteed the integrity of public deliberation, which yielded as law the best available approximation of justice and the common good.

The collapse of the French Revolution into Napoléon Bonaparte's empire tended to discredit popular sovereignty in Europe. This led to Benjamin Constant's famous (false) dichotomy between the liberty of the moderns and the liberty of the ancients.[21] Modern Europeans inevitably abuse political freedom, Constant argued, but still deserve personal liberty in their private affairs. So public and private liberty came to be separated, "liberalism" was born, and with it the question of how "liberty" and "justice" will be defined, in the absence of a valid democratic technique for discovering the deliberate consensus of the people.[22]

4. Civil society

Some now offer "civil society" as the new authority for a "law of humanity."[23] There exists no clear definition of what this might mean, but international "civil society" seems to imply (to those who promote it) an energized citizenry of the world, acting outside of normal governmental channels, to express the deliberate consensus of the people, while treating, as (Richard Falk puts it), "each person on earth a sacred subject."[24] Falk situates this general will in transnational non-governmental institutions such as Amnesty International, or internal social movements such as Solidarity in Poland, or Charter 77 in the former Czechoslovakia.[25]

If the "law of humanity" is to mean a "law that is enacted by and for the peoples of the world" it cannot rest on such self-appointed tribunals as these, or on the regional Watch groups, or Lelio Basso's Permanent Peoples Tribunals, or even on the Algiers Declaration of the Rights of Peoples. Such groups do not speak for the peoples of the world any more than most governments do. States exist to create and to apply laws for their subjects. Groups that claim to make or to determine the law are appropriating the attributes of states and, like states, gain legitimacy only to the extent that they properly reflect the deliberate consensus of the peoples of the world, or the regions that they presume to speak for. Civil society, properly understood, is a precondition of national statehood, just as statehood is a precondition of civil society.[26] Nations cannot fully express their deliberate consensus without the structures of a state. Justice and the common good cannot emerge outside the shared purpose of national institutions. Without guarantees of participation, free speech, and political checks and balances, "peoples" cannot enjoy the "self-determination" guaranteed by Article 1 of the Human Rights

Covenants.[27] "Peoples" only fully exist, and exercise self-determination, in the context of nation-states.

5. Popular sovereignty

This underlying semantic reality supports the conception of "civil society" only to the extent that civil society is also "republican," which is to say, committed to the common good, as discovered through public deliberation, under popular sovereignty structured to prevent domination by any single section of society.[28] The republican test of political legitimacy is service to the *res publica* or common good of the people.[29] Governments that are not republican cannot legitimately speak for the peoples that they presume to represent.[30] Reflective lawyers and philosophers have long endorsed a federation of such republics as the best basis for just law of nations.[31]

The republican argument for popular sovereignty runs as follows. People have different talents and life plans with differing perceptions of the common good. Private interests color human attitudes. Decent humility requires that citizens defer to a reasonable system for resolving conflicting perceptions of justice. Republicanism proposes that everyone is capable of perceiving moral truths. This makes popular sovereignty the best source of justice. If justice and the common good exist and all people have the capacity to perceive them, then the best route to a just society will be through public deliberation. To exclude any voices from the public debate would deprive society of their insights, and subject some private interests to the domination of others.[32]

Republicanism proposes a technique for creating and enforcing laws generally, including the laws of humanity. The persons affected, properly constituted into a civil society, become a "people" for the purposes of the relevant legislation, creating their own common good and common sense of justice. When popular sovereignty does not prevail, voices are excluded, the population cannot exercise its deliberative function, and the "people" no longer exist for the purposes of legislation. "*Res publica res est populi*," as Cicero first put it, (and many have echoed him since).[33] The lessons of the French and American revolutions demonstrate that for the purposes of republican government "the people" must embrace all permanent inhabitants of the territory in question.[34]

6. Peoples

"Peoples" in customary international law are the citizens of existing states. The history of decolonization, the Human Rights Covenants, and usage going back to Cicero demonstrate that the *populus* embraces all citizens. Modern republicanism and fundamental justice insists that the citizens should include all permanent residents of the state. Thus it is nonsense to maintain (as some self-styled "postmodern" scholars now do) that the Covenants' endorsement of self-determination for all "peoples" has "exploded once and for all" the notion of the nation-state. Such statements imply a confusion of "peoples," "minorities" and "nations." Stable peoples will evolve into nations. But not all minorities are peoples themselves (or states or nations).

The driving force exploding the "modern" interstate system owes less to the definition of a "people" (which has not and should not change) than to the concept of "self-determination". What is it for a people to enjoy its "right" to self-determination, or "freely" to determine its "political status" or "economic, social and cultural development" pursuant to United Nations Covenants? Plain English, and the history of the concept of self-determination going back past Woodrow Wilson to the American and other modern revolutions make it clear that there can be no self-determination without republican popular sovereignty, with all the rights to fair procedure and universal suffrage that entails.[35] To deny any segment or minority of the population basic rights and a voice in public affairs denies the people of that state their self-determination, in violation of international law.

Self-determination has long been recognized to embrace both "internal" and "external" popular sovereignty.[36] It requires that the people be free both of external interference and internal usurpation of government. Contemporary advocates of "democratically constituted geogoverence"[37] would do well to recognize the primacy of the most democratic of all legal systems, democracy itself, as a useful vehicle for providing a "government representing the whole people belonging to the territory without distinction as to race, creed or color," pursuant to the United Nation's Assembly's 1970 *Declaration on Principles of International Law Concerning Friendly Relations and Co-operation Among States in Accordance With the Charter of the United Nations.*

7. Nations

Nations were essential to the law of nations, and to the development of international law. But both categories (and particularly the latter) encouraged a false equivalence between nations and states. The proposed new "law of humanity" would avoid this mistake, at the cost of disregarding nations altogether. Instead, "postmodern" lawyers would elevate the authority of the United Nations General Assembly, or of

Nobel Peace Prize winners, or of the International Court of Justice, or of the media, or of other undemocratic or non-democratic forces in the best position to resist globalizing initiatives such as the World Trade Organization or the North American Free Trade Agreement. But why resist globalization if not in aid of local autonomy and national independence? The phrase "law of humanity" implies universal values and a world republic. The rhetoric of its advocates implies local interests and national particularity.

Both are desirable. Universal human rights provide the basic framework for local self-determination, and self-determination leads to local self-expression. Differences in climates, cultures, customs and history divide humanity into natural units. War, poverty and pestilence may force migrations and social discontinuity. But stable societies develop national attributes from the cultural capital of their constituent minorities. Stable states become nations. A world nation or world republic would not be desirable even if it were possible, because people properly savor the particularity of their own local circumstances. Nations benefit from the models that they provide each other. World government would risk universal tyranny through the single usurpation of an ambitious despot or self-important Caesar. National independence protects reservoirs of justice when the rest of the world becomes foolish or unlucky.

States properly follow the boundaries of existing nations, as nations themselves grow out of the peoples of existing states. Every people is a prospective nation. Given republican government, each people will become a nation. But in the absence of self-determination, oppressed minorities suffer (or sometimes majorities are oppressed), and secession may provide the best basis for developing the sense of justice and pursuit of the common good that leads to national identity and stable social institutions. As the United Nations General Assembly's 1970 *Declaration on Friendly Relations* strongly and correctly implies, the right to "territorial integrity" and "political unity" of "sovereign and independent states" depends on the representative nature of their governments, and the absence of discrimination on the basis of race, creed, or color.

8. The law of humanity

To speak of the "law of humanity" rather than the "law of nations" would be a mistake, because it understates the proper role of nations in human well-being. Speaking of "nations" rather than "states" usefully distinguishes "international" from "interstate" law. The law of nations is the law of humanity, discovered through the mediation of nations, or rather of peoples, treated as nations, even before they become so. The so-called "law of humanity" is not "post-modern" but pre-modern, harking back to when the Roman praetor's edict settled legal relations for all the Mediterranean world. The European Reformation put an end to any particular individual's or separate government's pretensions to universal authority. World-wide "civil society" does not exist, should not exist, and has not existed since Alaric sacked Rome.[38] The Secretary-General and United Nations General Assembly do not provide effective replacements.

The more law and justice change, the more they remain the same. Natural law was the basis of the old "law of nations." The United Nations confirmed the preeminence of what is now called "international" law. But both recognized the central importance of fundamental human rights. Civil society develops within nations, not between them. Every state should be a republic. This would make its people a nation, and self-determining nations still provide the best foundation for a just order of international law. Self-appointed "Watch" groups, "People's" tribunals, and scholarly gatherings may pontificate about the law of humanity, but they cannot determine its content without the mediation of self-governing national republics, based on human rights, popular sovereignty, and respect for the rule of law.

4
The Sources of International Law

Law must come from somewhere, and scholars and lawyers, to find law, and understand the law must know where to look for it, so from time to time writers and advocates have speculated about the sources of international law. The earliest modern advocate of the law of nations, Hugo Grotius, saw the ultimate source of law in humanity's natural need for social order, discovered and constructed by human intelligence.[1] Grotius observed that justice is approved, and injustice condemned, by good people everywhere.[2] So he sought evidence of the law of nations in unbroken custom and the views of skilled and reflective authors throughout the ages.[3] Just as municipal law arises from the mutual consent of individuals seeking the good of their community, so too, Grotius suggested, does international law arise from the implicit consent of states, seeking the good of the international community as a whole.[4]

Emmerich de Vattel also believed in natural duties to the universal society of the human race.[5] In his treatise on the *droits des gens*, that did as much as any other single volume to promote and to promulgate the modern law of nations, Vattel sought to clarify the proper role of consent. States may create and alter some of their duties by treaty or custom, but other laws remain immutable components of the "necessary" law of nations. Treaties or customs contrary to these provisions are unlawful and void.[6] Vattel identified the law of nations with the law of nature, applied to nations.[7] The greatest difficulty for international lawyers lies in discovering its content, which is why Vattel concluded that in making demands on other states, nations should restrict themselves to areas of general agreement.[8]

The Statute of the International Court of Justice reflects this same tension between immutable justice and its discovery by fallible human beings. Article 38 of the Court's statute recognizes four authorities to be applied in deciding cases according to international law: international conventions; international custom; the general principles of law recognized by civilized nations; and the teachings of the most highly qualified judges and publicists. Three hundred years of practice had not substantially altered the insights with which modern international law first sought the authority to find and to impose binding norms on independent states.

1. The international community

Both Grotius and Vattel spoke of creating and preserving the "international community" as a central purpose of international law. Christian Wolff, Vattel's main source, went further in identifying a preexisting world republic or "*civitas maxima*" as the source of the law of nations.[9] Some contemporary lawyers see the public interest of this "international community" as the central source of international law, without specifying too carefully who makes up the international "community" or why its interests should be paramount.[10] Traditional doctrine, going back to Grotius, described international law as regulating a community of states, just as municipal law regulates the separate national communities of citizens.

Vattel made the best argument for this conception of international law: "Since men are naturally equal, and a perfect equality prevails in their rights and obligations, as equally proceeding from nature, nations composed of men, and considered as so many free persons living together in the state of nature, are naturally equal, and inherit from nature the same obligations and rights."[11] It is an evident consequence of this liberty and independence of nations, that "all have the right to be governed as they think proper, and no state has the smallest right to interfere in the government of another."[12] The traditional conception of the international community has been of a community of states, regulating their external affairs in pursuit of justice and the common good of the nations and peoples that they represent.

More recently, a "realist" camp has arisen among some lawyers, which sees international law as a *modus vivendi* between competing sovereigns, serving their mutual interests without regard to justice or the needs of their people.[13] This view adopts Vattel's concept of a community of states, and sees each state's consent as the sole source of "law" regarding its own international obligations. John Austin's theories of legal positivism lent this attitude a certain respectability, by deriving all law from the will of "sovereigns," identified as the governments of individual states.[14] This differs from traditional doctrine in emphasizing the will of states as sources of law, rather than their shared perceptions of justice or truth, but both approaches agree in recognizing the importance of states for determining the content of international law.

2. International conventions

The emphasis on conventions in the Statute of the International Court of Justice, "establishing rules expressly recognized by the contesting states,"[15] follows naturally from Vattel's view of states as free and independent representatives of the peoples of the world. Treaties are the clearest possible expression of international consensus, and contract is one of the most basic components of universal natural justice. This is why so many since Grotius have endorsed his basic principle that *pacta sunt servanda.*[16] If states speak for peoples, then (a) their shared perceptions are likely to be true, and (b) their commitments should bind them.

To speak of treaties as binding would tend to vitiate the realist view of law as deriving from the will or consent of states. Treaties bind, under the usual doctrine, whether or not states still endorse their original agreements. There is an obvious utility in being able to rely on mutual commitments, which usually outweighs the harm caused by respecting ill-considered or unjust agreements. As with contracts between individuals, fundamental changes in circumstances diminish the obligation of the original pact. Even brigands can accept these principles, which serve a basic human interest in planning and coordination.

There will be limits, however, to the power of treaties as sources of law, if one looks beyond the pretense that states are free and equal representatives of free and equal citizens. Most states are not. Unequal treaties imposed by force do not reflect the views of the weaker party. Unjust treaties entered into by undemocratic governments do not speak for the peoples that they purport to represent. There may be prudential reasons for maintaining such treaties after power changes hands, but the ultimate source of "law" is not present to make such conventions genuinely binding.

3. International customs

Hugo Grotius[17] quoted Dio Chrysostom[18] for the proposition that time and custom create the law of nations. The reference in the Statute of the International Court of Justice to international custom "as evidence of general practice accepted as law"[19] reflects this very old observation that custom reveals a natural law proceeding from universal human characteristics.[20] Vattel added that it may also reflect tacit consent, or a tacit convention between states that observe certain practices toward each other.[21] Vattel considered this sort of customary international law useful and obligatory, if reasonable, but not obligatory otherwise, since nothing can oblige or authorize a state to violate the natural law of nations.[22]

Custom expresses the natural law of the community of nations because consensus naturally builds around rules made salient by universal human nature. Where several solutions could equally provide a viable rule, custom properly determines which rule will govern future conflicts. Here again custom does not express so much the will of nations as their mutual recognition of external and preexistent norms. Custom is very good evidence of natural law, applied to nations.

Custom need not be universal to bind states, even dissenters, when it arises from preexisting truths in the rational law of nature. Custom created by states to facilitate their social and mercantile interests derives its validity from consent,[23] and only binds those who benefit from the practice involved. So while it is true in a sense to say that customs, like conventions, are generally created by the international community to serve its own interests, the fundamental interest involved is the maintenance of social order[24] to the advantage, not of particular states, but of the whole society of states throughout the world.[25]

4. General principles of law

The general principles of law recognized by civilized nations take on a special significance for scholars who want to minimize the role of states in international law. This is because they arise among "nations" (not "states") and only "civilized" nations have standing to create them. In the Statute of the International Court of Justice, these "principles" would seem to be legal maxims accepted widely in the practice of more developed legal systems.[26] To these some would now add "proposals, reports, resolutions, treaties or protocols" debated and refined in modern multilateral fora, such as the United Nations.[27]

If all interested states participate in a discussion of some area of law and reach a consensus, or even substantial agreement, the standards thus generated would seem more likely correctly to reflect the social norms and justice that justify and create the law of nations than would most conventions or customs among states. The more open and self-conscious the process, the more valid the norm. Sometimes a short-term consensus will be able to generate norms that would be very difficult to achieve through gradual evolution, given the corruption and shifting self-interest of states.

This quasi-legislative process of creating general international law requires justification. Conventions and customs provide good evidence of international law because they reflect the consent and perceptions of states, which rest in turn on the consent and perceptions of their citizens and nationals. General principles of municipal law derive their validity in much the same way. Multilateral fora purporting to speak for the "international community" must offer some such theory to justify their claim of authority. Direct democratic participation through representatives who speak for the common good would supply the most compelling claim to moral accuracy and legal recognition. The smaller the democratic input, the weaker the validity of the norm.[28]

5. Teachings of the publicists

Judicial decisions and the teachings of the most highly qualified publicists of various nations might seem to fail this democratic test, even as a subsidiary means of determining the rules of international law. Their persistent importance, going back to Grotius, Wolff, Pufendorf, Bynkershoek, Wheaton and the Statute of the International Court of Justice,[29] among many other examples, reflects the weakness, incoherence, corruption, and democratic illegitimacy of most states during most of the world's history. If international custom, conventions and the deliberations of multilateral bodies derive their validity from the consent or perceptions of the peoples represented, then the participation of usurping governments and tyrants in creating such standards will undermine their legitimacy.[30] This creates the void that publicists have stepped forward to fill.

What judges and publicists offer in determining the content of international law is impartiality. Without a personal stake in the outcome of international conflicts, such figures may be franker and more objective in working out the obligations that arise from the community of states or universal human society. Their influence depends less on democratic legitimacy than on the ability to state truths clearly that, once uttered, cannot be easily suppressed. Judges and academics who owe their positions to the patronage or sufferance of government officials will not speak truth to power, and deserve little deference in determining the rules of international law.

It is doctrinaire nonsense to imagine that a strict system of autonomous states ever governed the creation of international law, and well-intentioned nonsense to suppose that the sources of international law have changed much in recent years. What may have changed is the efficacy of international law, and the frequency with which such sources are consulted. Claiming authority for international law has always involved assertions of truth about justice. The role of publicists may have decreased in recent years, as multilateral fora have proliferated, but the sources of their authority continue as before to be the truth of their doctrines and the democratic legitimacy of those who articulate them.

6. *Jus cogens*

The Vienna Convention on the Law of Treaties recognizes the long-asserted principle of international law that: "A treaty is void if, at the time of its conclusion, it conflicts with a peremptory norm of general international law." For the purposes of the convention, a peremptory norm of general international law ("*jus cogens*") is a "norm accepted and recognized by the international community of states as a whole as a norm from which no derogation is permitted."[31] This corresponds to Vattel's category of laws that no nation may create or recognize, because they violate the laws of nature.[32] The concept of *jus cogens* denies the possibility that international law ultimately derives in any significant sense from the simple will or consent of states. As described in the Vienna Convention, *jus cogens* creates a new category of non-derogable norms "accepted by the international community of states as a whole." This "international community" transcends individual states, and may encourage the development of multilateral fora to recognize and articulate inchoate standards of international law.

Difficulties arise in seeking to distinguish *jus cogens* norms from other less fundamental rules of international law, which states may restrict by agreement. The examples usually offered include prohibitions on genocide, racial discrimination, slavery, piracy, crimes against humanity, and the use of force.[33] All concern protecting individual rights against state malfeasance, with special emphasis on protecting personal security and bodily integrity against serious violations. Most proposed elements of the *jus cogens* protect what Vattel referred to as the "universal society of the human race."[34]

7. Erga omnes obligations

The "universal society of the human race" may sometimes find itself at odds with the "community of states," as is made most clear by the doctrine of *erga omnes* obligations advanced by the International Court of Justice in the *Barcelona Traction Light & Power Co.* Case (1970). In *Barcelona Traction*, the Court suggested that states owe certain obligations to the "international community" as a whole. These obligations are "*erga omnes*," according to the Court, and all states have a legal interest in their protection. *Erga omnes* obligations include acts of aggression, genocide, and violations of the basic rights of the human person, such as slavery or racial discrimination. States violating these norms offend the "international community," rather than the "community of states" and must accept certain limits on their own domestic autonomy.[35]

Human rights have played this overarching role in international law at least since the days of that first great promoter of state sovereignty, Jean Bodin, who admitted that rulers should be replaced by outside intervention when they cease to serve the common good of the people.[36] Vattel considered it an act of "justice and generosity" for William of Orange to protect the English against James II.[37] However much princes and the "community of states" may benefit from noninterference, international law has always recognized an obligation of the "international community" to liberate oppressed peoples from those who abuse them. The principles of self-determination and colonial liberation reflect this basic truth.

Attempts to corral international disputes into a purely bilateral framework ignore the principles that gave rise to international law in the first place. Certain obligations are *erga omnes* because they regard the very existence or basic justice of the international community as a whole. This is not strictly speaking a community of states, but rather a community of humanity acting through states to develop societies and protect their common good and basic freedoms. When norms are created to serve the international community, it makes sense that the international community as a whole should retain the right to enforce them.

8. The sources of international law

The primary source of international law has always been the law of nature, applied to nations. Conventions, custom, legal principles, and the opinions of publicists all seek to articulate preexisting realities, or new elaborations of what justice requires, made salient by historical circumstances. The recent turn to multilateral action through the International Law Commission and other United Nations agencies creates a new vehicle for systematizing this sort of deliberation. This is no departure, but rather a confirmation of the traditional sources of international law.

Recent scholarship has identified some confusion in the concept of an "international community."[38] Is it a community of persons or of states? The doctrines of *jus cogens* and *erga omnes* obligations also straddle this delicate issue. To justify international law its proponents have always assumed an underlying community of humanity. Grotius and Vattel supposed that the world's peoples would act through states. But states are means towards the realization of a just society, not ends in themselves.

The sources of international law in justice and the common good of humanity have not changed for centuries, since peoples first entered into commerce with their neighbors. New vehicles for discovering law's requirements do emerge, and are useful, most recently through multilateral fora such as those provided by the United Nations. Changed circumstances should never obscure the fundamental truths on which the law of nations rests, and without which international law would lose its efficacy and moral influence on states.

5
Why States Are Bound by Customary International Law

Any discussion of the sources of law must also consider when, if ever, the laws should be obeyed. What is the basis of law's binding force? The essential attribute and ultimate claim of all law is that, as law, it deserves the uncoerced obedience of its subjects. Customary international "law," to be law, must claim to bind the nations, states and peoples subject to its jurisdiction. To deserve obedience, customary law, like all law, must first substantiate the basis of this claim.[1]

Various explanations have been offered for why some customs bind as law. Positivists such as Hans Kelsen typically assert that states are bound by customary law because they believe themselves to be bound by customary law.[2] Others might say that states *choose* to be bound, because customary law serves their interests in peace and commerce.[3] The best and most accurate view is that customary law binds persons, states, and other subjects of international law, *whether they will or no*, for the same reason that any law binds anywhere, which is by providing the best available measure of what would be the right thing to do in a given set of circumstances. To the extent that proposed norms do not do this, their status as "law" is compromised, and they do not deserve the obedience of their supposed subjects.[4]

1. Evidence of law

Custom's status as international law was formally recognized by many states through the Statute of the International Court of Justice, adopted by reference through Article 92 of the United Nations Charter. Article 38 of the Court's Statute characterizes "international custom" as "evidence of a general practice accepted as law."[5] The Court also relies on international conventions "expressly recognized by the contesting states," on the general principles of law recognized by "civilized" nations, and on the judicial decisions and teachings of the most highly qualified publicists of the various nations, "as a subsidiary means for the determination of rules of law."[6]

These four methods of finding the law have deep roots in international legal theory. Hugo Grotius discovered the law of nations ("*jus gentium*") in custom ("*usus*"), the views of the learned, and the will ("*voluntas*") of states,[7] but explained that the underlying source of all law is the human need for society,[8] as explained by right reason.[9] Custom, will, and learning discover the dictates of reason to construct an international society of states.[10] Thus for Grotius, the customary law of nations corresponds to the *lex non scripta* of domestic legal systems.[11] Nations develop customs either by deduction from natural principles or from consent. In either case their customs should be binding. Emmerich de Vattel repeated and reformulated Grotius' observation,[12] but added that nations need society amongst themselves much less than individuals do.[13] Vattel insisted that customs and treaties both derive whatever binding force they have from antecedent natural law,[14] as deduced through the natural liberty of nations, the common welfare of states, and their interest in trade.[15]

The observations of Grotius and Vattel may not have much bearing on contemporary lawyers' sense of international custom, but they illustrate the purposes that international custom serves in determining the content of international law. As the Statute of the International Court of Justice indicates, custom has never been so much a source of law as it has been "evidence" of international law. When states make treaties, they indicate their belief that they ought to be bound in certain circumstances. When the subjects of international law develop and follow customs, they indicate their opinion that they ought to act in certain ways. When civilized nations recognize general principles of law, their agreement is evidence that such principles exist. When learned judges render decisions, they must claim that the law they have found requires the given result. The implication in every instance is that law exists, and that certain indicia give evidence of what the law is.

2. Positive law

To say that law exists to be found and obeyed is not to say that law cannot be made, or become more determinate, through the deliberate acts of those in authority (or others, in certain circumstances). Laws exist, in part, to clarify social relations when several equally viable arrangements would be possible, but one particular rule must be chosen. Domestic legal systems often do this by "positive law," which is to say by formal legislation, generated by a recognized process, and enforced by courts. Treaties offer a partial parallel in the international sphere. Between those party to them, treaties may be considered as "legislation," in the same way that contracts create "law" in domestic legal systems. Parties to treaties may be assumed to know best what should be done in their mutual relations, with certain restrictions to protect the general good, to prevent unconscionable results, or to proscribe violations of *jus cogens* and fundamental human rights.

Some "positivists" would look to legislation alone in determining the law.[16] The law (on this theory) is simply whatever those in authority say that it is, and the "sources" of law all derive from some determinate human will, without regard for the purposes that law exists to serve.[17] Such theories do little to explain custom, which has no determinate source. Positivists must view customs as tacit treaties, reflecting the will of those in authority, who tolerate their development, and suffer them to persist. In international law this would mean that customs bind states because those in authority intend that customs should bind states, and have legislated, in a sense, by allowing the custom to develop and survive.

Positive law certainly plays a part in international law, as when multilateral treaties clarify previously disputed legal issues, through quasi-"legislation," but most of international law has less obviously "legislated" origins. States can claim a certain authority, when they can agree, but often they cannot. Even when states do agree, their own legitimacy may be questionable. There is not enough positive law in the international sphere to constitute a coherent system of law. Legal theories based on authority need authorities to make them work, but international society has no universal authority, nor any prospect of finding one.

3. Obedience to law

International law, like all law, must claim to deserve obedience. The mystery is what supports this claim, without a recognized international authority to promulgate rules. Domestic legal systems rest on the government's claim to discover or to clarify law and justice through established structures of power and authority. No international authority can make this claim and enforce it. Thus international law must earn obedience by being persuasive or being right. States or others asserting principles of international law may persuade (1) by force of arms, or (2) by force of argument. When they persuade by argument, states evoke obedience by persuading themselves or others that certain rules deserve to be obeyed.

Custom generates laws, which should be obeyed when custom offers needed standards or rules to coordinate international actors in the service of justice. When several possible solutions exist to problems of international interaction, custom may identify the salient solution, much as a positive law or treaty would, if states had reached a more formal agreement.

Custom may also identify the substance of law in a deeper sense, by offering evidence of what would be the most just solution, based on the views of a wide variety of states and peoples. *Opinio juris*, or the view that something is law, and binding, offers very good evidence of what is law, and binding, if the opinion is widely shared and admitted. Some might consider it "circular" to say that the widespread belief that something *is* international law constitutes good evidence of it also actually *being* international law. This confuses the issue by considering custom as a *source* of law, rather than *evidence* of law, which derives its binding force from reason, applied to the purposes that international law exists to serve.

4. The purposes of international law

Like all law, international law derives its legitimacy from the purposes that it exists to serve and deserves obedience only to the extent that it is effective in doing so. One view might be that international law exists to serve the interests of peace and prosperity, through maintaining a system of states, that trade amongst themselves.[18] Such a system might avoid conflict by taking the most recent resolution to any dispute between states as the default norm, to be applied to the next similar conflict, unless one of the parties objects, in which case a different resolution could be sought. Trade maximizes prosperity, and peace maximizes trade. On this theory peace and prosperity both follow from respecting precedents in all disputes, thereby avoiding conflict, and maximizing opportunities to trade.[19]

Formulations such as this, that privilege peace and prosperity over other aspects of justice and the common good, slight some of the fundamental purposes that help customs and law to crystallize around determinate principles and rules. A dispute between two states may be solved at times by the application of rules that do not have much resonance elsewhere, as when the Pope divided the Americas between Spain and Portugal.[20] In such circumstances no customary rule emerges, and the law remains unchanged. Perhaps this example is a poor one, but it would be a mistake to say that "the governing rule that emerges from any international controversy is the birth of a rule of customary international law."[21] There would also need to be a widely shared opinion (or practice) indicating that this result was just and binding as law.

In the absence of an international legislature, inference from the purposes of international law (justice and common good), constitutes a much more direct source of law than would be the case in most domestic legal systems. Customary law, discovered in the views and practices of states, provides good evidence of law by revealing either (1) what states or others *have* agreed to, or (2) what all international legal actors *should* agree to, because it is widely recognized to be just. One might compare this to the old English view of the common law or *lex non scripta* as the embodiment of reason, applied to the necessities of human society, and worked out through generations of legal practice.[22] The opinions of judges constitute good evidence of the common law, but they cannot change or create law, only find it. The influence of their opinions depends on the truth (and so on the persuasive value) of their reasoning.

5. Treaties

Treaties can be evidence of international law in just the same way that customs can, so long as they reflect widespread recognition that certain standards are law and binding, or help to make one solution to an international coordination problem salient over others. Treaties can be sources of custom, to the extent that third parties observe or endorse rules that treaties recognize as having binding force.

Understanding the role that treaties and custom can play as evidence rather than as sources of international law makes it clearer how multilateral treaties may bind states and others even in areas where states have expressed reservations or opposition to the treaties in question. If the treaty reflects a binding norm of international law, widely recognized as law by the community of nations, this may be very good evidence that it *is* law, notwithstanding the reservations of even the most powerful states.

Treaties enter into what one might call the international "common law" or *lex non scripta* in much the same way that English statutes enter Anglo-American common law – through the widespread recognition that they capture fundamental elements of the developing law of nations. Just as Anglo-American common law after Coke "found" the law, and did not make it, so does international custom find the law (and does not make it), with or without statutory assistance. In the same way that chapter 29 of Magna Carta represents a central element of the common law, so fundamental that no statute or contract may alter it, so too *jus cogens* exists in international custom, when norms are so fundamental that no derogation should be permitted from their binding force.

6. The binding force of customary international law

Customary law is formed in much the same way that common law was formed, as common law was understood before the advent of legal positivism. No single holding can "change" or "make" the law, but taken together the customs and practices of states offer very good evidence of what the law is, which is to say, of right reason, in a given set of circumstances.

Whatever the resolution of an international dispute, by force or by agreement, by arbitration or by default, the bindingness of its "holding" depends on its being right. The greater the international consensus that a given result is binding as law, the greater the likelihood that the result is, in fact, binding as law. But determining the binding force of any "precedent" depends on examining the circumstances in which consensus emerged, and the nature, legitimacy and trustworthiness of those consenting. *"Opinio juris"* determines the content of customary international law, but it matters whose opinion is expressed, and why.

6
The Effectiveness of International Law

To be "effective" international law must be obeyed. Often law is obeyed, even by overwhelmingly powerful nations such as the United States of America. Why? Force and coercion cannot be the reason, but fear plays a role – the fear of appearing unjust in one's own eyes, or in the eyes of one's friends.

1. Blame

Greek kings in the Homeric age employed poets to praise themselves and to blame their enemies. Praise and blame set the parameters of acceptable behavior, which could be moved in one direction or another by clever verses and a loud voice, within certain external canons of plausibility. Some behavior simply is not praiseworthy. Some sovereigns deserve to be blamed.

These human universals of right and wrong made international law possible, when scholars such as Grotius, Pufendorf and Vattel first expressed their perceptions of the universal *jus gentium* – perceptions whose influence depended entirely upon the author's ability to convince readers of the justice and utility of their proposed standards of behavior. Some scholars had more persuasive power and authority than others, and could move law in one direction or another at the behest of their royal employers, just as a good poet could manipulate Hellenic public opinion with elegant verses or a memorable line of invective.

Human nature relies on the concepts of "right" and "wrong." As social animals human beings have a natural tendency to think in moral terms, to turn fiercely on others who violate their sense of propriety, and to feel shame when they themselves transgress, or others perceive them to have done so. As rational animals, humans naturally seek to turn these moral emotions to their private advantage, manipulating human feelings of indignation and shame to serve selfish ends, constructing conceptions of justice that harness public opinion to private interests, and cultivating self-righteousness in pursuit of personal appetites and desires.

2. Normative knowledge

Speaking in terms of "right" and "wrong" implies that some answers to moral questions are more "right" or "wrong" than others. Praise and blame depend upon claims of "normative knowledge" – the knowledge that one activity or attitude is "right" and praiseworthy and another is "wrong" or shameful.

Some types of normative knowledge are widely shared. The "golden rule," for example, has overwhelming resonance, as do its concomitant hesitations about homophagy, or the recreational deprivation of human life. But even these prohibitions are violated, with confidence, in societies that have constructed social realities to support their own moral obtuseness. People care a great deal about the views of others, and can be moved quite far even from quasi-instinctive moral knowledge by the pressure of social constructs, such as national identity or religion.

Nevertheless, the assertion of normative knowledge invites discussion of its content, and implies that grounds must be offered for any views advanced. Like other knowledge, normative knowledge rests on arguments about human perceptions, and is subject to change. Communities of discourse will tend to converge on certain answers to contested moral questions. Discussion and reflection lead to deeper and more accurate knowledge about norms. People find it very hard to maintain idiosyncratic personal "truths" in the face of steady interaction with others.

3. Epistemic communities

Human communities tend to converge on shared conceptions of moral and scientific "truth." But this fact of human nature need not always mean that social "truth" and reality coincide. Societies often construct moral conceptions to serve their interests, or the interests of those who dominate the social discourse. Powers that control the television and radio transmissions in a given territory, for example, will have a disproportionate impact on that specific society's outlook, and conceptions of moral knowledge.

Those interested in justice, which is to say, in real moral knowledge about the structure of political societies, will need a theory of valid epistemic community. For although it is natural that epistemic communities should converge on shared conceptions of "moral knowledge," these conceptions may be false or unjust. One advantage of international law in the pursuit of justice arises from its transcendence of numerous otherwise discrete epistemic communities, since international law must apply to diverse peoples, governments and nations throughout the world, and gain their acceptance.

This may also be a disadvantage, because so many governments serve the unjust and improper interests of their rulers, who are violent and self-interested local elites or individuals. Giving such figures a voice in international moral discourse corrupts the creation of moral knowledge about international law. When unjust regimes predominate, international legal discourse may even serve to encourage and validate injustice, putting democracies and liberal republics on the defensive, by allowing despots to reinforce and to justify each other's bad behavior.

4. Consensus

Consensus creates the international legal regime: consensus first about the principles of international law, and then about the details of their application. Widespread consensus creates compliance, even among regimes that may not fully share the consensus thus created. Human actors tend to internalize widely shared moral standards. Individuals find it personally difficult to maintain a separate viewpoint in the face of overwhelming agreement. Diplomats and politicians suffer shame at cocktail parties and academic conferences. Their children criticize them. They doubt their own convictions.

Who will have a voice in the international forum becomes immensely important, and one major task of detached or supposedly dispassionate analysis of international law in universities and elsewhere should be to determine which voices deserve to be heard. If participants in moral discussions tend to converge on a consensus, who should these participants be to create the most just or accurate conception of moral knowledge? Democratic republics rest on the principle that all voices should be heard that are willing to debate the creation of a shared or "common" good. According to this theory, justice best emerges from the widest possible discussion among the greatest number of sincere participants.[1]

Looking primarily to sovereign governments to represent the voices of their populations presents an obvious problem when most governments serve the narrow interests of a ruling elite. Non-governmental organizations, the media and other self-appointed and self-regulated groups also suffer from a lack of democratic accountability. Their motives may be purer than those of most governments, but their value lies more in the information that they bring to the discussion, such as on-the-ground experience or scientific studies, than it does in any legitimate claim to be heard or respected about the emerging content of moral knowledge about international law.

5. Operational systems

Joaquín Tacsan has distinguished "myth systems" of normative knowledge from the "operational systems" that apply them.[2] "Myth systems" will be more or less appealing depending on the quality of the norms that they embody. Operational systems develop the consensus that make these norms effective. Operational systems may be more or less successful (1) in achieving consensus and (2) in finding justice. Both attributes are important. The ideal operational system will create consensus about real normative knowledge – will help people and nations to find and to agree upon normative truth. Experience has shown that democratic republics make the best operational systems for discovering legal norms, and that a republican federation of democratic republics will be the best operating system for authorizing or legitimating moral knowledge about international law.[3]

6. Democratic republics

"Democratic republic" signifies a state committed to finding the common good (*res publica*) for its inhabitants through public deliberation in which all citizens have a voice. A republican federation of democratic republics is a federation of states that observes the same rules of participation and deliberation among the representatives of its component peoples that they observe internally among their own citizens. Such states and federations will more likely discover valid normative truths than other epistemic communities, because they involve the moral perceptions of wider groups of people, under conditions of mutual cooperation.

The best epistemic community for discovering international law will include only those voices that seek the common good, and respect the democratic process. Other voices, be they governments, publicists, nongovernmental organizations or the media should carry weight only to the extent that they convey useful information to democratically validated participants in international normative discourse.

The substance of international law depends on consensus, and consensus depends in turn on the identity of those who forge it. Democratic republics deserve deference in this process, and should not themselves be swayed by the views of non-democratic or non-republican voices. International law does not deserve to become effective unless it is just, and it will not be just if its epistemic community embraces too many corrupted or usurping speakers.

7. The rule of law

The rule of law ideal constrains decisions made in democratic republics more than in other states, because only through the rule of law can democratic decisions ever successfully guide government officials in serving the common good. This makes the concept of "law" a powerful tool in international relations for moving democratic republics toward conformity with justice. Republics blame themselves for legal transgressions. Successfully label something as a "law" and the battle for effectiveness is already half-won, at least among the democratic republics.

Tribunals such as the International Court of Justice derive improper influence from this analogy with domestic legal institutions. One must examine the provenance of would-be lawgivers before deferring to their rulings. Did they arise from a democratic process? Who had a voice in the decision? The authority of the International Court of Justice is diminished by its derivation from the Security Council and General Assembly of the United Nations, which contain many corrupt and despotic governments, and by the limited terms in office of the judges themselves, which leaves them subject to outside influences.[4]

International law derives in part from universal perceptions of normative reality and in part from the expression of that reality by authorized speakers. This latter process posits specific rules of law, and the claim that states should respect them. "Extrinsic" factors about the structure of international discourse may have as much influence on state behavior as the "intrinsic" validity of the norms proposed. The more the standards advanced can be made to look like law, the more likely it is that they will be obeyed.

8. The effectiveness of international law

The effectiveness of international law rests on two pillars: the desire to respect its norms and the ability to do so. Ability depends primarily on the existence of a functioning bureaucracy, fostered through education and the rule of law to create the discipline and intelligence without which obedience cannot occur. Desire is more complicated, and grows out of either "normative knowledge" or the threat of violence. The first is more significant in international law, since powerful states can safely disregard most external sanctions.

"Normative knowledge" may be manipulated by eloquent arguments and the structure of the relevant epistemic community. Consensus creates international law, but consensus will be mistaken when the wrong actors play too large a role in its elaboration. Yet truth has special resonance. Those who would subvert normative reality find their task more difficult once morally significant truths enter into the conversation.

Scholars should see to it that this happens and strive to bring international institutions into line with democratic and republican imperatives. International lawyers who wish to measure, to monitor, or even to predict the effectiveness of international norms should look first to each norm's validity and then to its foundations in democratic discourse. The sounder this basis the longer the law will survive to influence the actions of the international community.

7
The Right to Republican Government Under International Law

The fall of the Soviet Union and the liberation of East and Central Europe have emboldened international lawyers to reassert the principles of human rights and democracy that intermittently inspired their predecessors over the last four centuries. Some rely on state practice to justify democratic norms,[1] by pointing out that many states now formally recognize some sort of individual or collective right to self-government.[2] This is the "positivist" argument for liberal democracy.

Other scholars make the same argument from a "naturalist" or "deontological" perspective, identifying human rights that exist whether or not states recognize them as binding in practice.[3] This more direct approach more accurately reflects the moral truth that obligates states to obey international law, but understates the value of their agreement or deliberation about the content of legal standards, and the specifics of how to enforce them. A better (intermediate) position would recognize the right to republican government, which is to say to government for the individual and collective good or well-being of all citizens, as realized through the organized and balanced structures of the republican form of government. Bald assertions by scholars of detailed lists of individual rights are only slightly more likely to be correct than bald assertions made by the governments or foreign ministries of existing non-republican states.

1. The positivist mistake

Self-styled "positivists" in international law mistakenly derive international obligation from state consent, or recognition.[4] This confuses power with authority, by attributing binding force to the views of various despots or tyrants, whose actual influence depends on terror, force or usurpation. Such sovereigns' "consent" obligates no one, nor do any existing human rights become more (or less) binding on states because such governments have agreed (or not) that particular rights should apply to them or to others. In practice, states will be more likely to implement rights that they have recognized publicly to exist, but even this is only sometimes true. The existence of rights influences state behavior with or without agreement, and governments often violate rights whether or not they have endorsed them in formal international instruments.

States do often maintain legal systems that operate to some extent independently of the immediate desires of the leaders that they serve. To the extent that states have "law," they recognize legal principles of general application, which they claim to be morally justified. States which recognize preexisting human rights thereby make it more likely that their own legal systems will recognize and apply these rights in practice. To this extent it makes a difference whether states recognize universal human rights, and states should be encouraged to do so.

In fact, as many scholars now understand,[5] democracies are more likely to recognize human rights than other states are, and having recognized them, are more likely to implement them in practice. This stands as a powerful argument in favor of democracy. Positive law in municipal legal systems can strengthen the application of justice to particular persons in particular cases. States earn their legitimacy by serving the individual and collective good of their subjects. Since democracies serve fundamental human rights better than other types of government, they are more legitimate than other types of government, and their directives are more binding.

2. The Rousseavian mistake

The value of democracy in protecting fundamental human rights has misled some of its advocates into endorsing democratic institutions as the sole or final arbiter of international legitimacy. Just as positivists view the consent of existing governments as decisive in measuring the validity of international norms or standards, so some democrats treat majority votes as the sole conclusive measure of obligation under international law. This loses sight of the purposes that justify democratic voting in the first place. Universal participation in voting prevents self-interested elites from running the state in their own interests. It does not license the majority to usurp state power in pursuit of their own oppressive agenda.

Some types of coordination problems may best be solved by the essentially random (or even somewhat self-interested) procedure of majority voting. The maximum width of the juridical continental shelf may be settled, perhaps, by the vote of all states. The direction of traffic may be settled by plebiscite, or votes may settle the distribution of executive authority. These sorts of questions do not necessarily admit of "right" or "just" answers. They do need *some* answer, so that matters may move forward. On other questions, such as human rights or the definition of crimes, getting the right answer determines the legitimacy of the government concerned. Democracy is required under justice and international law, because non-democracies usually get such questions wrong, in pursuing the self-interest of their rulers.

This does not mean that democracies always get such questions right. Democracies do not constitute republics unless they serve the collective good of the people, in preference to that of a majority, or of elected elites. All republics are democracies, but not all democracies are republics. The rule of law, an independent judiciary, respect for fundamental human rights, the separation of powers, bicameral checks and balances, representative government, and other republican safeguards must be in place, before democracies will serve the republican purposes that alone confer legitimacy on the coercive power of the state.[6]

3. The liberal mistake

The excesses of certain democratic regimes have caused some liberals to denigrate democracy itself, or to minimize its importance under international law. Liberals rightly view universal human rights as fundamental to human well-being, and condition all governments' legitimacy on their respect for human rights. But liberal scholars and lawyers often do not understand democracy's centrality in achieving this goal. Many liberals value democracy for the equal concern and respect that it shows citizens, for its generally peaceful attitude toward foreigners, and for its usual support for human rights, but question its role in the "deliberative process" of discovering human rights and protecting them.[7] Liberalism emerged as a distinct philosophy by setting aside democracy and political science in the wake of Robespierre's Terror, when many blamed unfettered democracy for the degeneration of France.[8] Fear of democracy has weakened liberalism ever since.

The problem with liberalism's agnosticism about political procedures lies in the danger that rights face without general agreement about when to recognize or enforce them. Non-republican governments will neither readily recognize rights nor protect them. While individual scholars may assert the existence of certain rights, these will not enjoy widespread recognition or legitimacy until they are tested by public deliberation. Non-democratic governments simply will not respect or even accurately identify which fundamental human rights exist or what they entail. States without independent judges, the rule of law, the separation of powers, a mixed and balanced bicameral legislature, and an elected representative assembly will not defend human rights, or treat all citizens with equal concern and respect, or show restraint in their international affairs, because they lack the republican defenses that would help them do to so.[9]

Liberalism requires republican institutions, including democracy, in order to realize its goals. Liberals who assert the primacy of certain rights, without subjecting them to the test of public reason in a republican deliberative process, will often make mistakes, pursuing unwarranted interventions in the frenzy of their own self-righteous self-importance. Decent humility demands that would-be arbiters of international obligation test their convictions against the best available procedures for taking everyone's insights into account, treating every person and people's well-being with equal concern and respect. Such republican procedures go beyond democracy in their search for universal human rights, but also respect the separate needs of different nations and cultures, which liberal universalism may sometimes violate and overlook.

4. The right to republican government under international law

International law derives whatever binding force it has from its ability correctly to determine the international rights and obligations of states and individuals. Positivists overvalue the importance of existing state governments in making these determinations. Democrats overvalue the importance of simple majority decisions. Liberals overvalue their own standing to dictate rights to the world. Republican government satisfies the needs of all three viewpoints by showing how states may earn the legitimacy democratically to determine the human rights due to all of their citizens. Without the support of republican institutions and principles, international law would become the nebulous assertion of rival moralities, without authority to control state behavior or to limit individual self-interest in any specific situation.

Only republican structures of government can legitimately determine the content of international law sufficiently accurately to deserve deference from actors in the international arena. Republican deliberation confirms the nature of existing international norms. Neither treaties, nor practice, nor democratic majorities, nor academic declarations of rights can stand as proxies for real moral discourse in settling the content of the law. The right to republican government under international law is the ultimate source of all international obligations, just as the right to republican government is the only real source of obligation in domestic systems of law. Governments exist for the collective and individual well-being of those subject to their control. When they violate human well-being, states forfeit their authority to rule.

8
International Relations and International Law

The most obvious difference between students of international relations and students of international law arises from the subjects of their inquiry. International relations scholars consider the relations between states. International law considers the norms that govern these relationships (and many other important transactions). Some have characterized this distinction as the difference between "realism" and "idealism," the difference between what actually is done and what *ought* to be done by states.[1]

When international relations specialists encounter international law, their response has been to ask: "how important is persuasion on the basis of norms in contemporary world politics?"[2] Such scholars seldom inquire about the norms themselves, but generally assume that all international law rests on "legal agreements" between governments or "treaty rules" established by states. This conception of international law reflects the international relations community's special interest in *state* action, and corresponds to the political theory of Thomas Hobbes, who derived legal obligations from contracts between individuals or states.[3] This reduces international law to a single principle, the rule that "*pacta sunt servanda.*"

1. Treaties

Few states always respect their treaties. Nor should they, under international law. Just as written contracts bind individuals in some situations, but not others, so states have obligations that may override treaties. The Statute of the International Court of Justice mentions "international custom," "general principles of law recognized by civilized nations," "judicial decisions," and "the teachings of the most highly qualified publicists of the various nations," as the basis for judicial decisions in accordance with international law, in addition to "international conventions" and "rules expressly recognized the contesting states."[4] Treaties are *evidence* of the law of nations, inasmuch as they reflect a consensus about international norms, but they are not the sole *source* of law, which rests instead upon fundamental truths about basic questions of right and wrong.[5]

Political scientists often study elites, who seek to acquire and to maintain power by invoking and manipulating international law to support their interests. This "instrumentalist" approach reflects a familiar facet of human nature. People often take the law as they find it, to serve their private agendas. Structure the rules correctly, and such private interests will serve the public good, or at least inhibit excessive private depredations. This was the doctrine of Madison in the *Federalist*, following Adams, Montesquieu and Cicero before him.[6] International relations theory suggests how to manipulate rules and "regimes" to control the operation of "politics" among states. Multilateral treaties provide a tempting vehicle through which social scientists may impose their theories on reality.

International lawyers and political scientists converge in this desire to influence the real world. They also share a "scientific" interest in clarity and quantification, through which their disciplines build credibility in the academy. Treaties serve the dual role of providing concrete objects of study, and solid vehicles for influencing future doctrine. International relations studies offer lawyers most when legal scholars engage in self-conscious attempts to create new law. Lawyers need theories of human behavior to legislate effectively, which they borrow from political scientists' ideas about human nature in international relations.

2. Human nature

International law grows out of human nature, and above all out of the overwhelming human need for approval. People value their reputations, not just to facilitate future transactions, but also (and more importantly) as an independent good. People like to be well thought of. This explains why governments such as those in China and the former Soviet Union (for example) care so deeply about Western criticism of their human rights violations when there is no prospect of outside intervention or any other substantial material consequences. Criticism is harm enough in itself. Yet to suffer criticism, one must hear it. The single greatest constraint in international relations, beyond the bare balance of military power, is the profile of its public critics – the people whose voices are heard in discussing the actions of others.

The founders of international law as a modern discipline considered their subject to consist in explicating the law of nature, as applied to states. Grotius, Pufendorf and Vattel described what would be just, and generals applied their strictures.[7] Monarchs hired famous scholars, ostensibly for advice, but also to influence the course of future scholarship. Scholars provided the most detailed and articulate descriptions of international law, which politicians read and followed. The teachings of the most highly qualified publicists formed the relevant community of opinion, and governments deferred to their holdings.

Criticism is not all that governments fear. They also worry about what other governments will take offense at. Obvious rules of right, wrong and fairness determine this to some extent, but well-known writings and conventions also play a role. Rules governing prisoners, envoys and prizes all developed largely through the writings of European publicists. Any government seeking to manipulate law to its own advantage must consider not only the obvious strictures of fairness, but also what has been written on a given issue, and which writings had the greatest effect. International law as such, often has less influence on state action than states' perceptions of what opinion leaders will criticize as violations of international law.

3. Realism

How states and others experience the constraints imposed by international law will vary depending on the sources and nature of the rules involved. The most accurate "realist" test of such rules is not whether law "persuades" states,[8] but rather which norms actually influence behavior. The more widely accepted the rule, and the more clearly it is stated, the more likely that powerful states and their officers will defer to public opinion.

"Realist" scholars who deprecate the importance of rules, and stress the centrality of self-interest in all state actions, make their arguments more true simply by stating them, because stating such views alters the climate in which government officers make their decisions. Similarly, "idealist" scholars who discuss the content of international law and assume its relevance improve the likelihood that states will obey the law, simply by disapproving of those who do not. The more prominent the voices that pontificate about international law or international relations, the greater their likely influence on state practice.

People want to be good, to think well of themselves, and for others to approve their actions. This means that instrumentalists, seeking to manipulate international relations, will have to take into account what people believe to be right and wrong – the ultimate sources of international law. Such beliefs are manipulable, within limits, but determinate. People or states with shared interests can create their own interpretive communities, to reinforce self-interested misconceptions, but their discourse will be normative, even when it is insincere.

4. Effectiveness

Normative discourse is most effective when it clarifies rules that actually apply, or creates a climate of acceptance for rules that may (or may not) apply in fact. This is not the same as legitimacy. "Legitimate" rules actually apply. "Effective" rules may not actually apply, but are widely accepted anyway. Effectiveness is evidence of legitimacy, but not conclusive. Situations often arise in which all nations will benefit from a given rule. This makes the rule legitimate and usually effective too. But groups of nations may sometimes impose rules for their own benefit, which are the illegitimate product of "effective" normative discourse.

Principled beliefs have as much impact on international relations as mere interests because they provide the framework through which interests express themselves. What elites want out of life reflects what they believe a good life to be. How elites act in their dealings with others reflects what they believe that others will think of what they do. Effective normative discourse depends on these background realities. To manipulate international law one must understand its sources. Instrumentalists will not be effective until they understand the power of norms.

To suppose that instrumentalism and normative thinking are two optics, each incomplete without the other, mistakes their true relationship, which is hierarchical. "Realists" and "idealists" operate at two different levels of consciousness. Strong normative assertions (idealism) will have significant (realist) effects on international relations. Avoiding normative discourse has real (and unfortunate) consequences. The purpose of international institutions should be to support the open, free and independent discourse that produces legitimate effective legal norms.

5. International relations and international law

The fields of international relations and international law diverged because some doubted the efficacy of norms in the international arena.

After decolonization, the Second World War, and two centuries of European revolutions, such doubts betray a very shallow sense of history. Once the power of ideology is admitted, its sources must be examined even when it is insincere. Truth and the semblance of truth about justice can have tremendous influence over human behavior, but public consensus is decisive. People care about what other people say and think, which explains the power of international law. There can be no cooperation without norms, no laws without a sense of justice.

International law coordinates international behavior by providing the framework through which private interests express themselves. Much more than the positive law of states, international law evades definitive interpretation. This gives scholars a considerable voice in its development, and corresponding influence over international affairs. Their discourse helps to shape the perceptions of governments, to create new constraints on those pursuing international goals. What a shame it would be if scholars squandered this influence in a discussion of tactics and state interests without considering the rules that make sense of public lives, and bring order to international affairs.

9
Justice and the Rule of Law in International Relations

No inquiry into international law, and its place in the international order, can get very far (or make much sense) without a theory of what law is, and what makes the law worthwhile. The answer to both questions is this: the central element of law in every legal system – what makes law "law" as distinct from other systems of rules or coercion – is law's claim to codify justice. All laws and legal systems claim to realize justice. Rules that do not claim justice cannot claim to be laws.[1] This is not to say that all laws are just, but rather that all legal systems claim to be just, or to realize justice better than other available systems for mediating conflicts and regulating human society.

Applied to international relations this means that international norms always claim to be just when they seek recognition as "law" to govern the actions of states (or other international persons or behavior). For example, a hegemonic power might seek to impose its own world-view as "law" on other, less-powerful states, but in doing so would also claim to be enforcing "justice," which is to say, enforcing norms that ought to be obeyed, even without coercion. Such norms may not be just, but they must claim to be just. The frank imposition of unjust norms on subservient populations would not be law, without the claim of justice to support it.

1. The rule of law

The rule of law is the system, much praised since antiquity, in which "*imperia legum potentiora est quam hominum*" – "the rule of law is more powerful than the rule of men." The value of this method of government, as advocated by Aristotle, Livy, and their successors in Italy, England, France and the United States of America,[2] depends on the assumption that law serves justice, which is to say the common good of all those subject to its rule.[3] If the law serves justice, then the rule of law will realize justice, while rule by the will of individual men or women would serve private interests, against the common good of the community as a whole.

The value and desirability of the rule of law depends entirely upon its efficacy in securing justice. While all law claims to be just, not all laws always are just. One could easily imagine a legal regime in which laws claiming to be just in fact systematically advanced the unjust ends of a ruling elite or dictator. This makes the actual success of any legal system's service to justice the only effective measure of its value and binding force on any supposed subjects of its legal control. Unjust legal systems do not deserve deference, although prudence may dictate circumspection in defying their power, so long as they enforce their will.[4]

The rule of law secures predictability, even in unjust regimes, by providing known regulations in advance. When laws rule, and not men, people can plan their actions, based on the law's known provisions, even when these are not just. Since laws always claim to be just, the identification and application of law may tend to soften the rule of even very unjust regimes. By seeking to present their edicts as "law," and therefore deserving respect, even despots and oligarchs must claim concern for the general welfare and common good of the people. This may encourage or at least allow some judges and others to apply the law more justly than insincere and self-seeking legislators had intended them to.

2. Natural law

Law that actually would be just in a given situation may be thought of as the "natural law." This natural law is the law that all legal systems claim to seek and to impose, although none will ever fully do so. Some may claim simply, with Thomas Hobbes, that natural law requires no more than to know one's superior's will, and to follow it.[5] This claim, like all other assertions that any system of norms should be recognized as "law," amounts to an assertion of justice. Thomas Hobbes believed "justice" to be whatever the sovereign desires (short of mandatory self-immolation).[6] Few other theorists would be so bold, but anyone who speaks of "law" makes an implicit assumption that the system in question claims to realize the natural justice that all law necessarily claims to serve.

The actual validity[7] and legitimate authority[8] of any system of law depend on that system's usefulness in discovering and enforcing the natural law of any given situation. Supposed standards of international law (for example) deserve deference and obedience only to the extent that they either actually implement justice or (and this is the important point) represent a system of legislation more likely to realize justice than would unregulated conflicts, in which every individual simply decided for her- or himself what justice requires in any particular case.

International law differs from most other law in that its content is relatively unsettled. Most legal systems have widely accepted mechanisms for determining what the law requires when different views conflict. International law has no obvious legislature, judiciary or executive power. This means in many cases that disputes over issues of international law provoke direct appeals to natural law, because the mediating institutions that would settle disputes about the content of natural law are weak, missing or controversial. If international law is "the law of nature applied to nations" (as all law is, or claims to be) then the direct study of nature (i.e. human nature and needs) will be the best method for finding out what international law requires, when other methods fail.

3. The positive law

Legal systems exist to preclude the necessity of direct appeals to natural law in resolving disputes. Given human self-interest, self-righteousness, and the natural capacity for self-deception, perceptions of the natural law will often (perhaps usually) vary, whenever conflicts arise. Legal systems and the rule of law offer objective methods for determining what justice requires, so that one claimant can defer to the other, without trying the relative accuracy of their perceptions with violence or battle, (which the weaker or unluckier party will lose, whatever the actual merits of the claim). Legal systems produce "positive law" to clarify the content of natural law when different perceptions of justice collide.

Not all positive law will actually embody the natural law of the case, although positive law will always claim to do so. In fact, positive law may be mistaken, unjust, and unfair. If so, the legal system has failed, on its own terms, because all legal systems claim to find justice. The natural measure of any legal system's value, validity, and worthiness to be obeyed is its efficacy in doing what it claims to do – in realizing the justice of the case. If a legal system finds and enforces the just result better than would have happened in the absence of that legal regime, then its rule deserves deference, until a better system can be found to take its place.

The binding force and proper position of the "positive law" of international relations depends entirely upon its ability to implement a just world order to resolve international conflicts and controversies. Different proposed sources of law should be evaluated according to their usefulness in finding and maintaining a just world order, or as just a world order as will be possible, given the circumstances. This requires taking into account the world order that already prevails, to the extent that one does. If, for example, widely recognized positive law already exists in the form of "international custom" or treaties, then this "law," and the system that supports it as "law," must endorse it as "just." Whether such international "law" deserves deference will depend on whether this claim to establish justice is actually true (or not).

4. Justice in international relations

International law, like all law, claims to codify justice. Codifying justice is desirable because it precludes or settles conflicts, and prevents the imposition of the unjust desires of one state or person on another. The rule of law keeps those with power honest, by guiding their activities to serve the common good, rather than their own private interests or desires. This only works so long as good law rules. Not all laws serve justice as well as they claim to. The greater this gap between "natural" and "positive" law, the less the validity or legitimacy of the legal system in question, and the less it deserves to be obeyed.

International "law" is unusually vague in prescribing its positive laws. Debates about the content of international law often reduce themselves in the end to conflicts about natural law, or different possible conflicting sources of positive law, which may yield different results. Real benefits will follow when states establish a just system of positive law to resolve their international conflicts. No such system fully governs every conflict (yet). Until it does, states and scholars should seek to encourage the development of just institutions of international adjudication,[9] without relinquishing their direct commitment to natural law and justice. Those charged with interpreting international law should remember that all law claims to be "just" and frame their decisions accordingly, to secure the eventual rule of law in international relations.

10
The Elements of International Law

Henry Wheaton is the Blackstone of international law. By giving lawyers a simple, clear and convincing description of international law, as he understood it, Wheaton shaped the law of nations for his contemporaries, and their successors for at least half a century after his death. Wheaton's *Elements of International Law,* first published in 1836, went through many editions, culminating in the canonical eighth edition, with notes by Richard Henry Dana, Jr., published in 1866. Dana's became the most frequently cited version, and was selected by the Carnegie Endowment for reproduction in its series on the Classics of International Law. Wheaton' s *Elements of International Law* presents the classic statement of international law doctrine, as it was understood for most of the nineteenth century.

Wheaton's ideas still permeate the international legal order that they did so much to establish, but Wheaton himself is largely forgotten. Mentioned (if at all) only in quotations from nineteenth-century court decisions, Wheaton is seldom read and almost never cited. Yet no subsequent treatise has reached the same level of influence as Wheaton's *Elements,* and much of Wheaton's thinking remains embedded in the institutions of contemporary international law. Wheaton's arguments are worth reviewing and evaluating for their own sake, but also for the insights that they give into the philosophical foundations of the international legal order.

There has been a tendency among some recent scholars to exaggerate the separation between law and morality, even in international law.[1] A close look at Wheaton confirms how late and incompletely (if ever) this doctrine infiltrated accepted international law doctrine. Just as lawyers since Cicero have understood that states should be communities of free and equal citizens, associated in pursuit of the common good, so

Grotius, Wolff, Vattel, and Wheaton saw international law as supporting a community of free and independent states, associated together in pursuit of justice. The nature and moral independence of states requires a well-established set of laws to govern their community, just as human nature requires certain laws to regulate human society. The measure of both is justice.

This does not mean that people or states receive justice unmediated, directly from nature. They must turn instead to the evidence of history, public opinion, judicial decisions, custom, and other institutions that reveal justice through human behavior. Wheaton understood the value of collective perceptions in clarifying the details of international law. *The Elements of International Law* includes many specific precepts of international legal doctrine, supported by extensive citations to publicists, to decisions by various courts, and to other expressions of human opinion that show where history, morality, and universal consensus have generated specific rules of international conduct.

1. The sources of international law

Henry Wheaton identified justice as the ultimate arbiter of international law,[2] making use of those principles "which sound policy dictates as necessary to the security of any state."[3] Europeans first recognized these maxims through their study of the canon law and Roman civil law, as revived by Spanish casuists and learned professors at the University of Bologna. The Professors of Roman law were the public jurists and diplomats of their age and continued to be so even after the Protestant Reformation of Europe. Naturally, such learned men looked to well-recorded Roman civil law precedents to discover the basic requisites of justice, and to settle international disputes.[4]

The value that Wheaton saw in Grotius and other public jurists[5] is the benefit that he himself offered to statesmen by writing impartially to clarify justice, as revealed through reason and experience. What Wheaton's treatise on the "reciprocal duties of sovereign states" lacked in the force of "positive law," it gained through the moral sanction of enlightened opinion, responding to truth and sound reason.[6] Wheaton's concentration on the relationship between states might seem at times to endorse the positivism that he elsewhere explicitly rejected,[7] but Wheaton always measured international law according to "the principles of justice" which "ought to regulate the mutual relations of nations."[8]

Wheaton adapted his formal definition of international law from James Madison, believing that: "international law, as understood among civilized nations, may be defined as consisting of those rules of conduct which reason deduces, as consonant to justice, from the nature of the society existing among independent nations; with such definitions and modifications as may be established by general consent."[9] Wheaton sought specific evidence for the content of international law from (in order of importance): first, the writings of publicists; second, treaties; third, the ordinances of particular states; fourth, the adjudications of international tribunals; fifth, private government archives; and finally, from history itself, of how states have behaved in the past, and what they recognize as justice.[10] The primacy that Wheaton gave to publicists, and their views, in determining international law, depended on their impartiality, as recognized by statesmen, and so ultimately on reason itself.[11]

2. States

Wheaton's treatise concerns states, and their mutual relations.[12] States, in this context, constitute separate political societies, supreme in their own spheres, and independent from outside authority.[13] Wheaton posited a "great society" of states, with determinate rights and duties between them.[14] Membership in this society depended on mutual recognition,[15] with sanctions enforced by opinion.[16] But the fundamental rights which all states enjoy with regard to each other derive from their separate existence as independent moral beings. Wheaton calls these basic rules the "absolute" international rights of states.[17] There are also "conditional" rights, derived from particular conditions and circumstances.[18]

The "absolute" rights of states include self-preservation, self-defence, peaceful expansion, peaceful internal development,[19] and all the other ordinary processes of self-realization naturally due to independent moral actors living in a "state of nature."[20] International law depends for its efficacy entirely upon "moral sanctions," not including the resort to arms, except in exceptional circumstances.[21] Wheaton hesitated to articulate the particular conditions of any specific "right to intervention," for fear that states would abuse it, as a pretext for invasion.[22] He approved Britain's vigorous resistance to any overarching world government, that might presume to regulate the internal affairs of other states.[23] This policy of non-interference extended to protecting the independence of Spain's former American colonies, which Wheaton approved.[24] Wheaton supposed that the principles of international law might sometimes justify interference to *support* wars of national liberation "when the general interests of humanity are infringed by the excesses of a barbarous and despotic government"[25] or the "general peace" and "balance of power" are threatened.[26] This despite every state's right "as a distinct moral being" independently to alter or abolish its own municipal constitution of government,[27] without the interference of others.[28] The difference here lies in Wheaton's distinction between "barbarous" and "civilized" governments. "Civilized" governments, established for the good of their own citizens, enjoy a right to autonomy which "barbarous" governments, acting despotically to dominate and exploit their own subjects, do not.[29]

This illuminates the circumstances in which independent states may properly enforce the universal law of nations. Wheaton suggested (for example) that piracy was a crime by the universal law of nations, while slavery was not.[30] The "general, ancient and admitted practice" of states, their treaties, and various transactions of civilized nations had once accepted slavery and the slave trade. To make these crimes "by the universal law of nations" (Wheaton believed) would require a treaty, or universal change in state practice.[31] Notwithstanding that the slave trade was, as John Marshall observed (and Wheaton admitted), "contrary to the law of nature," nonetheless the enslavement of those defeated in lawful wars was an ancient practice, still widely recognized in Africa, where many European states had been willing to purchase such slaves. Universal practice and opinion had once supported the slave trade and so (Wheaton supposed) must the law.[32]

3. Jurisdiction

The law of nations, as recognized in Wheaton's day by "all civilized and commercial states throughout Europe" was in part unwritten, and in part conventional. Wheaton sought the unwritten law first "in the great principles of reason and justice," but then also in the judicial decisions of various tribunals in every country, which tend to make the unwritten law more "fixed" and "stable."[33] The mutual independence of states leaves them without any common arbiter or judge, and so each must, in the end (of necessity) become a judge for itself against the others, whenever they disagree.[34] The rules of law that Wheaton laid down tried to restrain this discretion and prevent the "clear and open denial of justice."[35]

Wheaton understood that older and less humane rules of international conduct had gradually been replaced by newer and better principles, when publicists such as Grotius and Vattel articulated new standards. The law of nature often supplies a rule (such as proportionality) which publicists and practice make more complete.[36] This "progress of civilization" (as Wheaton recognized) was not complete in his own time,[37] despite the efforts of enlightened statesmen,[38] nor is it even now. In many cases justice fails from an absence of reciprocity. For one state, unilaterally, to embrace the just rule might leave it defenseless against the others.[39] When one state exercises its jurisdiction unjustly, to harm another's nationals, Wheaton believed that the second state may respond with reprisals, to prevent "the denial of justice."[40]

Wheaton explained that the jurisdiction to legislate and to enforce the law in each separate and independent state properly extends throughout that state's own territory, to its own nationals (wherever situated), to offences committed on its vessels on the high seas, and "to the punishment of piracy, and other offences against the law of nations, by whomsoever and wheresoever committed."[41] Regarding pirates and other international criminals,[42] Wheaton believed that since these are "common enemies of all mankind," all nations have an equal interest in their apprehension and punishment.[43] Wheaton did not accept that the international law of his period extended to the punishment of ordinary murders on the high seas,[44] or to preventing the African slave trade,[45] except as between nations that had mutually agreed to do so.[46]

Here Wheaton' s commitment to "reason" and to "nature" gave way to a positivistic doctrine of previous consent. When states had first consented to the slave trade, a right had vested, such that states could not now withdraw their consent, to reflect their new sense of justice.[47] Wheaton elsewhere accepted that "the progress of civilization" can change international law to support "the serious interests of mankind,"[48] so Wheaton's views on slavery stand revealed as products of his own moral blindness. His position would seem to have been that once universal consent has recognized a doctrine of universal international law, that doctrine may not be superseded, except by subsequent universal consent.

4. The elements of international law

The relationship between Wheaton's fundamental principle of international law ("justice") and his subsidiary measure ("consent"),[49] depends on a belief (borrowed from Grotius) that justice itself requires good faith, even in war.[50] Thus treaties and agreements become binding, even when unjust, through the underlying moral obligation to keep one's word (with certain obvious exceptions).[51] Wheaton accepted a doctrine of "moral impossibility," which sometimes limits this binding influence of treaties. "Moral impossibility" arises when fulfilling a treaty engagement would injure third parties.[52] Coerced consent would also void treaties, because coercion violates justice.[53]

The value of Wheaton today lies less in the specifics of his explanation of international law (as it existed in his day), than his underlying conception of where law comes from, and the purposes that law serves. If international law consists in "those rules of conduct which reason deduces, as consonant to justice, from the nature of the society existing among independent nations,"[54] then the justice and nature of this international society will merit close attention. Wheaton's work should remind contemporary scholars of international law that there can be no law without justice, no justice without community, and no international community without reflection about the underlying purposes which all states exist to serve.

The greatest weakness of Wheaton's *Elements* lies in his overwhelming commitment to states, as the sole and unique subjects of international law. States provide a useful vehicle for codifying and enforcing international law, but not to the exclusion of individual justice (as Wheaton himself admits). The strong analogy made in international law from Grotius to Wheaton between the liberty and equality of the individuals within the state, and the liberty and independence of the state within international society, breaks down when states deny their citizens' rights at home. Wheaton's commitment to justice in international society offers a vehicle for correcting despotic states, which contradicts his occasional moral obtuseness. His emphasis on "civilized" states disparages "barbarism" and injustice.

Wheaton's distinction between "civilized" and "barbarous" nations lies at the heart of his practical legacy. Both terms seem crude and impolitic to modern sensibilities, but they capture important truths about the structure of international society, still recognized in the Statute of the International Court of Justice.[55] Not all states deserve a place in the community of "civilized" nations, because not all states meet even the minimum requirements of justice. Standards of membership can and should rise, as enlightenment advances, just as it has since the twelfth century in the context of a civilian tradition, derived from Rome. Wheaton understood the purposes of international law better than many contemporary lawyers, but also its nature and sources. "Le droit international, ou droit des gens positif, est fondé sur la morale internationale, qu'on a ordinairement appelée le droit des gens naturel."[56]

11
Universal Human Rights

One central measure of a government's legitimate membership (or not) in the international community of nations is the respect that it demonstrates (or not) for fundamental human rights. Human rights are justified moral claims that human beings make on other human beings on the basis of their common humanity. Universal human rights are an important measure of any government's legitimacy, because they apply in all societies everywhere. This does not mean that all peoples should demand exactly the same structure of rights in their different communities. Circumstances differ from place to place and are never exactly the same. But sincere deliberation about the application of universal human rights to a particular set of circumstances yields remarkable consensus across cultures. Circumstances vary, but human nature does not. Disagreements about the sources, application, enforcement, and limits of universal human rights usually turn on private interests, rather than real differences of perception or understanding.

1. The nature of human rights

Human rights arise from human nature, in that the concept of human rights assumes certain similarities between human beings that justify their moral claims on each other. Like other sorts of rights, human rights depend upon the existence of a shared community, whose membership justifies claims against other members. In this case, the community in question embraces all of humanity. The concept of human rights rests on the assumption that in some relevant respects all human beings deserve equal consideration and dignity. To deny this premiss would be to deny the existence of *human* rights and to substitute a more limited conception of rights and community, excluding some part of humanity.

Moral claims, such as human rights, are claims about which standards of behavior *ought* to be respected and obeyed. Morality in this context means something more than the customs of a particular society. Moral claims assert an ethical obligation of obedience. They concern human duty, and in the case of human rights, general duties toward all of humanity. These duties derive their binding nature from underlying commitments to fundamental values. The value that supports the concept of human rights asserts the equality (in certain respects) of all human beings. As articulated in the Universal Declaration of Human Rights, the United Nations General Assembly has embraced, without dissent, the fundamental assumption that "all human beings are born free and equal in dignity and rights."[1]

The fundamental moral claim to a "right" to equal dignity as a human being is the parent of all the other human rights. Put in another way (as elaborated in the Universal Declaration), since all human beings are "endowed with reason and conscience," they should "act towards one another in a spirit of brotherhood."[2] Brothers care for each other's mutual welfare, and so (up to a point) should all human beings. Self-interest dictates this search for a formula through which all humans could live together in peace. The fraternity of all humanity should lead human beings to respect the liberty and equality which all deserve as members of the human race. Rights and liberty derive from the equal moral status of all human beings, which entails an equal moral claim to live worthwhile and rewarding lives.

The equal moral claim that all humans possess to live worthwhile and rewarding lives reveals other human rights, as the cosmopolitan community determines the necessary preconditions of worthwhile human existence. These rights are "natural" and eternal in the sense that they exist whether or not they are recognized by particular societies or individuals at any given time. Human rights derive directly from the circumstances of human existence. But they are also transient and mutable in the sense that the circumstances of human existence themselves can change. Different circumstances require different rights, although some "fundamental" rights may have very broad application. What does not change is the independent origins of universal human rights, and their common origin in the equal dignity of all human beings.

The universal rights that all human beings should enjoy in any given set of circumstances are "natural" rights because they derive from universal human nature. To deny human nature would be to deny human rights. But not all aspects of human nature can be fully realized in any given human being. Proposed enumerations of universal rights will have to temper the universality of human dignity with the particularity (and desirability) of a wide variety of different individual lives. The more basic the human need, the more fundamental the right. "Life, liberty and the pursuit of happiness" offer a well-known trinity of fundamental human rights,[3] to which the International Covenants added prohibitions such as those against torture, slavery, the denial of legal personality, and state interference with the freedom of thought, conscience or religion.[4]

Not all human rights are so fundamental as these, but the stipulation that human rights should be universal keeps the list from getting too long. All human beings desire the security of their persons.[5] But they also desire property,[6] work,[7] leisure,[8] and a reasonable standard of living.[9] These are universal human rights because they relate to universal needs, which humans wish equally to enjoy. Canonical lists, such as the United States Bill of Rights, the French Declaration of the Rights of Man, the Universal Declaration of Human Rights, and the international rights Covenants, all depend on the usually secularized assumption that "all men are created equal" and "endowed by their creator with certain unalienable rights" inherent in their status as human beings.[10]

Human nature determines the content and scope of universal human rights because rights exist to honor the equal dignity of all human beings. Since human nature is always and everywhere the same, or changes at the extremely slow pace of evolution through natural selection, the fundamental human rights can be determined with some precision. Human rights arise from human needs and desires, and one of the most fundamental human needs is the desire for the society of other human beings. The requirements of human society include the necessity of rights to control the incursions that human beings and their societies make upon individuals or disfavored groups, in constructing their common identity.

2. Tensions in universal human rights

Human rights arise from the contemplation of human nature in society, in pursuit of a community in which all human beings can live worthwhile and rewarding lives. This leads to two types of conflict in particular communities. First, the rights themselves may conflict, in the sense that the moral claims necessary to develop different aspects of human nature may be difficult to reconcile with one another. Second, the application of such rights to specific societies may differ, given their different histories and circumstances. The fact that all human beings enjoy universal human rights does not mean that human beings will or should enjoy identical rights in practice, within their different societies.

Difficulties emerge in trying to determine the application of universal rights to particular communities. Even when international consensus exists (as it frequently does) about the nature and content of universal human rights, observers may disagree sharply about how these rights should be implemented in practice. This gives a necessary primacy to certain procedural rights, which is to say, to rights concerning the procedures by which other rights will be recognized and applied. Governments should respect these necessary conditions of social cooperation. Societies that do not respect just political procedures are not legitimate, and do not deserve political respect themselves. Since social recognition is a necessary precondition of the actual enjoyment of universal human rights, the political structure of society will ultimately determine rights' actual existence in practice.

Democracy offers the central example of a procedural right that protects the realization of other rights, without supplanting them. The people who best understand the circumstances of any given society are its citizens. Decisions about the application of universal rights in practice should be in their hands, or subject to their control, because citizens know their own needs, and the nature of their own society. To deny any citizens a voice in this deliberation would deprive society of their insights, and result in mistakes that could have been avoided. The collective self-development of citizens also has an independent value, beyond the determination of rights and justice. But democracy is only one of several procedural mechanisms for making rights more certain in practice. Representation, elections, checks and balances, the separation of powers, bicameralism, and the rule of law are all at least equally important and equally constrained by the underlying purpose of human well-being.

Democracy makes mistakes in implementing human rights, because democracy favors majority views or the views of dominant political factions, above the common welfare. Women, for example, have never fully enjoyed their human rights, because they have been underrepresented in the governments of almost all human societies. Representation and inclusion will be necessary at all levels of politics and power, for women and other distinct groups in society, before rights can properly be implemented, or recognized in practice. All political actors and institutions should adopt an ethic of listening, through which they consciously recognize and accommodate the widest possible range of perspectives and experiences. All societies contain cultural or intellectual minorities, whose rights should be extended to reflect their own traditions and circumstances.

Governments and institutions have positive duties to realize the rights of citizens and individuals, just as they have negative duties not to violate individual rights. For example, the right to democracy requires governments to provide periodic and genuine elections to their citizens, but it also requires foreign governments to respect the results of such elections, and other institutions to support the people's right to vote. This does not mean that the right to democracy will require the same institutions in all societies. Democratic rights, like economic rights, require progressive development to achieve their full potential. But institutions and governments have a duty to take steps that will lead people towards a greater realization of their democratic and economic rights. The tension between universal rights and existing institutions should lead to institutional change within cultural traditions, to help them better to support the human rights of their subjects.

The limitations of human perception determine the procedural rights through which other rights should be recognized in practice. These procedural rights constitute the basic requirements of political legitimacy, because they supply the conditions of a just accommodation between rights and reality. Just procedures resolve tensions within and between universal human rights, both by reconciling conflicting rights that arise from different aspects of human well-being, and by adapting universal rights to specific societies, in the light of their own particular traditions and circumstances.

3. Enforcing universal human rights

Even rights that are well-known and well-adapted to existing societies will require enforcement. International consensus may exist (as it does) about the content of rights, or even that rights have been violated in particular instances, without offering an obvious remedy or punishment for transgressions. For centuries humanity has divided itself into states, and separate political communities. Within these societies citizens should have the power to vote and the other procedural guarantees of universal human rights. Sometimes they do not, or the procedures are incomplete or unsuccessful. This calls for outside enforcement, but in the absence of a functioning world government, it is not entirely clear how enforcement should take place. In practice, effective enforcement will depend upon the intervention of persons, organizations, or states, who seldom have the clear authority to do so.

States enjoy a peculiar status as the primary vehicles of human authority in the legitimate exercise of military and police power. States deserve their legitimacy because worthwhile lives develop best in civic communities. But this remains true only when communities respect the political rights (and therefore other rights) of their subjects. When states respect the political rights of their subjects, states constitute the best (and most legitimate) vehicle for realizing and enforcing their citizens' other rights and duties. States that disregard their subjects' political rights will also violate their subjects' other rights out of ignorance if not by design. In such cases states lose their legitimacy, and enforcement must come from somewhere else, outside the structures of ordinary state power.

Revolution provides one remedy for the enforcement of rights and duties in the absence of legitimate state power. The oppressed subjects of an illegitimate government may properly replace their rulers and reform their institutions when the state denies them their fundamental political and other rights. The legitimacy of revolution turns on the severity of the oppression and likelihood of peaceful reform. When unjust institutions have already set out on the path toward just reformation, the cost of violent revolution will be too high. Would-be revolutionaries should measure the possible benefits of force against the seriousness of the government's transgressions, and the likelihood of their revolution's eventual success.

The same is true of outside intervention, when undertaken by other institutions or states. Outsiders have less cause to intervene than internal revolutionaries, because their understanding of local circumstances will necessarily be clouded and incomplete. Nevertheless, human rights violations will sometimes reach levels that justify outside intervention. Humanitarian intervention to enforce universal human rights should be proportionate to the offense, in the sense that intervention should not cause more harm than it prevents. Outside enforcement through humanitarian intervention should take into account the expectation of resistance, which raises the cost of interfering. Would-be enforcers of universal human rights should also consider the danger of creating a precedent for officious intermeddling in other nations' affairs.

The primary danger of relying on foreign humanitarian intervention to enforce universal human rights is the possibility of mistake about the necessity of using force, based on incomplete information, self-interest, or both. The best guard against such mistakes are the same procedural techniques that guard against mistakes within the borders of legitimate states. Democracy, checks and balances, the rule of law, the separation of powers, broad participation, and other procedural protections should control outside decisions to intervene in much the same way that they control and justify the actions of legitimate states – by being more likely to answer fundamental questions correctly than other forms of political deliberation would be.

The best enforcement mechanism for universal human rights and duties when states forsake their responsibilities would be an international police force, under the direction of a procedurally legitimate international federation or organization, leading to trial before a legitimate international court. The source of legitimacy in such cases would be the same procedural protections that should be enjoyed within states in implementing the rights of their citizens. Existing international institutions fall far short of this standard, but may in some cases be sufficiently more legitimate than existing national institutions to warrant intervention, to prevent particularly egregious human rights violations.

The International Criminal Court provides one recent example of an international institution intended to facilitate the enforcement of international human rights standards against the most flagrant abuses. The Rome Statute of the International Criminal Court establishes a tribunal of last resort to enforce prohibitions against the most serious international crimes. When member states fail impartially to enforce international prohibitions against war crimes, genocide, and crimes against humanity, the International Criminal Court can assert jurisdiction to punish violations. The Court's authority derives from the status of its signatory member states. To the extent that they are not democracies or in other ways legitimate themselves, the Court loses its derivative claim to legitimacy.

The United Nations Security Council, the North Atlantic Treaty Organization, the European Union, the Organization of American States, the United States and other sometime would-be enforcers of universal human rights, derive their authority to intervene (or not) through the same procedural tests that apply within states. The broader the federation and the more democratic and otherwise procedurally legitimate its processes of internal deliberation, the greater an organization's authority to intervene to prevent human rights violations. The authority to intervene is always greatest when rights violations occur within a federation's own territory, as in the American South during the Civil War, but democracies may also have the authority to intervene against very serious external crimes, such as genocide and the slave trade.

4. Rights *in extremis*

The claim that human rights are universal implies that they should never be denied. This cannot be true to the extent that different rights may sometimes conflict, nor is it absolutely true even after such conflicts have been resolved. The International Covenant on Civil and Political Rights recognizes, for example, that "in times of public emergency which threatens the life of the nation and the existence of which is officially proclaimed, the States Parties to the present Covenant may take measures derogating from their obligations."[11] The covenant also enumerates a shorter list of rights from which there should never be any derogation in any circumstances,[12] such as the right to life,[13] the right against torture,[14] the right against slavery,[15] the right of legal personality,[16] and freedom of religion.[17]

The supposition that there are certain fundamental rights from which no derogation should ever be permitted, even by formal consent, has played a large role in the development of international law,[18] but even these fundamental precepts of humanity may sometimes seem unduly restrictive, *in extremis*. History reveals several instances in which the bombing of cities, the destruction of agriculture, and the indiscriminate slaughter of civilians have been justified by their perpetrators as necessary to prevent even greater violations of fundamental human rights.

Terrorists have suggested that the purposeful slaughter of civilians may in some cases be the only defense available against powerful adversaries, who enjoy an enormous military advantage. Terrorist attacks against democracies are particularly effective, because terrified ordinary citizens in democracies have the ability to influence national policy, and share a part of the national guilt, when democratically adopted policies are unjust. The greater the transgression against ordinary norms of humanity, such as those that protect women, children, and noncombatants against attack, the greater the impact on public opinion and possible effectiveness of terrorist tactics. Non-state terrorism would be on this theory more justified than terrorism by states, because states have other effective methods at their disposal to achieve their ends, that smaller, less powerful groups do not.

Responses to terrorism raise precisely the same set of questions from the opposite perspective. Since terrorists are willing to slaughter innocents in large numbers to influence public policy, states sometimes claim a reciprocal license to disregard fundamental human rights to life, against torture, or other rights which make it difficult to stop terrorists who are willing to exploit the moral fastidiousness of liberal societies. Suicidal terrorists are particularly difficult to deter, and capable of particularly serious attacks. Terrorists successes lead to loss of life so large that governments have been tempted to disregard rights against torture and incarceration without trial, in order to preempt the terrorists before they strike.

Deliberate contemplation of the role of human rights in extreme circumstances makes it clear that there is a hierarchy of rights, which citizens hold not only against their governments, but against each other. The right to life is more important than the right to vote, which is more important than the right to a free press, which is more important than the right to leisure. A well-adjusted polity will protect all four, but in certain extreme circumstances protecting lives may require restrictions on speech, or free movement. All such restrictions reflect failures in social organization. The central concept of a right implies a justified claim that one citizen can make against others. When balancing rights becomes necessary, the structure of rights will be weakened. Any deprivation of rights without the due process of a just legal system destroys the superstructure of human dignity that justifies societies to their subjects.

The rights to life, against torture, against slavery, and to legal personality, should never suffer derogation, because they set minimum standards below which human welfare becomes impossible. Terrorism, torture, and slavery should never be tolerated, whether practiced by states or individuals, because they violate the fundamental presumption of human dignity, from which all other rights derive. All necessary exceptions to this fundamental rule are captured in the right to self-defense, narrowly construed. Even *in extremis*, the shared community of human nature remains, to govern the claims that humans make against each other, on the basis of their common humanity.

5. Universal human rights

Universal human rights arise from the attributes in which all human beings are alike, which includes their fundamental need to live together in the society of other human beings. Natural morality grounds rights in society, because human nature grounds individuals in societies. Rights arise from the social necessity of taking the needs and dignity of others to some extent into account. Discussions across cultures quite readily achieve a substantial consensus about the nature, scope, purpose, and vindication of universal human rights. This consensus mirrors and elaborates a similar consensus among states. Once a person or a government grants the premiss that human beings belong to a single species, the whole superstructure of rights follows, on moral, practical, and prudential grounds.

The nature of universal human rights arises from similarities between universal human needs and abilities throughout the world. If human beings deserve some measure of equal concern and respect everywhere, then their moral claim to certain equal rights should follow. All humans have an interest in living together in peace. Respect for universal rights will make this happy result possible, by constructing societies in which all members can live worthwhile lives. Oppression, exclusion and other violations of fundamental rights lead to conflict and violence, by destroying the common purpose that holds human communities together. Rights, like societies, exist to serve the common good, which embraces the separate welfare of all members of the group.

Tensions in universal human rights reflect the differing circumstances of different individuals and communities. Some human needs and abilities are difficult to reconcile with one another, and various places and their histories give rise to variant types of society. Procedural rights reconcile the tensions that arise in applying universal rights in practice, by providing just techniques for reconciling rights to reality. Diversity within and between societies provides humanity with a valuable range of perspectives and experiences. Procedural rights to democracy, the separation of powers, the rule of law and other political checks and balances protect minority cultures and traditions, as well as the common good. Rights protect diversity and minorities against the tyranny of majority opinion.

Enforcing universal human rights requires the same respect for diversity and difference between political societies and states that should exist within them. States that respect the procedural and other rights of their citizens should not usually be subject to outside interference, even when they make what seem to be mistakes about individual rights and justice. States and governments that disregard political rights deserve less deference, but should not be subject to interference without good reason. The best test of the value of international intervention to enforce human rights against illegitimate states would be the widest possible democratic deliberation, through the same set of procedural safeguards that should have existed within each state in the first place. The best enforcement mechanism for universal human rights would be just political structures within the world's separate societies. Just international institutions should intervene to enforce rights only when existing national institutions have failed.

Extreme circumstances may modify the application of universal human rights, by altering the moral calculation that supports them. The standard example concerns fundamental threats to the existence of society, which justify derogations from some individual and economic rights. The more fundamental the right, the harder it becomes to imagine circumstances that would justify its suspension, but even the most important rights may have limits. For example, self-defense may justify the taking of life, when innocent lives are in danger. Terrorism against civilians will almost never be justified in this way, because civilians seldom have responsibility for or control over sufficiently large-scale threats to human life, but attacks against public officials might be justified when the danger they pose to others is proportionately severe. The test of proportionality should always restrain any derogations from human rights, since human rights supply the ultimate basis of society.

Universal human rights derive their existence from human nature, overcome their tensions through balanced deliberation, deserve enforcement through international cooperation, and should apply even *in extremis*, because they constitute the foundation of every just society. Human rights impose moral order on a divided world, by appealing to the needs and abilities that every person shares. That is why rights have proved so hard to deny, once they have been articulated, even in the most unjust states. Human rights are justified moral claims that human beings make on other human beings on the basis of their common humanity. Each of us would wish to enjoy such rights, and most of us can understand the benefit of recognizing similar rights in others. It is to secure these rights that governments should exist, and when universal rights are not protected, new institutions will be needed, to restore the people's safety and happiness.[19]

12
International Legal Personality

One frequently mentioned right, guaranteed by the Universal Declaration, is the right to legal personality. Everyone has the right everywhere to recognition as a person before the law.[1] Many legal systems also recognize some non-human "persons" as legal persons under law. International law usually views states as "persons" in this sense, which raises the question which other collectives deserve to receive a similar status, and whether any real persons should ever be denied full legal personality in any circumstances at all.[2]

The concept of international legal personality is parasitic upon the concept of real human personality, which is to say, upon the actual existence of sentient human beings. "Personality" in its strictest sense signifies the separate existence of individual human characters, with their own emotions, desires, intentions, and ideas. Personality implies consciousness, and indeed, self-consciousness, in the possession of mental and moral qualities. The attribution of "legal" personality is a metaphor through which non-human, non-conscious entities, usually collectives, are described in the discourse of law as if they had mental and moral consciousness. "International legal personality" applies to those entities which international law regards as if they had independent personality. States are the paradigmatic example of this. Modern international law developed primarily through viewing states as if they were individuals, and elaborating the "natural law" which ought to apply between them.[3]

The metaphor of legal "personality" has always been and remains at the foundation of the international legal system. Hugo Grotius wrote of a great society of states maintained for the mutual advantage of all.[4] Christian Wolff described nations as "*personae morales*,"[5] associated in a great "*civitas maxima*," just as individual persons unite into their own particular polities.[6] Vattel understood nations or states to be moral persons, with their own will and understanding, as well as rights and obligations.[7] "Because nations are made up of men who are by nature free and independent ... their nations or sovereign states must in turn be regarded as free persons living together in a state of nature."[8] The moral authority of the state derives from the natural rights and freedom of the citizens it represents.[9] This justification of the power of states in international law, by derivation from the people that they represent, provides the primary basis for all treaty law, including the United Nations Charter, which presumes to speak on behalf of "We the peoples of the United Nations."[10]

The strength of this rhetorical device depends upon the perception that both law and states exist to serve the people, which is to say, real persons. The collective "people" evokes flesh and blood individuals, possessed of hopes, fears, desires, needs, and a set of rights and duties protected by the legal system under which they live.[11] Legal "persons" in any given legal system necessarily include all the real persons subject to that system, but often also some class of fictive "persons," which is to say, associations or groups of real persons, given collective rights and duties by the governing legal regime.[12] Sometimes animate creatures or inanimate objects also enjoy rights and duties, and so a sort of anthropomorphic personality, as when rocks or dogs are put on trial for murder or given legal protection against cruelty and thoughtless exploitation.[13] International law confers legal personality on states, giving them "rights" and "duties" in much the same way that real persons enjoy rights against injuries or assaults, and duties not to commit them.[14]

The existence of states as "juristic" or "moral" persons should not be allowed to obscure the purposes for which international law, like all law, exists, which is to say, for the common good and regulation of real persons.[15] States and other corporations act, if they act at all, through and upon real persons. German theorists sometimes speak in a disconcerting way, of the "collective will" ("*Gesamtwille*") of a corporate body or the state.[16] But no one can deny the culpability of statesmen who violate international law, or the rights of those that they oppress in violation of international protections.[17] Some legal systems limit the capacity of certain persons, such as minors, to act in certain ways. This does not diminish their personality, but rather their ability to act independently from those who have care of their interests.

The very name of "international law" was coined to emphasize the personality of states, and the power of governments to express the collective will of their subjects.[18] Henry Wheaton articulated the nearly universal nineteenth-century consensus when he described international law as "consisting of those rules of conduct which reason deduces, as consonant to justice, from the nature of the society existing among independent nations."[19] This passage describes a "*ius inter gentes*" (law between nations) rather than "*ius gentium*" in the older sense,[20] and much of international law has come to reflect this statist way of looking at things. (Human rights law necessarily retained a more direct concern for the real human persons.)[21] The Charter of the United Nations still takes states as its primary constituency,[22] while also recognizing the importance of international "human rights" and "fundamental freedoms,"[23] which members must promote and respect.[24]

The role of international legal personality in conferring legitimacy upon the power of states in international affairs has obscured the significance of personality, the purposes of international law, and the legitimacy of international institutions by focussing on the circumstances in which non-human entities can achieve juristic personality, rather than the value of real human personality in justifying international law. The most famous case on international legal personality, the *Reparation for Injuries* case, concerns the right of non-state international organizations to raise claims for injuries before the International Court of Justice.[25] The International Court of Justice exists primarily for the purpose of adjudicating disputes between states,[26] so it should not be surprising that its jurisprudence on personality tends to focus on the extent to which other legal persons resemble states in their ability to bring international claims. But this should not be allowed to obscure the central element of legal personality, which concerns the rights and duties of real persons.

International legal personality differs from the artificial legal personality of other legal systems, not in the nature or even (usually) in the identity of persons, but rather in the mechanisms through which their rights and duties can be vindicated. Thus those who would deny individual persons "or particular organizations" standing to vindicate their rights in international tribunals have often phrased their objections in terms of "legal personality," when what was really at issue was whether the legal system did or should give a direct cause of action to a particular person before a particular court. Just as in the old common law a woman had legal rights and duties, but the power to vindicate them rested, when she married, entirely in her husband, so persons and corporations may have rights or duties under international law which only their national government can vindicate in international tribunals.[27]

This does not diminish individual legal personality, but rather the power to take legal action in certain circumstances.

The confusion between personality and standing may lead to injustice, when the absence of standing is taken as the absence of enforceable rights. Personality concerns the possession of rights and duties. Standing concerns the vindication of rights and duties. The absence of standing should not be understood to imply the absence of rights (or personality). As the *Mavrommatis* case makes clear, lacking the power to act in certain international tribunals does not negate the underlying rights which others may raise (or not) in defense of one's interests. Standing is a question of systemic utility and representation. Personality is a question of identity and morality.

The international legal system is justified (or not) by the justice and accuracy with which it recognizes and protects international rights and duties. The first consideration concerns legal personality and the second concerns standing. There is no question that individual human beings, as well as many sorts of artificial persons, have rights and duties under international law. If they have rights or duties, then they have legal personality, because legal personality signifies nothing more than to have interests which the community recognizes as deserving of social protection, or abilities which the community supposes to require restraint. International prohibitions against war crimes, for example, recognize the personality *both* of the victims *and* of the perpetrators of the prohibited acts.

Some would say that to have personality means also to have the power personally to vindicate one's rights,[28] but this is a simple confusion between the possession of a right and the protection of a right. The protector or administrator of a right is conceptually separate from the subject of the right. Much of modern international law rests on the possibility of making this distinction. States in modern international law claim to act on behalf of (and in vindication of the rights of) their citizens. If their citizens did not have rights, and therefore personality, the state would lose the primary justification for its existence.

The move to deny individual persons their legal personality is also a move to deny them their rights. Governments that wish to avoid their international obligations have challenged individual legal personality, but this is a self-defeating tactic, because the state's own claim to legitimacy under international law rests on the separate (and collective) personalities of the persons subject to its rule. More sophisticated states admit individual personality but deny their subjects the separate capacity to vindicate their rights themselves, as parents speak for their children, or guardians act for the mentally impaired.

This sort of paternal relationship may be appropriate in certain circumstances, but it runs the risk of mistaking the real needs of its subjects. Just as coverture in the common law contributed to the subordination of women, so unfettered power to speak on behalf of the collective may lead governments into injustice. Those with the power to make decisions on behalf of others will tend to favor themselves, which is why there has been a trend toward the emancipation of subject classes, giving them a right to speak for themselves. Persons without the legal capacity to protect their own rights have found their rights more often overlooked, than those who could assert their rights directly in courts.

People prefer to have the capacity to vindicate their own rights, through access to courts, rather than leaving the protection of their rights in the hands of others. State-centered courts, such as the International Court of Justice, or state-based institutions, such as the United Nations, necessarily privilege the interests of governments over those of their people, because the people have no direct access to court proceedings. The most vigorous enforcement of individual rights under international law has historically taken place in national courts, which are more accustomed to considering the status of individuals. Individuals not only have rights and duties, and therefore legal personality under international law, they also have standing to vindicate their rights in some courts, including national courts, as in the United States. Individuals who can vindicate their own rights in court will be more likely to enjoy their rights in practice than those who cannot.

This brief review of the nature of personality clarifies the relationship between real persons and artificial persons in international law. The artificial personality of organized groups of individuals, such as corporations or states, exists to expand individual rights by allowing individuals to act collectively. States and other collectives can defend and enhance the rights of their members, which is why they deserve the protection of law. This should not be taken to diminish the concurrent personality of real human individuals. To do so mistakes the purposes and justification of law, which is to enrich the lives of its subjects.

States and international lawyers should wish all individuals to enjoy their rights in practice, because the legitimacy of government depends upon this result. International law as a Benthamite *ius inter gentes* rests on the metaphor according to which the state subjects of international law resemble the individual citizens they rule and claim to represent. States derive their just powers from the needs of their subjects. This has led many states ro recognize that individual citizens have legal rights and duties, which is to say, legal personality. States also assert their own fictive collective legal personality, on the basis of the persons that they serve. To deny the legal personality of individuals would threaten the legal personality of the state. Scholars and judges who carelessly do so, are undermining the foundations of public international law.

13
What Are Peoples and Nations?

Words mean what we want what we want them to mean (as Humpty Dumpty once observed), "neither more nor less."[1] This gives meaning a certain fluidity,[2] since what one wants or needs from words can change. Yet words also represent ideas about reality, and are more or less useful as they capture and perpetuate useful ideas with language.[3] This pushes meaning towards stability, resting on history and experience. Some tension will always remain between what words have meant, and what words might usefully come to mean, to serve new circumstances. "Truth consists in the right ordering of names in our affirmations" (as Hobbes so sensibly recognized), so that those who wish to pursue the truth will have to decide what the words that they use will mean, or find themselves eventually "entangled in words, as a bird in lime twigs; the more he struggles, the more belimed."[4]

"Peoples," "nations," and "states" have evolved through so lazy a muddle of mangled usage and etymology that none developed their meanings unobstructed, without some negligent author's careless definition to mar and confuse them. Bad definitions have led to such absurdities that reason cannot repair them, "without reckoning anew from the beginning, in which lies the foundation of their errors."[5] The best way to distinguish the three separate concepts of "people," "nation," and "state," will be by looking at their etymologies and dominant usage over time, beginning with their origins, to establish the central and distinct separate zones of meaning at the heart of each of these frequently overlapping concepts.

All three words developed out of Latin political vocabulary left over from the turbulent history of Rome. The people or "*populus*" first signified the citizens of a common territory, country or state, with common laws and a common system of justice.[6] The nation or "*natio*" first signified an ancestral tradition or shared hereditary culture among people who might (or might not) also share a common country or citizenship.[7] The state signified the form of polity or government established in a country, and hence the supreme civil power in that country, ruling over a particular people or *populus*.[8] Finally, as a necessary modern appendage to these preceding definitions, "country" has been used to signify a region, district, or (more usefully) the land territory of a political state, or territorial homeland of a non-political nation.[9]

The relationship between peoples, nations and states follows naturally from each word's central political meaning, or definition, as derived from usage, etymology, and justice. Each state has a people and a territory, subject to its ultimate coercive control.[10] From these stable foundations, states usually aspire to create nations among their citizens, bringing the people together with a common sense of purpose and fraternity. Sometimes the people and nation do not coincide, when one nation oppresses or dominates another, within the confines of a single state. Then the dominated or subordinate nation may wish for independence and a separate state of its own. Whether this should happen (creating two new peoples or *populi* from one former *populus*) will depend on circumstances, determining which constitution better suits the mutual needs of all the parties and separate members of society.

1. Nations

The very term "nation," deriving from *natus* ("born"), implies a common birth and cultural unity between co-nationals. Nations arise by nature from stable human cohabitation. Neighbors develop customs, a common language, shared habits, and cuisine through imitation and intermarriage over centuries. Within the natural borders of rivers, mountains, deserts and seas, nations have always emerged and adapted to suit their common country best. All known history consists of a series of examples of disparate individuals, brought together for whatever reason, gradually developing their common culture and nationality until some cataclysm of famine, invasion, war, immigration or disease tears the culture apart, to begin the evolution again, until the next disruption.

Nations once preceded states as society precedes the state, being simply earlier in time. Nations existed before states existed, and helped the first states to form, by providing a common identity to support them. Later, when the idea of statehood became more established, new states could form new nations, as in North America, England, Italy, France, and many former colonial possessions, where administrative boundaries fostered new cultural identities. Nations such as the French, British, and Pennsylvanians share largely invented identities, which finally became real through the common experiences of their peoples, promoted by government policy. Nationality strengthens statehood, and statehood nurses nationality, so that one would expect in a peaceful, stable world that all states would eventually become nations, and all nations gradually conform themselves to states.

As it happens the world has never stayed stable or peaceful for long, through misfortune, malevolence, and natural human aggression, cultivated by avarice and ambition. Passions have scattered the nations, as tyranny and conquest drove Scots to America, Huguenots to England, and Jews to Italy and France. Or as starvation and poverty drove Irish to America, Saxons to England, and Gauls to Italy and France. Or as thirst for wealth and plunder brought the Spanish to America, French to England, and Germans to Italy and France. Slavery and abduction, ethnic cleansing and genocide, conquest and corruption all drive nationals from their native countries to new homelands, where migrants retain for a while the national characteristics of their former lives, expressed in separate ethnicities or tribes.

The diversity of migrant nationalities contributes innovations and curiosities to the recipient culture, as immigrant identities gradually fade, creating a new community. Sometimes, however, discrimination and xenophobia prevent the natural assimilation of neighbors, by maintaining an exclusive citizenship that rejects immigrant nationals. Exclusion perpetuates differences by investing them with political significance. Discrimination by nationality sustains national differences that normally would not survive transplantation to new countries and circumstances. Parties within peoples often look for trivial differences of appearance or origin, around which to organize factions, for the elevation of some few citizens, to expropriate the liberty and property of the rest.

2. Tribes and ethnicity

Non-geographically based political subdivisions of citizens within the state are known as "tribes," a word derived from the Latin "*tres*" ("three"), reflecting the threefold ethnic division of Rome's original population. Sometimes national divisions among citizens survive as tribal affiliations, which distribute power and offices by ethnic and hereditary criteria, rather than by competence or geography. Tribes perpetuate separate national identities by naturalizing differences within the structure of the state. Sudden and uncontrolled incursions of population may require tribal recognition to prevent civil war. Fortunate or well-managed states gradually translate their tribes into regional identities wherever possible, to forestall dissension and maintain the equality of citizens before the law.

Tribes threaten national unity by maintaining separate public identities around which citizens can organize factions to dominate other citizens and plunder the state. Human nature structures social and moral life through unity and exclusion, encouraging altruism within and ruthless self-interest against those outside the group (howsoever constructed). This emotional adaptation that well-suited the mutually hostile nomadic gangs of early human evolution, encourages self-seeking dissension and violence in large multicultural states. Self-righteous group identity can strengthen the nation when generalized at a high-enough level, to bring all citizens together in peace. When citizens construct their group identities too narrowly, excluding their neighbors, they will find it much easier to hurt and to expropriate the "others," to serve their own selfish needs.

The warmth and fellowship of small ethnic groups fulfill the strong human urge to associate, when states or nations become too large, and can no longer fulfill this important social function. The emotional attraction of ethnic solidarity seems to be unavoidable, frequently reinforced by familial or religious allegiances. Such private associations may be helpful and comforting, so long as they remain private, personal, and elective. Public recognition of private ethnic affiliations threatens non-members by dividing the people as citizens, who should be working together for justice and peace. Forcing citizens into non-geographic tribal categories by the exclusion or inclusion of some citizens (and not others) constitutes oppression, since it discriminates on non-functional grounds, in what should have been a public function of the state.

Tribes should be restricted to a purely private status as ethnicities, expressing personal identity, without dividing the people. Unlike families and geographical communities[11] (from which tribes sometimes develop), tribal feelings should neither be recognized nor regulated, but simply allowed to develop into ethnic identity, as individuals choose (or choose not) to maintain hereditary affinities. Such ethnic identities contribute spice and diversity to national life, so long as no one imposes membership without consent. Overlapping ethnic and cultural identities create nuanced lives, and shades of meaning in individual experience. Tribal feeling is natural, but dangerous, when tribes abuse public power to promote their private interests or agenda.

3. Peoples

As tribes are (or should be) transformed into private ethnicity, so peoples are public, as history and etymology reveal. Cicero observed that "*res publica*" means the "*res populi*," organized to find justice.[12] The words are nearly synonymous, but "public" (as an adjective) clarifies the proper business of government, which is to serve justice and the common (or "public") good of its citizens.[13] The people are the citizens of a given state, or rather, the inhabitants of a given state's territory, since justice requires that all permanent residents within each state's jurisdiction should also be its citizens, with equal rights and duties to the rest.[14]

The United Nations Charter confirms the primacy of "peoples," as the union of all citizens in any given state, by asserting the Organization's power through the voice of "We the Peoples of the United Nations," in a document actually ratified by states. The United Nations Charter seeks to unite all nations, by uniting all peoples "based on respect for the principle of equal rights and self-determination of peoples,"[15] to encourage "respect for human rights and for fundamental freedoms for all without distinction as to race, sex, language, or religion."[16] The International Covenant on Civil and Political Rights and the Covenant on Economic, Social and Cultural Rights reiterate the international consensus that "all peoples have the right to self- determination. By virtue of that right they freely determine their political status and freely pursue their economic, social and cultural development."[17]

The Civil and Political Covenant also confirms that all persons should be equal before the courts and tribunals,[18] and that every citizen should have the right and opportunity "to vote and to be elected at genuine periodic elections which shall be by universal and equal suffrage" and "held by secret ballot, guaranteeing the free expression of the will of the electors."[19] This right of "peoples," which is to say, of all citizens in any given state, to political self-determination, does not and cannot apply to all "nations," which may transcend jurisdictional boundaries, and certainly does not extend to "tribes" or ethnicities, except in their members' separate capacities as citizens, in perfect equality with the rest.

The United States Declaration of Independence asserts the right of one "people" in certain circumstances to "dissolve the political bands" that link them to another.[20] This raises the question of precisely what constitutes a separate "people" within a larger political entity or empire. The prototype would seem to be colonial situations of geographical separation, when subordinate peoples occupy wholly distinct and somewhat distant countries under some limitation of sovereignty, as "trust" or non-self-governing territories. The United Nations General Assembly recognized the separate identity of such colonial "peoples" in its "Declaration on the Granting of Independence to Colonial Countries and Peoples."[21]

The obvious justice of "recognizing the passionate yearning for freedom of all dependent peoples"[22] forces consideration of which territories should count as dependencies subject to "alien subjugation, domination and exploitation,"[23] with a consequent right to popular "self-determination,"[24] which are therefore not part of an integral "country," whose "national unity" and "territorial integrity" should be rigorously maintained.[25] Actual subjugation, domination or exploitation through the denial of civil or political rights provides very good evidence of a subgroup's separate identity as a people, even in the eyes of its own oppressors. But oppression is not enough. There must also be a geographical separation, along recognized borders, which is why the doctrine of "*uti possidetis juris*" (recognizing old administrative boundaries), has played such a large part in the liberation of subject peoples throughout the world.[26]

4. Countries

The separate identity of territorially based "countries," each with its own separate people, with a right to independence and self-determination, has been confirmed through decolonization and the break-up of empires in the Americas, Asia, Africa, and most recently the former Yugoslavia. The doctrines of self-determination and *uti possidetis juris* formed the basis for the lawful secession of Slovenia, Croatia, Bosnia and Macedonia, where existing frontiers at the time of independence divided the old federation without regard to actual ethnic or national boundaries.[27] Each country emerged as a separate state, without revising existing borders, despite the Serbian nation's strong desire (and violent attempt) to change boundaries to their own private advantage.

The examples of Yugoslavia, and of African countries such as Nigeria, illustrate the difficulties that arise when peoples, countries and nations do not coincide. Traditional countries, within reasonable geographic boundaries, such as Bosnia or Macedonia, may contain a melange of different but overlapping nations. Or recent history and colonial inattention may create a state (and therefore a people), as in Nigeria, embracing several natural countries, and many different nations. Peoples accommodate themselves to their countries best, and become nations, when boundaries remain stable over time. Thus history may define a country as much as natural geography does. The Mason-Dixon Line between Pennsylvania and Maryland, or the border between New York and Québec, that began as arbitrary constructions, now divide two separate countries, which history has established as permanently and properly distinct.

The permanent recognition of separate clearly delineated and geographically defined "countries" is the first and strongest foundation of peace and justice within and between nations, peoples, and states. So long as boundaries seem to be contingent, parties will arise to contest them, manipulating inevitable differences to construct rival factions and new tribal claims. Once boundaries have been established, and populations become stable, inhabitants will adapt themselves to their countries and neighbors, as they must to time and nature, to construct worthwhile lives.

Well-defined, stable countries provide the basic conditions for peace and justice without necessarily securing either. Countries begin to create nations by providing the permanent communities within which cultures can evolve, but nations have been built on injustice, or grown through domination and empire. Countries provide the homelands of nations, the identity of states, and the matrix of peoples, without directly shaping their cultures, beyond the brute exigencies of physical geography and nature. Real justice depends on political institutions, to guide human interactions towards harmony and peace.

5. States

States define peoples (their citizens) and rule countries (their territories), for which states supply the political institutions that help to create nations, and maintain peace and justice. As countries supply stable geographical boundaries, within which individuals cohere into nations, so states supply stable political institutions, that serve the same purpose. States help to form nations, but also to constrain them, by protecting the equal citizenship that makes nations just. States properly exist only to serve the common good or public business (*res publica*) of their people, and will therefore necessarily be more changeable in their structures than the countries that they rule, or the peoples that they serve. Bad states should be reformulated to serve justice and their peoples better.

States are essentially political institutions, while countries and peoples are essentially geographical, and nations essentially cultural constructs. As political institutions, states form and maintain communities, which exist at various different levels of intimacy and abstraction. "State" signifies civil power, but does not preclude overarching federations or alliances, which may confuse terminology by exercising significant powers of their own. For example, the constituent "states" of the United States joined themselves into a larger federation, which in turn attached itself to the United Nations. Locally, within each of the United States, smaller counties, cities, townships and so forth also exercise important political functions. Different entities exercise "supreme civil power" for different purposes, in different circumstances, within (and above) the state.

"State," then, will be used most properly to describe the basic unit within which most power *should* reside, which is to say the largest viable cultural unit or country, within historical borders. States are properly the governments of nations, or should aspire to become so, while federations are international, and counties or cities sub-national administrative units, To make the state too large, embracing more than one geographically distinct country and nation, would institute an empire, with the consequent oppression of some nations by others. Making the state too small frustrates the public purposes for which states exist, by denying the basic resources that make a common culture worthwhile.

Regional federations and overarching organizations of states serve the useful purpose of constraining the national consensus that makes states in some circumstances so valuable. The same consensus that creates inspiring national enterprises may also lead to internal injustice and oppression within states when minority interests run counter to the majority will. Some areas of life properly belong more to the individual (or private), rather than to the communal (or public) sphere. Unified nations will trespass on individual and minority rights, but larger multi-national federal governments can overcome this natural prejudice, born of national unity and enthusiasm. States protect cultures and unity, while multi-national federations protect individuality, and universal human rights.

6. What are peoples and nations?

"Peoples" and "nations" are two distinct social categories referring (in the first case) to political and geographical associations and (in the second) to cultural affinities. Peoples inhabit known territorially defined political "states" or geographical "countries," while nations (like "ethnicity") may straddle political and geographical boundaries. Keeping these categories distinct clarifies the laws, morality and justice of human interaction. Peoples gradually construct their common cultural identities as "nations" to support their own political and geographical union. States exist to maintain justice and the common good within and between peoples, and to develop nationality among fellow citizens.

Each state has its own country and its own people. Stable states foster nations, by bringing neighbors together toward a new synthesis of common interests and culture. Tribes disrupt this march toward national unity by claiming separate political power without regard to geography. Private ethnic, religious or other non-political associations can add beauty and diversity to a state's national development, to everyone's benefit, but tribes (in their strictest sense, as political units) will always threaten the state and the nation, by setting some citizens against the rest. Peace and justice depend on the social solidarity of peoples and states, to develop national harmony from diverse individuals and interests.

Life and society have natural structures and consequences that exist whether we name them or not, but giving cultural artifacts and realities clear names will influence their development, and help to maintain human harmony and justice. Humpty Dumpty's philological attitude, while true (in a sense), was foolish, since what matters is not so much how words *can* be used (however we want), but rather how words *should* be used, to find a just and better world, through cooperation and knowledge. Contingency and license may seem very appealing to professors sitting on top of the wall. People who fall will want some clarity and effectiveness among the King's horses and men, to make each citizen (and society) whole, despite their inevitable misfortunes.

14

The Law of Peoples

Modern international law began in the seventeenth century as "the law of nature applied to nations." Lawyers and philosophers studying the natural rights and duties of persons had developed an equal concern for the rights and duties of states.[1] States and persons are not the same, as clear-headed advocates of international law such as Emmerich de Vattel readily admitted, but the temptation to recycle good philosophy as law was very strong, some parallels between persons and states are legitimate, and most lawyers have spent as much time representing individuals (not states) as philosophers have spent thinking about individuals (and not states), so the habit of translating doctrine from one sphere to the other remains very strong.

John Rawls presents a recent example of this ancient phenomenon. Having refined his elaborate *Theory of Justice*,[2] for constitutional democracies in his book on *Political Liberalism*,[3] Rawls has now applied his conclusions to international relations. The subjects of Rawls' *Law of Peoples* are members of what he calls the "society of peoples," which is to say, those states that meet his test as "decent" societies. Rawls published his *Law of Peoples* bound together with an essay on *The Idea of Public Reason Revisited* (discussing domestic political discourse) to underline the intimate connection between his "liberal" theories of domestic and of foreign politics. Both depend on a "public reason" that avoids questions of truth to construct a "political zone," within which government can take place.[4]

1. International law

Rawls' "law of peoples" recycles his domestic conception of right and justice to reconstruct the principles and norms of international law.

Rawls proposes that the "society of peoples" should embrace all "decent"[5] states, that follow the ideals and principles of his law of peoples in their international relations. Rawls' concept of "decency" corresponds loosely with the concept of "civilized" nations perpetuated in Article 38(c) of the statute of the International Court of Justice. "Decent" states would seem to be those states whose views are worth taking into account in constructing the law of nations.

Rawls' study of international law offers a new method for discovering the requirements of international justice to complement his liberal technique for finding justice within states. The concepts of "decency" (between states) and "reasonableness" (within states) define whose views will count, and in which circumstances, when deliberating about justice. But Rawls' concept of "decency," as applied to states, is broader than his concept of "reasonableness" as applied to persons. "Decent" states also include "decent hierarchical peoples" (he means governments), whose public officials "consult" their subjects, without giving them any real voice or power.[6] Such governments are not "reasonable" in their internal politics, but still manage to be "decent" in their external relations.

This curious gap between "decency" and "reasonableness" reflects Rawls' recognition of a difference between "ideal" and "non-ideal" theory. In a perfect world, all states would be "reasonable" liberal democratic societies, as described in Rawls' book on *Political Liberalism*. He developed his general "law of peoples" to serve this ideal situation. But because not all states really are liberal democracies, Rawls has extended his liberal law of peoples as much as possible to embrace non-liberal non-democracies, at least to the extent that they are still "decent" enough to participate in international relations.[7]

2. Realism

Rawls sets out to construct what he calls a "realistic" utopia, in which reasonably just constitutional democratic societies can participate in a broader international society. This society must be "realistic," in that it takes the world and human nature as it is, which is to say, imperfectly democratic. Rawls' proposal is still "utopian" because it seeks to construct an international social structure that realizes political right and justice for all "decent" peoples.[8] Political injustice leads to other evils, so Rawls believed that establishing better basic political institutions will put an end to unjust war, oppression, religious persecution, and other unpleasant byproducts of human nature, on both the domestic and the international levels.[9]

Realism means pushing the acceptable range of basic social institutions as far as possible in the direction of actual institutions as they presently exist, without sacrificing the ultimate ideal of liberal justice. At the beginning of his essay on the social contract, Jean-Jacques Rousseau wrote of taking men as they are, to construct laws as they might be.[10] Rawls took states as he imagines them to be, to construct international law as he would wish it to be. He sets aside questions of war, immigration and nuclear weapons on the assumption: (1) that democracies and decent authoritarian states will not fight each other; (2) that immigration need not be permitted; and (3) that nuclear weapons are only necessary to keep outlaw states at bay.[11]

Rawls' "realism" lies in his willingness to extend the "original position," in which all states determine the rules of justice between themselves, to include non-liberal non-democracies. In his earlier discussions of the *Theory of Justice* (1971) and *Political Liberalism* (1993), Rawls proposed an "original position" for designing the basic concept of justice in liberal constitutional democracies. This original position was designed to take the religious and philosophical beliefs of all "reasonable" people equally into account in constructing the basic rules of justice. "Reasonable" people in this context included only those people whose philosophy or religion left them willing to take other people's "reasonable" views equally into account. Applied to states, Rawls' "realism" in designing his new original position means taking the interests and views of all "decent" governments equally into account at the international level, including many that have *not* adopted the original position conception of justice to govern their domestic affairs. Rawls gives the views and desires of "decent" non-liberal non-democracies the same weight as the views and desires of reasonable democratic states.[12]

3. The fact of pluralism

This "realistic" theory of justice in both its domestic and its international versions develops from what John Rawls has called "the fact of reasonable pluralism."[13] This "fact" as Rawls imagines it in constructing his domestic and international constitutional ideals assumes the persistence of an inevitably permanent and unavoidably conflicting plurality of "comprehensive" conceptions of the good, which people and peoples will neither change nor compromise in the face of reasoned arguments or truth.[14] Rawls constructs his theories of justice and international relations on the basis of reciprocity between the holders of these mutually incompatible and non-commensurable "comprehensive" moral views.[15]

This fundamental assumption of the "fact of pluralism," as Rawls understands it, is simply false as applied to normal political relations, which vitiates his concept of "political liberalism" in domestic politics. The "fact of pluralism" may be better supported in international relations, but not as the basis of any "just" law of peoples. The "fact" of pluralism is false as applied to normal political relations because very few individuals have "comprehensive" conceptions of the good. Most people have partial conceptions of the good. To the extent that people do hold comprehensive views, reasonable people (in the word's usual sense), will be willing to modify their opinions when faced with cogent arguments for changing their minds. People who cling to non-revisable conceptions of the good, refusing to engage in reasoned argument, are not "reasonable," despite Rawls' appropriation of that term. Their refusal to reason makes them unreasonable, and discounts the moral relevance of their views.

Rawls' concept of pluralism may apply better to states, because states are inherently less reasonable than individual persons engaged in public deliberation. States are less reasonable than individual persons because states are not real persons, and cannot reason, except to the extent that the particular persons or representative structures that govern states at any given time reason on their behalf. To the extent that states represent real persons deliberating in good faith about justice and the purposes of government, they may usefully be considered sometimes to be "reasonable" (or not). Non-representative, non-democratic state structures represent nobody, except their government's interest in power, wealth and self-preservation. Such attitudes generate an inevitable pluralism and incommensurability of views between states, but these differences are not "reasonable." Sometimes each self-seeking government's relatively equal power forces a *modus vivendi* in which each government leaves the others free to exploit their own subjects. This self-interested stand-off has no rational connection with either law or justice.

4. Reason

Rawls' conception of "reason" means the willingness to get along. "Reasonable" people, as Rawls understands the term, are people who do not challenge their neighbors' fundamental beliefs. No moral questions are open for discussion beyond the purely political arrangements of basic governmental procedure.[16] Extended to create a "reasonable" law of peoples, this strategy determines that the governments of states should not challenge the fundamental commitments of governments of other states, until these cross some ultimate threshold of "decency."[17] Rawls' sense of "reasonable" implies the necessity of never contradicting someone else's views. Rawls' sense of "rational" means pure and undisguised self-interest.[18]

The idea of public reason in Rawls' "society of peoples" parallels the idea of public reason in his domestic democratic constitutional model.[19] Rawls avoids confrontation because he fears the fanaticism of religious conviction.[20] The over-confidence of irrational faith does often lead to persecution, but not simply because "comprehensive" beliefs are too deeply held. What makes such views dangerous is their irrationality. Defining "reason" to avoid reasoned discussion of fundamental moral questions strengthens the power of irrationality and therefore the threat of violence. Rawls advocates the maintenance of formal respect for and deference to irrationally held comprehensive views, when he should have prescribed humility in the application of reasoned discourse to reduce the dangers of religious and philosophical oppression.

"Reasonable" peoples, according to Rawls' theory of reason, are peoples willing to offer "fair" terms of cooperation to other peoples, just as reasonable citizens in domestic society should offer to cooperate with fellow citizens.[21] This formula would be perfectly acceptable if Rawls had a more robust conception of fairness. Rawls' sense of "reasonable" is too far removed from actual reason to offer any useful measure of what should count as "fair" between peoples. Assuming a plurality of equally "reasonable" yet "comprehensive" doctrines traduces the normal sense of both words, by assuming that persons, behind a veil of ignorance, not knowing which views they will hold, would agree equally to honor all views, and would not prefer to encourage those moral views that are actually correct.[22]

5. Peoples

Rawls speaks of "peoples" rather than "nations" or "states" to convey the need for community among the inhabitants of a given territory, whatever their origin may be.[23] "State" implies sovereignty and a certain separation between the government and people that Rawls strongly disapproves.[24] By writing of "peoples" rather than "states" in the second-level "original position" in which states determine their mutual duties, Rawls implies that states in a sense do (or should) speak for, embody or represent the peoples that they rule. This introduces a spurious impression of consent into Rawls' broader society of "decent" peoples, which includes the governments of authoritarian and non-democratic states, who have no legitimate authority to deliberate or to consent on behalf of their subjects.

By using the word "peoples" in writing of governments, Rawls hopes to convey the "reasonable" values of reciprocity that ought to exist between states.[25] Reciprocity between peoples would be desirable, but should not necessarily extend to the governments of all states, whose interests may be quite different from those of the peoples that they rule. By obscuring the difference between peoples (subjects or citizens) and states (governments), Rawls gives states a spurious legitimacy, and too much authority in speaking on behalf of the peoples that they rule. Just as liberal governments view their subjects as free and equal citizens (according to Rawls' theory), so he believes that international society should view all states as free and equal in constructing international law.[26] But many states are neither free nor equal. Some are authoritarian non-democracies. Such governments do not deserve an equal voice.

Perhaps at this point one might argue that even when the governments of states deserve no equal voice, their peoples do, which is certainly true. In constructing rules of international justice, some imaginary pre-political "representative" of the people may need to be constructed to express their interests and views.[27] Rawls would picture this representative as also speaking for the state. The difference between "states" and "peoples" is not for Rawls, as it would be in ordinary discourse, the difference between governments and their subjects, but rather the difference between two types of government. Governments that respect the dignity of other governments are "peoples," in Rawls' terminology, and governments of "states" are those that do not.[28]

6. States

"State," as the word is usually understood, signifies the government of a determinate territory, with its own population ("people") and political independence, confirmed through recognition by the governments of other separate (and "sovereign") states. Rawls speaks of "peoples," but he means states when he writes that they should be: (1) free and independent; (2) bound by treaties; (3) equal; (4) committed to non-intervention; (5) pacifist, except in self-defense; (6) respectful of human rights; (7) humanitarian when forced into war; and (8) committed to helping less fortunate states to achieve prosperity and good government. These are the basic tenets of the "law of peoples" that Rawls imagines that the representatives of states ("peoples") would embrace in an original position, behind the veil of ignorance.[29]

Rawls assumes stable boundaries between states. However historically arbitrary a state's geographical boundaries, Rawls would maintain them in perpetuity to give each people a clear sense of property and responsibility over its own national territory and fate.[30] Governments would insist on their mutual equality,[31] in the original position, (Rawls believes) to protect any state's interests from being short-changed to serve the happiness of others. This leads to the familiar and largely traditional "law of peoples" that Rawls adapts from long-established usage in international law and practice.[32]

In the first instance, Rawls' "law of peoples" applies only to liberal democratic states, such as those constructed behind the "veil of ignorance" in his first (domestic) "original position." His law of peoples emerges "politically," and not as an expression of the comprehensive doctrines of truth or right that might hold sway in any particular society.[33] As extended to "decent hierarchical peoples," Rawls' rationale must be somewhat different. Principles that would be accepted from the standpoint of liberal democratic peoples acting behind a veil of ignorance must be shown also to be valid from the standpoint of authoritarian hierarchical states that reject the principles of liberal democracy.[34]

7. Toleration

Rawls proposes to extend the benefits of the law of peoples to non-liberal governments, by applying the principle of "toleration." By "tolerate" (contrary to ordinary usage), Rawls means not simply to put up with, but fully to include non-liberal governments in his society of peoples.[35] Rawls would "tolerate" (in this broad sense) all "decent" peoples,[36] including certain non-liberal governments, because he believes that the dignity of their subjects would be compromised by any measures taken to encourage "decent" authoritarian governments to become more democratic and liberal. Here again Rawls equates disrespect for governments with disrespect for peoples.[37] By confusing peoples with states, Rawls diminishes the power of peoples against their own governments. There may well be non-liberal states that deserve the protection of Rawls' eight principles of international law, but their governments should be tolerated (in the ordinary sense of the word), not praised. Contrary to what Rawls' believes, states that disenfranchise their peoples should be stigmatized as wrong, even when they must be tolerated, for prudential reasons.

Toleration implies error, as Rawls well understands. His broad conception of toleration is tactical, like his domestic strategy of reasonable pluralism. Rawls believes that if liberal peoples pretend that authoritarian governments are fully acceptable, and act as if authoritarian leaders were fully respectable, then eventually authoritarian states will move towards liberalism. This reflects Rawls' fundamental beliefs: (1) that all criticism is counterproductive; and (2) that all moral change comes from within. Rawls opposes challenging false moral beliefs or bad government practices directly because he does not think that criticism will persuade. Rawls would like governments to reform themselves in their own way. Recognizing authoritarian governments as part of a decent society of peoples will encourage them to reform.[38] Rawls believes that peoples will lapse into bitterness and resentment when liberal governments criticize the authoritarian masters of non-democratic states.[39]

Rawls' conception of toleration as full inclusion and respect weakens the persuasive value of good institutions by forcing good governments to pretend that bad governments are equally respectable. This deprives bad governments of the truth, which might have encouraged reform, and perverts international discourse, to the extent that non-representative governments have an equal voice in international affairs. True toleration includes a measure of disapproval. Hiding this disapproval, as Rawls suggests that one should, will dispirit reformers within authoritarian regimes, and betray the aspirations of their peoples. Rawls' conception of toleration betrays the oppressed by denying the reality of their oppression. It encourages liberal peoples to collude with foreign injustice.

8. Decency

Rawls defends himself against this charge of collusion by insisting that his law of peoples extends its benefits only to "decent" authoritarian regimes.[40] These regimes count as "decent," because they have a "decent consultation hierarchy,"[41] they do not harbor aggressive aims,[42] they respect human rights,[43] they view all members of society as decent and rational, and their judges and public officials sincerely believe that the law serves the common good of all those subject to it.[44] The main difference between "decent" authoritarian regimes and liberal states lies in their different conceptions of the subjects of the law. Liberal governments respect their subjects as free and equal citizens. "Decent" authoritarian regimes regard their subjects as members of groups,[45] and consult only with officially recognized group "leaders" in deciding public policy.[46]

Rawls' eight laws of peace apply only to "decent" peoples, which makes his criteria of decency both too narrow and too broad for the different purposes they serve. Rawls' standards of decency are too narrow, because governments that do not meet his requirements of human rights, the common good, and judicial sincerity[47] may still deserve protection against aggression and other violations of international law. Rawls' standards of decency are too broad, because he insists on respecting all "decent" states equally, as if they were fully liberal and democratic, which they are not. No government that denies the political equality of its citizens will ever fully respect their human rights, or seek their common good. Rawls' fantasy of "consultation" through group leaders[48] will only entrench certain "leaders" in power, and coerce citizen membership in artificially perpetuated groups.[49] Denying the equal citizenship of any member of society is not "decent," and future subjects of the law would not accept authoritarian government behind a veil of ignorance, as Rawls himself must recognize.

Perhaps governments may properly be considered to be "decent" when they *try* to serve the common good of their people.[50] But governments are not fully worthy of respect unless they also actually *realize* the common good to some extent, and this will never happen under authoritarian regimes. By putting the rulers of authoritarian governments into his inter-state "original position," alongside the representatives of liberal democracies,[51] Rawls pollutes his contractarian model. Authoritarian governments cannot speak for their subjects because they do not represent their subjects. Governments that claim equality in the international arena should first concede equality to their subjects at home. Rawls' conception of a "decent consultation hierarchy"[52] cannot replace the direct representation of citizens, because authoritarian systems delegate authority without consulting the citizens themselves.[53] Self-appointed or government-selected group "leaders" can only represent their own interests, not those of other citizens or groups.[54]

9. Human rights

Rawls' two primary tests of "decency" are respect for the common good, and protection of the most basic universal human rights. Defining either too broadly would assimilate decency to democracy and liberalism, which is not Rawls' purpose. Instead, he restricts the human rights requirements of "decency" to a short list of "fundamental" rights[55] against military aggression, slavery, religious persecution, and genocide.[56] Rawls suggests that governments respecting these minimum rights should be immune from economic sanctions or other interference designed to protect or to encourage their subject peoples.[57] Outlaw states that violate fundamental human rights may be sanctioned or invaded,[58] but Rawls would respect authoritarian non-democracies, even though they deny the more refined human rights of constitutional democracies.

Despite his Kantian antecedents,[59] Rawls disavowed the immediate recognition of any world-wide "cosmopolitan" justice, that would respect the equal rights and liberties of all persons, without discrimination.[60] Respecting the universal and equal dignity of all persons would threaten the power of "decent" authoritarian governments, by undermining their authority. Beyond the absolute minimum of a "common good" attitude, "reasonable" consultation, good-faith judges[61] and minimum human rights, such as those against slavery and genocide,[62] Rawls refused to endorse any values that authoritarian governments could not themselves accept.[63] Even to offer incentives, in the form of foreign aid, for governments to respect human rights, would violate Rawls' policy of "respecting" authoritarian regimes.[64]

Rawls' deferential attitude toward existing regimes seems unnecessary to his basic theory and fundamentally unjust to the subjects of authoritarian governments, whose rights Rawls disregards. His argument has three parts, (1) describing the law of peoples that would prevail between liberal states; then (2) extending the same rules to "decent" authoritarian governments; and finally (3) protecting "decent" non-liberal non-democracies against criticism. The first step is reasonable, the second excessive, and the third pernicious. Deliberative, democratic and rights-respecting governments (1) should defer to each other in ways that non-democratic or non-liberal governments (2) do not deserve, and certainly (3) should not accept without criticism. By putting non-representative governments into an equal position "behind the veil of ignorance" (and in the community of states) as just and representative democracies,[65] Rawls minimizes the protection of human rights in his unnecessarily illiberal "law of peoples."

10. The basic requirements

The eight principles of Rawls' law of peoples,[66] regarding states' (1) independence, (2) respect for treaties, (3) equality, (4) non-intervention, (5) pacifism, (6) respect for rights, (7) humanitarian attitude to war, and (8) generosity, are all constrained by, and to a large degree derived from, or subordinated to, his fundamental commitment to the sovereign power of "decent" governments, against their own subjects. Rawls' proposals mirror standard nineteenth-century international law doctrine (1–3 and 7), slightly modified by post-second-World War pacifism (4–5) and the Western charitable impulse (8). Rawls' weak commitment to human rights deprives his doctrine of the only transformative element (6) that might have challenged existing authoritarian structures and orthodoxies.

Universal human rights to personal security and political participation have a stronger position in contemporary international law than they do in Rawls' "law of peoples."[67] Had Rawls understood the duty "to honor human rights"[68] more robustly, his proposals might have strengthened international law. As it is, Rawls' "law of peoples" will encourage oppression, by protecting the independence and equality of oppressive governments without restraint, so long as they avoid chattel slavery, ethnic genocide or other violations of what Rawls calls the most "urgent" human rights.[69] Only then would Rawls permit liberal societies to begin to encourage certain "outlaw" governments to reform.[70]

Rawls overlooks important distinctions between the different situations in which just societies may: (1) criticize unjust governments; (2) impose non-military sanctions on unjust governments; or (3) take military action to correct international injustice. His curiously broad conception of toleration would seem to imply that authoritarian governments may not be (1) criticized or (2) sanctioned until they may also (3) be corrected by military force. The choice of means becomes entirely prudential. Rawls presents governments as either "decent" or "outlaw" states. Decent states must deliberate among themselves to decide the best means of correcting outlaws.[71] Throughout his argument, the standards of intervention and criticism of injustice under Rawls' "law of peoples" become increasingly strict, until even human sacrifice may be to some extent protected, so long as outlaw states do not export it.[72]

11. The law of peoples

John Rawls' "law of peoples" goes wrong by extending the title of "decency" too far among illiberal non-democratic states. By giving illiberal non-democracies an equal voice in determining international law, Rawls replicates the worst elements of existing international practice. Like the older conception of "civilized" nations, which Rawls' theory reproduces for the modern world, "decency" is both too broad and too narrow as applied to states under international law. Too broad, because it gives unrepresentative governments an equal voice in determining the law of nations. Too narrow, because it deprives subject peoples of any voice at all, when their governments oppress them.

Rawls' concept of the "original position" might have been useful in reforming international law, if applied from the standpoint of all human beings, to regulate state structures and interstate relations. Or the governments of just states, as constructed by their future subjects from the standpoint of the original position, might usefully have entered into a second-tier inter-state "original position" to construct international institutions. By putting non-representative non-democracies into his own international original position, however, Rawls would simply perpetuate the interests of illiberal elites against their unfortunate subjects. States are not people, and unless governments actually speak for peoples, Rawls' technique of imagining a non-liberal interstate "original position" is dangerously misconceived.

The fundamentals of a just law of peoples hover somewhat obscured in the midst of Rawls' overextended conception of "decency." The "common good idea of justice" and "basic human rights"[73] deserve a more prominent place at the center of any just law of nations, which Rawls denies them by minimizing rights, and overstating self-interest. At times in his argument, Rawls seems to contemplate a more robust world order,[74] only to retreat in the end[75] to the defense of authoritarian governments, and excessive deference to established power.[76] Had he drawn his conception of "decency" more narrowly, Rawls' argument would have made more sense.

15
Perpetual Peace

Immanuel Kant seems so often to be right, in the eyes of contemporary philosophers and legal academics, that his writings have taken on a nearly scriptural authority. To find one's views in Kant confirms their validity. To challenge Kant implies reactionary prejudice, or pointless iconoclasm. John Rawls has made so many new "Kantians" in the academy that every scrap and letter of the great Königsberger's work has got its own scholiast, and school of eager exegetes. Finally the commentators have turned even to Kant's short last essay on *Perpetual Peace* (1795),[1] which closely follows a tradition of proposals deriving through Kant's model Jean-Jacques Rousseau (1761)[2] from the Abbé de Saint Pierre (1713)[3] and William Penn (1693).[4] The question addressed by each of these illustrious men was how the different nations of the world can live together in peace.

Kant's proposals deserve serious consideration, both in their own right, and because of the influence that they have had on others. To what extent are they applicable to contemporary relations between states? Kant proposes six preliminary articles of a perpetual peace among states, and three definitive articles, supplemented by a guarantee, a secret article, and two appendices, designed to establish and to maintain a universal community ("*Gemeinschaft*") of political, international, and cosmopolitan right.

1. Kant's preliminary articles of perpetual peace

Kant's six preliminary articles of perpetual peace are practical and prospective. They set out basic rules through which existing states may bring an end to hostilities and develop the basis for creating perpetual peace. Kant intended that several of his proposals (2, 3, and 4) should admit some flexibility or subjective latitude, so long as their ultimate purpose remained in sight. Kant's six preliminary articles of perpetual peace propose that: (1) "No conclusion of peace shall be considered valid if it was made with a secret reservation of the material for future war"; (2) "No independently existing state, whether it be large or small, may be acquired by another state by inheritance, exchange, purchase or gift"; (3) "Standing armies will gradually be abolished altogether"; (4) "No national debt shall be contracted in connection with the external affairs of state"; (5) "No state shall forcibly interfere in the constitution and government of another state"; and (6) "No state at war with another shall permit such acts of hostility as would make mutual confidence impossible during a future time of peace."[5]

The first preliminary article forbidding the secret reservation of material for future war reflects the republican commitment to honesty. Honest states that agree to peace would relinquish their capability for war. This preliminary article will be impractical in a multipolar world of mutually distrustful powers. Full disarmament requires universal compliance and trust. In the absence of either, prudent states will retain their capability for war, while working to create the necessary conditions for peace. Perhaps Kant's first provision will be a necessary preliminary to "real" peace in the sense that complete and permanent "peace" (in its strongest sense) cannot exist without disarmament. As applied to contemporary international relations, the trusting renunciation of all material for war would be unwise, and likely to provoke avoidable conflicts between states.

Kant's second preliminary article of perpetual peace, forbidding exchanges of national territory, recognizes the fundamental principles of self-determination and cultural stability. Each society has its own life and history, which would be destroyed by transfer or amalgamation. Kant recognizes the folly of a single consolidated world empire. This clause is elegant, convincing and true, but should not be read to prevent federation. Kant simply endorses the stability of existing administrative borders and the doctrine of *uti possidetis juris*. Each community or separate republic must develop its own sense of the common good and consensus about justice, standing on its own cultural history. This does not preclude a broader cosmopolitan citizenship that encompasses of all humanity.

The third preliminary article of perpetual peace, proscribing standing armies, follows from the first, concerning material for future wars. Standing armies exist to fight, provoking apprehension in others, expensive arms races, and the danger of prophylactic or preemptive aggression. The coercive power of professional armies can also become a threat to the citizens they serve. Kant proposes a gradual disarmament, which might be possible in a just world of legitimate states, provided that they disarm together. Kant's further prohibition on the accumulation of public currency reserves (which he sees as equivalent to armies, since wealth can hire arms) makes little sense. Governments need wealth and reserves of wealth to serve their citizens. Converting wealth to arms takes time, and even poverty cannot prevent rearmament, when states are determined to do so.

Kant's fourth article, forbidding a national debt, follows from his fear of public wealth. Such prohibitions would impoverish the state, without preventing war, and reflect a naive unreasoning fear of finance. Kant's subsidiary point, that foreign debts may lead to war when debtor nations cannot pay, has a kernel of truth in it. His solution – that states should band together to prevent foreign borrowing – seems unnecessarily harsh. Some states and populations may benefit from timely borrowing, to fund the development of their local resources and economies. Kant's view of debtors as improperly enriched would-be imperialists reveals his conception of Britain as the typical debtor nation. Regulated international borrowing, by satisfying and empowering the poorer nations, may be an important force for world peace, because it promotes a greater equality among states.

The fifth preliminary article of perpetual peace comes closer to the substance of contemporary international law by banning forcible intervention in the constitution or government of another state. Kant's reasoning reveals his conception of states as moral persons, with their own political autonomy comparable to the private autonomy of real human individuals. This analogy supposes that just as every individual may foolishly harm herself or himself, without legitimating someone else's intervention, so every state or people may freely harm itself, so long as it does not injure others. Accepting any intervention in a state's internal conflicts would (Kant supposes) make the autonomy of all states insecure.

Kant's attribution of moral identity and autonomy to states would be justified, if one's aim were simply to establish a peace between states, preliminary to a more definitive permanent settlement. Looked at from the standpoint of justice, however, the equivalence would fail. Just as individuals deserve liberty and moral autonomy, so too nations deserve liberty and moral autonomy, but only so long as states stand in the place of the individuals that they represent. State autonomy is derivative, and depends (as Kant recognized) on the collective right to independence and self-determination of the people or citizens behind it. Oppressive states that disregard their citizens' welfare cannot claim to speak for the citizens, or vicariously to enjoy their citizens' collective right to independence. In such circumstances, other states may sometimes legitimately respond directly to appeals for help from subordinated populations, against their government oppressors.

Kant's confusion between the moral autonomy of individuals and the moral autonomy of states carries over to his prohibition of certain excesses or dishonesties in war. The sixth preliminary article of perpetual peace rests on Kant's assumption of a state of nature between nations, which share no common court of justice to legitimate their wars of punishment (*bella punitiva*) against illegal behavior. In such circumstances, Kant suggests, wars represent a form of trial by battle, resolved by the judgment of God. Kant insists that such wars must follow civilized procedures, to avoid a descent into total destruction through escalating mutual atrocities.

This last point makes a powerful argument in favor of the laws of war, rendered almost ridiculous by Kant's rhetorical reference to the "so-called judgment of God" (*sogenannt Gottesgericht*). War is not a trial, but mutual destruction, to be avoided at almost any cost. Different parties to the conflict will be more or less at fault, and more or less to blame. Victory goes to the stronger (and often less justified) party, without any reference to justice. Justice plays a part in appealing for allies, or justifying measures taken to win the war. Kant's sixth article misses the decisive importance of justification (which he recognizes elsewhere). When states are at war, the more justified party may legitimately take much stronger measures to win or to resolve the conflict than the less justified party, whose duty lies more in submission and restitution, than in vigorous pursuit of war.

Kant's preliminary articles look less to justice than to the stabilization of existing situations. Taken separately and individually, his articles hardly apply to contemporary international relations, when international institutions and finance have evolved beyond the structures of Kant's simpler era. Taken collectively, however, Kant's preliminary articles indicate a useful strategy for achieving perpetual peace, by first stabilizing the current administrative boundaries of states, then moving toward justice. Peace precedes justice, in Kant's formulation, but justice justifies and perpetuates peace, when peace between states facilitates their mutual reform, and the establishment of definitive articles of perpetual peace.

2. Kant's definitive articles of perpetual peace

Having established what he considered to be the minimum preliminary foundations of a perpetual peace in his initial proposals, Kant described his three definitive articles of perpetual peace, which establish the formal relationships between nations, without which states must necessarily regard each other as enemies. Kant takes it as given that only a lawful ("*gesetzlich*") state can be trusted. Only states that share a legal civil state of government ("*bürgerlich-gesetzlich Zustand*") can live in peace. Otherwise their neighbors must suppress them as law-abiding citizens properly suppress those individuals who refuse allegiance to the common civil society. Kant envisioned three types of legal ("*rechtlich*") regimes, depending respectively on civil right ("*Staatsbürgerrecht*" or "*ius civitatis*"), international right ("*Völkerrecht*" or "*ius gentium*") and cosmopolitan right ("*Weltbürgerrecht*" or "*ius cosmopoliticum*"). Persons without such constitutions live in a state of nature with respect to each other, Kant believed, and so of perpetual war.

Kant's three definitive articles of perpetual peace follow from his conception of "*rechtlich*" or "*gesetzlich*" institutions, without which there will be no peace. First, all states' civil ("*bürgerlich*") constitutions must be free or "republican." Second, international right ("*Völkerrecht*") must derive from a federation of free or republican states. Finally, the requirement of cosmopolitan right ("*Weltbürgerrecht*") will be limited to conditions of universal hospitality. All three of these "lawful" regimes depend on Kant's conception of freedom, in its older "republican" sense. For Kant rightful freedom ("*rechtlich Freiheit*") requires submission only to those laws to which one could actually give one's consent. Rightful equality requires that all legal obligations apply equally to all persons. These innate and inalienable rights ("*angeborne, zur Menschheit notwendig gehörende und unveräusserliche Rechte*") forbid all relations of unequal power among citizens, Kant insists, except for distinctions derived from merit alone.

Kant's powerful commitment to this natural law of reason determines his conclusion that only republican constitutions can sustain a perpetual peace. Kant's conception of the republic depends on the equal freedom ("*Freiheit*") of all members of society; their equal dependence upon the civil law ("*Gesetz*"); and their equality ("*Gleichheit*") as citizens. Republican constitutions are the only constitutions that equal citizens could agree upon, because republics spring directly from the concept of right ("*Rechtsbegriff*"), and require the consent of their citizens to any public decision. Kant believed that republican citizens armed with the vote would reject war as pernicious to their own well-being, while non-republics embrace war, to enrich those in charge.

These last remarks might lead some readers of Kant to confuse the republican constitution with democracy. To do so would be a mistake.

Kant followed Rousseau and his classical sources in believing that democracies will always be despotic, unless they separate their legislative and executive powers. Republics, Kant believed (in common with his contemporary James Madison and most other self-styled "republicans" of the period), will combine the separation of powers with representation through the election of executive magistrates, so that each public officer remains a servant of the state. Kant suggested that the absence of representation will always result in despotism of one, a few, or the many, which amounts to a state of war, in which no one's rights are observed.

Kant's first definitive article confirms his commitment to justice as the basis of perpetual peace. Kant rightly conceded that there will be no peace or safety for the subjects of any state that disregards the inalienable republican civil rights to freedom, equality, and law. This adds very little to his underdeveloped concept of republican government, which is restricted (in his discourse on *Perpetual Peace*) to requiring representation, the separation of powers, and implied doctrines of popular sovereignty and the rule of law. Kant's contemporaries John Adams, Alexander Hamilton, and James Madison gave much more nuanced descriptions of the republic,[6] as did earlier authors such as James Harrington and the baron de Montesquieu.[7] Nothing Kant says contradicts their more detailed republican prescriptions for checks and balances, elected senates, and life terms for judges. Kant simply does not address the details of republican government, in an essay dedicated to the relationship between states.

The position of the republic as the basis of world peace becomes much clearer in Kant's second definitive article of perpetual peace, basing his *ius gentium* on a federation of republics or federal "free states." This international constitution would mirror the civil constitutions of its several member states, by securing the rights of each state against the others. Kant emphatically rejected the possibility of an international or world state. He preferred a *"Völkerbund"* to a *"Völkerstaat."* The difference lies in maintaining each people's separate identity in separate republics. Each republic must be an equal member of the international federation of peoples, just as every person must be equally a citizen of her or his separate component nation, within the federation.

Kant had no patience for disorganized (*"gesetzlos"*) peoples, without republican government, and did not see why he should accord any respect to disorganized states, that reject the republican federation. Lawless states like lawless persons naturally express the inborn depravity of universal human nature (*"Bösartigkeit der menschlichen Natur"*). Kant believed that only republican structures of government will bring out the moral capacity of human nature sufficiently to overcome this natural propensity to vice. Even after peoples acquire a lawful internal constitution ("*eine rechtliche Verfassung*"), Kant believed that they would continue to need a permanent overarching pacific federation ("*foedus pacificum*"), to preserve each state's proper freedom, as a separate lawful republic.

This idea of federalism, gradually extending to encompass all states, seemed attainable to Kant, if ever a powerful and enlightened nation could form itself into a republic, as a beacon of justice to the world. The recent examples of France and the United States may have given some encouragement to Kant's expectation that other states would flock to form a federation around powerful republics, if given the chance. In any case, Kant firmly believed that reason mandates free federalism ("*frei Föderalism*") as the ultimate shield of individual rights. Just as individuals must renounce their savage and lawless condition through public coercive laws, so states must accept an enduring and gradually expanding republican federation to prevent war.

Kant's proposal may seem somewhat unrealistic, in the midst of global lawlessness and war. In fact, Kant contemplated an arrangement considerably short of his ideal world republic ("*Weltrepublik*" or "*civitas gentium*"). Kant's second definitive article of perpetual peace clarifies the first by extending republican principles from individuals to peoples. Ideally the international federation should have its own enforcement mechanisms, and public coercive laws. Lacking these, Kant hoped that a weaker federation would at least limit the force of universal human inclinations to disregard law and injure other persons.

The third definitive article of perpetual peace concerns cosmopolitan right ("*Weltbürgerrecht*" or "*ius cosmopoliticum*"), which is to say, right growing out of the relationship between individuals (and states) as citizens of the universal "state" of mankind. Kant would restrict cosmopolitan right to the rule of universal hospitality. This requires non-hostility to foreign states and foreign nationals, so that no one kills, enslaves or maltreats them, without good reason. Kant believed that foreigners may legitimately be excluded from entry into independent republics (unless their lives are in danger), but expected that friendly overtures would lead to commerce, and so gradually to a cosmopolitan constitution ("*weltbürgerlich Verfassung*").

Kant's conception of right thus depends on three imagined "codices" of unwritten law, concerning the *ius civitatis, ius gentium,* and *ius cosmopoliticum* respectively. Natural law implies fundamental human rights, which only a republican civil constitution can secure or maintain. This constitutes the *ius civitatis*. Protecting these republican states against outsiders (and each other) requires an international federation of republican peoples, to govern their mutual relations. This determines the *ius gentium*. Finally, this republican federation will not develop or survive without an attitude of universal hospitality, which is the very least that all states and persons owe to all others. This represents the *ius cosmopoliticum*, that underlies the rest.

These three categories of natural law or right ("*Recht*") do not represent three levels of duty, as one might expect, but rather two related systems of obligation, overlayed (or undergirded) by a separate and dominant requirement, applicable to both. The *ius civitatis* (concerning the right of citizens), and the *ius gentium* (concerning the right of peoples) contain within them the universe of public obligations. The *ius cosmopoliticum* embodies the one simple rule that leads (in the end) to developing the rest. Not doing harm to others by simply avoiding hostility will lead to community, Kant believed, as people naturally seek the mutual benefits of commerce and association. People will wish to interact, and doing so without hostility will produce all the benefits of natural right, within and between peoples.

Kant's Definitive Articles of Perpetual Peace constitute the essence of his proposal, unrestricted (unlike the preliminary articles) to specific circumstances of time and place. The threefold project of (1) republican constitutions, (2) republican federation, and (3) general (arms-length) non-hostility between states provides a convincing model for developing peace and justice from a common foundation of republican politics. A *weltbürgerlich* attitude on the part of persons and states will lead to better mutual understanding, interdependence, and peace. Whether such an attitude will ever actually develop remains to be seen. Kant's republicanism is convincing and morally sound (though politically underdeveloped), but the non-republican institutions of existing states, and their less than *weltbürgerlich* attitudes, make it seem a bit utopian, so long as existing regimes fall short of republican political attitudes and institutions.

4. The guarantee of perpetual peace

Kant would have responded to this observation by reiterating his argument that peace and justice both depend, and will in the end both arise and prevail, from the inborn structures and desires of ordinary human nature. Human nature must supply what Kant identified as the ultimate guarantee ("*Garantie*") of perpetual peace. Kant supposed that inherent structures of nature would bring humans into concord, even against their will, so that the moral ends which people *ought* in any case to pursue, as prescribed by reason, will also naturally result from their self-seeking greed and ambition. Kant suggested that all three types of public right – *ius civitatis, ius gentium,* and *ius cosmopoliticum* – will follow eventually from nature, with or without any deliberate human commitment to justice.

In order to secure their own ambitions, with mutual protection against each other's avarice and self-interest, people will form states (Kant supposed) with civil laws to bind them. To strengthen their own state's interests against the rest, even wicked citizens and states must seek republican confederation. Kant embraced the republican conclusion, already well articulated by James Harrington,[8] John Adams,[9] and many others, that even a nation of devils would gradually establish the checks and balances of republican government, to control each other's self-interest by setting each devil to watch the others, so that ambition would counteract ambition, and the public interest would rule, despite the avarice and bad intentions still eagerly raging in each private devil's own secret heart.

This mechanism of nature ("*Mechanism der Natur*") by which selfish inclinations are naturally opposed to one another, compels submission to coercive laws, which in turn preserve peace (as Kant believed), both within and between states. Good morals follow good laws, and dissipate without them. Thus nature irresistibly determines that right will (eventually) gain the upper hand. ("*Die Natur will unwiderstehlich, dass das Recht zuletzt die Obergewalt erhalte.*") Virtue and good will do not matter so much, according to Kant's conception of nature, because right follows from selfish conflict, through an equilibrium of power among vigorous rivals, within and between states. Thus nature wisely separates the nations, and Kant would keep them separate, to maintain justice through balance, in perpetual peace.

As separation prevents despotism, Kant believed, so commerce assures unity and peace among nations, by offering an economic incentive against war. These two forces supply nature's guarantee of lasting peace. Using rivalry and self-interest (to support *Staatsbürgerrecht* and *Völkerrecht*) and avarice (to support *Weltbürgerrecht*), nature maintains peace by the universal mechanism of natural human inclination. This is not to say that justice and peace now actually exist (or ever have). Rather, Kant suggested that nature supplies the materials for perpetual peace, to be gradually channeled and implemented, by those who have the wit to do so.

This constitutes Kant's "secret" article of perpetual peace. Philosophers have studied and explained the mechanisms of peace in government and international relations. Kant proposed that governments should secretly make use of this wisdom. He never advocated philosopher-kings, or even king-philosophers, but rather that kings should secretly implement the philosophers' insights, in pursuit of perpetual peace. Power corrupts, and corruption misleads the public councils of state. But philosophers have no power, which frees them to think, and to understand better the real mechanics and purposes of government.

Kant's secret article supplies some of the deficiencies of his earlier guarantee, by acknowledging the extent to which nature requires guidance in realizing its ends. The whole history of the world reveals a procession of violence and injustice so seldom interrupted, as to undermine the plausibility of natural providence, or nature's benevolence to humanity. Nature supplies the materials for human felicity without creating the political structures to support them. The science of politics determines the best system of political checks and balances to harness nature in pursuit of republican government, and social justice for all. Creating just constitutions requires active philosophy and human intervention. The greatest weakness of Kant's proposal for perpetual peace is his lack of specificity about what structures will be needed to secure and to preserve a lawful republican state.

4. The identity of international law, morals, and politics

Kant's sanguine reliance on nature's "guarantee" of perpetual peace reflects his greater interest in moral than in political questions. Both appendices to his essay on perpetual peace explain all politics (national and international), as applied branches of right or justice, for which morals supply the theoretical foundation. This means that morals and true politics never conflict. Politics, properly understood, realize the absolutely binding moral laws by which all actions *ought* to be governed, so that anyone who wishes to know her or his own civic duty may do so, simply by consulting the inborn reason that all of us possess. Kant knew that practical political maxims must consider the actual structure of human nature, including its weaknesses. Good Kantian politicians and statesmen will continuously examine their political institutions, to bring them into conformity with natural law or right ("*Naturrecht*").

Kantian politicians will not, of course, destroy the existing bonds of any political or cosmopolitan community before they have something better to put in its place, but they will always continue to maintain a course toward eventual reform, to realize political justice (*"die nach Rechtsgesetzen beste Verfassung"*). Kant hoped that politicians would rule as much as possible in a republican (*"republikanisch"*) manner, while adjusting the constitution gradually to be itself more republican, and just. Kant concluded that any natural-law-respecting constitution (*"rechtliche"*), even if it is not very lawful (*"rechtmassig"*) itself, will be better than no constitution at all. Revolutions and invasions should not occur, unless they will make things better.

Kant observed that international society does not possess and should never obtain the despotic right to formulate coercive laws for mechanical application by lawyers. Nations must rely instead on the application of reason to universal principles of freedom to justify their public actions and political constitutions to others. This follows the normal international practice of public argument by reference to public right (*"öffentlich Recht"*). Even when states and lawyers argue insincerely, their insincere references to public right and justice confirm those concepts' irreducible value as sources of international obligation, applying Kant's fundamental principle of right, which is always to act in such a way that you could wish your maxim to be the universal law.

Kant's conceptions of political, international, and cosmopolitan right are the moral constructs of reason, and universally binding. He considered that genuinely republican (*"echt-republikanisch"*) government will best secure the obedience and prosperity of the people so long as politicians introduce it gradually, seizing upon favorable circumstances to advance the republican agenda, without recourse to hasty or violent innovation. Kant expected that peace would follow justice, when the general will (*"allgemeine Wille"*) discovers the concept of right (*"Rechtsbegriff"*), among or between peoples, on the basis of freedom and equality. *"Fiat iustitia, pereat mundus"* – for Kant justice came first, and everything else would follow.

Kant's formula for perpetual peace required first that the state should have an internal constitution organized in accordance with pure principles of right (*"eine nach reinen Rechtsprinzipien eingerichtete innere Verfassung des Staats"*) and second that it should unite with other states to form some sort of federal union (*"allgemein Staat"*). Morality, law, and politics go together. Without justice, there will be no peace. Kant was confident that human reason will gradually apply moral principles to secure justice, helping right to increase, since all right comes from justice (*"Gerechtigkeit"*).

This identity between international law, morals, and politics demands a more detailed description of republican institutions, at both the national and the federal level, than Kant was ever willing to provide. To claim (as Kant did) that republican institutions will find and implement justice, requires some description of what republican institutions would look like. *Perpetual Peace* avoids these specifics. Kant's specificity lies instead in his moral formula or calculus, "to act in such a way that you could wish your maxim to be the universal law." This leaves the politics too vague to reach any definite understandings, or to resolve any disagreements about justice, which may arise between citizens or states.

5. The transcendental concept of public right

Kant concluded his essay on perpetual peace by supplying a new and more detailed formula with which to calculate the content of public justice or right, which forms (as Kant explained it) the only lasting basis of peace. Kant's conception of public right depends on publicity as the final measure of law and justice. Kant's rule holds that all maxims of action that cannot be made public are wrong, while all maxims that require publicity in order to succeed must be right, in morals as well as politics.

This formal attribute of publicness ("*Publizität*") epitomizes in a single phrase all Kant's philosophy of right, both ethical and juridical. Kant argues that every claim of right must have this public quality. Concerning the "*Staatsrecht*" or "*ius civitatis*" (for example), Kant denies the right of rebellion against unjust tyrants, because such a principle could never be openly accepted, as part of a civil constitution. Similarly, in the case of "*Völkerrecht*" or "*ius gentium,*" Kant denies that states can ever legitimately renounce their commitments within the pacific federation, because no state would willingly have joined the federation in the first place, knowing that others could withdraw. Kant explained that "*Weltbürgerrecht*" or the "*ius cosmopoliticum*" follows the same principles, by close analogy with international law. Kant did not imagine that everything public is necessarily just, but rather that nothing political can ever be just, that cannot be publicized, or acted on openly.

Publicity discovers morality or "rightness" best (including international right), only when a lawful ("*rechtlich*") state already exists. Kant's conception of public right ("*öffentliches Recht*") requires this lawful state or republic. Since Kant believed that only a federative association of states can lawfully support freedom, he concluded that politics and morality will never agree, until the federative union ("*Verein*") is in place.

Kant's transcendental concept of public right, requiring publicity, captures a central element of republican justice, which recognizes the importance of public debate. Republics test ideas by deliberation, and confirm them by votes. Governments that act without submitting their policies to public examination will make mistakes about justice, by misunderstanding the common good. Public deliberation clarifies moral error by bringing all citizens' experience and observations into play. This true and convincing argument for popular sovereignty becomes nonsense, however, when Kant twists it to protect despotism. To publicize one's planned revolution against non-republican tyrants would be suicide. This does not mean that revolutions should never happen. Secret plans against oppression will be justified, when republican deliberation would be subject to retaliation and violence.

6. Kantian theory of international law

Reviewing Kant's arguments on *Perpetual Peace* reveals the extent to which his conception of right depended upon natural law. Kant's two maxims of universality and publicity provide the natural-law basis for all legitimate government policy. The only legitimate governments (Kant believed) will be those that implement republican institutions, as part of a republican federation, to realize the moral rules that Kant's moral maxims endorse. Some preliminary articles would be necessary to make the world ready for republican government, but even without them Kant expected that justice would eventually prevail.

The central element of Kant's essay on perpetual peace – his list of definitive articles – is also his best and most convincing argument. Kant believed that *ius civitatis* should rest on whatever political institutions (including the rule of law) will best realize objective morality and justice. This is true. He argued for a *ius gentium* that would protect and coordinate these republics in one large federation. This seems sensible. Kant suggested that the *ius cosmopoliticum* should encourage mutual non-hostility between states. So it should. What Kant lacks is any workable description of what should count as republican forms of government, when applied to the actual constitutions of states.

In this Kant resembles John Locke – useful for the principles, but not for forms of government. When Kant does offer specifics, they are weak and unconvincing (as in his preliminary articles), or pernicious (as in his strictures against revolution, forbidding secrecy against tyrants). Kant's argument for republican government is just and convincing, but never supported by sufficient details about what a republic should look like. This leaves would-be Kantians strangely at sea, committed to principles of liberty and justice, without clear techniques for making them real. To find the "*rechtliche Verfassung,*" republican internationalists most look to other sources, which is why they so seldom agree on what their master would have wanted. The Kantian Theory of international law is a republican theory of natural law, left deliberately vague, to encourage the gradual development of republican institutions, in a world of illegitimate despots, and lawless tyrannical states.

16
International Humanitarian Intervention

Humanitarian intervention has always played an important part in international relations. States intervene in each other's affairs to promote justice, to advance their own interests, or both – but usually call on justice and human rights first in justifying their actions. Even the most extreme apostle of sovereignty, Jean Bodin, conceded that one sovereign may intervene to punish another who governs without regard to the common good of his subjects.[1] Some level of interference by governments or individuals to prevent the abuses of others must be tolerated in any case, whatever one's views, for the same reason that some interference with others must always be legitimate under any legal system: because it cannot be totally avoided. Any action by a state, individual, group of states or group of individuals will have an effect on others, and to that extent interfere with them. The question for lawyers and philosophers cannot be *whether* intervention is legitimate (because a total prohibition on interference would preclude all action) but rather *when* intervention is legitimate and when it is not. Law sets limits on how much one person, group of persons, state or group of states may intervene to influence others, and establishes procedures to support official interventions (enforcement), or to prevent improper interventions (delicts or crimes). Some level of interference must be tolerated because all action is intervention, and total inaction would not be practical.

Philosophers and lawyers who have sought to limit "intervention" by one person or state in the "internal affairs" of others are not engaged so much in promoting a prohibition as in drawing a line – the line between what will count as forbidden "intervention" and what will not. Those actions of a state that we view as "internal" (or "private," when speaking of individuals) will be protected from "intervention" or outside scrutiny. Those that we choose to count as "external" (or "public") will not. When the Charter of the United Nations discourages United Nations intervention "in matters which are essentially within the domestic jurisdiction of any State" (Art. 2.7), the protected zone extends only so far as our conception of the state's "domestic jurisdiction," however we choose to define it.

Theories of law provide definitions for terms such as "intervention" and "domestic jurisdiction" that practice and treaties leave vague. Like all law, international law claims to deserve obedience, which (like all law) international law actually deserves only to the extent that it is just, or at least more just than other available options. Most legal systems have a legislature to make laws, courts to interpret them, and systems of enforcement to make their laws effective. But international law finds its content primarily in considering what *would be* just, and its obedience primarily in convincing states that international law *is* just and deserves to be obeyed. Drawing the line between a state's protected "domestic jurisdiction" and its unprotected "human rights violations" depends largely on what would be just, and which line captures justice best.

1. Sovereignty

The "sovereignty" of states, like the "liberty" of citizens, is the bundle of rights that all states deserve as members of the international community. The United Nations Charter (to give one recent example) begins with the fundamental principle of "sovereign equality" among its members.[2] This implies that members shall settle their disputes by "peaceful means" (in accordance with justice)[3] and refrain from "the threat or use of force against the territorial integrity or political independence of any State."[4] Later United Nations documents such as the 1970 General Assembly *Declaration on Principles of International Law Concerning Friendly Relations and Cooperation Among States* reaffirm the basic importance of the sovereign equality of states, based on the principle of "equal rights and self-determination of peoples," as established by the Charter of the United Nations[5] and customary international law.

The *Declaration on Friendly Relations* illustrates the process by which governments justify their power under international law, by connecting their national "sovereignty" to indisputable moral truths. The Preamble to the Charter of the United Nations declares the "equal rights of men and women and of nations large and small." All men and women deserve equal rights, and therefore so do the nations into which they have associated themselves. From this it follows that the "peoples" of these nations should develop mutually "friendly relations," on the basis of their "equal rights and self-determination."[6] Peoples deserve equal rights because people deserve equal rights. The *Declaration on Friendly Relations* "bear[s] in mind" the values of "freedom, equality, justice, ... respect for fundamental human rights," and the "rule of law"[7] while asserting a norm of non-intervention "in the affairs of any other state."[8] This juxtaposition is designed to imply that the two principles are inseparable.

The Declaration on Friendly Relations goes on to denounce any form of "coercion" aimed at the "political independence or territorial integrity" of any state, [9] as being (by implication) contrary to that state's "sovereign equality."[10] The Declaration strengthens the Charter's prohibition on the "use of force" by forbidding "political" or "economic" coercion. States should not be "coerced," because their peoples deserve "freedom and independence."[11] The *Declaration on Friendly Relations* properly criticizes "the subjection of peoples to alien subjugation, domination and exploitation,"[12] while prohibiting intervention "directly or indirectly, for any reason whatever, in the internal or external affairs of any other State."[13]

2. Non-intervention

The *Declaration of Friendly Relations* provides a useful starting point for discussing the international norm against intervention, because it supplies the most extreme recognized elaboration of the non-intervention norm. The *Declaration* prohibits even "indirect" intervention "for any reason whatever" in any "affairs" of state. Yet in order to justify this standard, and to secure compliance from states, even the *Declaration on Friendly Relations* must relate non-intervention to "liberty," to "justice," and to "fundamental human rights." The *Declaration* must condemn "subjugation, domination and exploitation" and maintain the "equal rights and self-determination of peoples." These qualifications help to clarify what will count as "intervention" and which are properly a state's own internal "affairs" for the purposes of international law. Violations of liberty, justice and fundamental human rights, or other subjugation, domination and exploitation of a people, or the denial of the rule of law or of a people's right to self-determination, cannot fall within the zone of a government's private affairs that are protected against inter-state "intervention," because sovereignty and self-determination themselves cannot be justified as law, without reference to the universal principles of non-domination and fundamental human rights.

The Institute of International Law recognized the borders of states' protected "affairs" and the limits of their inviolable "domestic jurisdiction" in its resolution on *"La protection des droits de l'homme et le principe de non-intervention dans les affaires intérieures des Etats,"* adopted on the thirteenth of September, 1989 at Santiago de Compostela. The Institute considered that human rights, having been given international protection in the Charter of the United Nations and other charters and constituent instruments of international organizations, and commonly understood as including the rights described in the United Nations General Assembly's *Universal Declaration of Human Rights* of December 10, 1948, are therefore legally subject to "international protection" and not "matters essentially within the domestic jurisdiction of states."[14]

The resolution of the Institute of International Law is not important so much as an authoritative statement of international law (although it is very good evidence of widely accepted principles), as it is as a clear illustration of the reasoning that supports the international legal order. Although "intervention" in a state's domestic "affairs" would be improper, "measures" taken in response to violations of international human rights law are perfectly acceptable and indeed sometimes required by each state's duty of international solidarity in defense of human dignity throughout the world. Under ordinary international law, as it has existed for centuries, states are entitled to take diplomatic, economic and other "measures," individually and collectively, against states that have violated their international obligations. Legitimate countermeasures in the form of retorsion or reprisals are not forbidden "intervention" under international law.[15]

3. Humanitarian intervention

Humanitarian "intervention" (to use the word in its ordinary sense) is not prohibited international "intervention" (in the legal sense) because it does not trespass on a state's protected "affairs." The Institute of International Law recognized human rights as a direct expression of the dignity of the human person, and therefore the subject of each state's *erga omnes* obligation to every other state, so that "every state has a legal interest in the protection of human rights" everywhere. The Institute referred to the "duty of solidarity among all states to ensure as rapidly as possible the effective protection of human rights throughout the world"[16] and noted that a "state acting in breach of its obligations in the sphere of human rights cannot evade its international responsibility by claiming that such matters are essentially within its domestic jurisdiction."[17]

Human rights violations cannot be considered as essentially within a state's domestic jurisdiction, because doing so would discredit the underlying concept of "domestic jurisdiction" in international law. States exist, according to the theory of international law advanced by the United Nations Charter, to secure economic, social and cultural advances, to guarantee human rights and fundamental freedoms, and to implement national self-determination.[18] Releasing states from these obligations would undermine the foundations of their sovereignty by discrediting the concepts of freedom and autonomy on which state sovereignty depends. Without individual rights there can be no states' rights. Governments deserve deference only to the extent that they serve the common good of all the citizens subject to their rule.

Humanitarian intercession cannot be prohibited "intervention" in a state's internal "affairs," because human rights violations are never wholly "internal" or "private" in the necessary sense of those words. This does not justify indiscriminate or excessive humanitarian countermeasures to correct all human rights violations, whatever the circumstances. Like all other international measures, humanitarian countermeasures must be proportionate to the gravity of the violation, taking into account the interests of individuals and of third states, and all of the relevant circumstances.[19] The proper limits on humanitarian intervention to enforce international law against human rights violations depend less on the limits of "intervention" and "domestic affairs" (since human rights are never purely domestic) than they do on questions of proportionality, objectivity, and enforcement.

4. Enforcement

Measures or countermeasures against human rights violations may sometimes be justified as necessary for the enforcement of international law. But not all enforcement measures are justified. Different responses will be appropriate to different violations, and some violations will have to go unpunished when no appropriate remedy can be found. The International Law Commission's *Draft Articles on State Responsibility* suggest some of the limits to measures that states may take in response to other states' violations of international law (or of obligations that "may be owed to another State, to several States, or to the international community as a whole)."[20] In their current form, the *Draft Articles* would preclude the threat or use of force in countermeasures "in a manner contrary to the Charter of the United Nations," or other measures in violation of fundamental human rights; in violation of humanitarian law; in violation of peremptory norms of general international law; or in violation of diplomatic inviolability.[21]

The *Draft Articles on State Responsibility* recognize that countermeasures "must be commensurate with the injury suffered, taking into account the gravity of the internationally wrongful act and the rights in question."[22] This reflects the obvious truth that the punishment should fit the crime, but also raises pervasive problems of judgment in enforcing international law. Sanctions against human rights violations will have negative effects, not only on the governments that have violated international law, but also on the subjects that they rule. Military interventions will often hurt oppressed peoples. Economic sanctions almost always harm citizens and subjects far more than they harm oppressive governments. Indeed, rights-violating regimes often profit (as in Yugoslavia and Iraq) from economic sanctions, while their peoples starve.

The notion that subjects are in some sense collectively responsible for their government's violations of international law is particularly ill-considered in the case of human rights violations, when the citizens themselves are victims of the state. In such cases swift overwhelming military interventions may be more justified than drawn-out economic sanctions, so long as military interventions act quickly to restore or to establish democratic institutions and respect for international law. The less democratic the government that violates human rights, the less appropriate economic sanctions will be for enforcing international law. Sanctions were more appropriate (for example) against Serbia, whose people were united in oppressing ethnic minorities, than against Iraq, whose dictator never enjoyed popular support.

5. Objectivity

The examples of Serbia and Iraq, whose governments suffered for violating international law, while other equally culpable governments in Russia and China (for example) did not, raise the question of objectivity in humanitarian interventions. Large powerful states that violate international law do not face the same levels of enforcement that smaller weaker states do. Small weak states can seldom act to prevent human rights violations from occurring elsewhere. Large powerful states sometimes intervene. This raises two problems of objectivity. First, the problem of impunity, because the large states are immune from serious punishment. Second, the problem of poor judgment, when powerful states act alone. Given the absence of any legitimate international government, enforcement of international law will necessarily be partial, uneven, and favor the strong.

Some scholars suggest that *de facto* impunity for strong governments justifies an equal impunity for the weak, but this does not follow. Punishing weak oppressors establishes principles that also apply to the strong, and may sometimes be enforced against them. The problem of poor judgment raises greater difficulties. Powerful states may make mistakes, or use human rights as pretense to dominate their neighbors. Given the *erga omnes* nature of human rights violations[23] and every state's right to respond proportionately to violations of international human rights law, states must be constrained so that they judge violations and impose their sanctions correctly.

The test of veracity in international law is consensus. The greater the consensus, the greater the likelihood of truth. Like other foundational doctrines of international law, this doctrine of legal clarification rests on the enlightened premiss that people (and peoples) everywhere possess reason. If international law consists of rules of conduct deduced by reason from the nature of the society of nations,[24] then consensus clarifies the dictates of reason, and consent may modify them, in certain circumstances. This doctrine has two implications: first, that governments may act with greater certainty in enforcing international law when other governments agree with their judgments – multilateral decision-making is more accurate than unilateral action; second, that the views of non-democratic governments count for less in establishing the requirements of international law. Non-democracies speak only for their rulers, and not for the captive subjects of their power.

6. The use of force

"Intervention" in its strongest sense implies the use of force, which has a special status under the United Nations Charter. In Article 2, section 4 of the Charter, the members of the United Nations renounce "the threat or use of force against the territorial integrity or political independence of any State, or in any other manner inconsistent with the Purposes of the United Nations." This language would seem to imply that the use of force consistent with the purposes of the United Nations would be acceptable (Article I purposes include protecting human rights and the self-determination of peoples), but the Charter also puts the use of force into a special category, as being inherently threatening to international peace and security, and contrary to the principle that disputes should be settled by "peaceful means."[25]

Reason and the nature of the society of nations indicate that force should be avoided as much as possible in resolving international disputes.

The members of the Institute of International Law discouraged "the use of armed force in violation of the Charter of the United Nations" to enforce international human rights law.[26] The Third *Restatement of Foreign Relations Law* endorses "all remedies generally available for violation of an international agreement,"[27] but limits its conception of human rights enforcement to states that have exhibited "a consistent pattern of gross violations."[28] *The Draft Articles on State Responsibility* restricts its discussion of *erga omnes* violations to "serious breaches" involving "gross or systematic" harm,[29] and provides that countermeasures shall not involve any derogation from the "obligation to refrain from the threat or use of force as embodied in the Charter."[30]

The United Nations Charter offers a mechanism through the Security Council for coordinating "measures" to be taken to maintain or to restore international peace and security,[31] which may extend to enforcing human rights norms, to the extent that such violations threaten international peace and security. The General Assembly of the United Nations also provides a vehicle through which states can reach consensus about the maintenance of international peace and security, and may make recommendations,[32] as the General Assembly did to encourage intervention against the "subjugation, domination and exploitation" of colonialism.[33] Not all human rights violations necessarily threaten international peace and security, however, and the United Nations is not the only instrument for enforcing international law. The long-established practice of bilateral enforcement by military force remains available in response to serious and systematic violations of humans rights law, such as slavery and genocide.

7. Humility

The guiding principle in determining the existence of and proper response to human rights violations under international law should be humility on the part of the governments involved. Those with the power to intervene or take measures to enforce international law should act with humility, understanding the limits of their objectivity and judgment. The chance of mistake and the costs of intervention favor overlooking minor or anomalous violations of human rights law. Even serious or systematic violations should be studied with care, and due deference to the judgment of others. Sometimes the costs of humanitarian intervention will outweigh the benefits to those oppressed.

Humility in judging violations encourages democratic techniques in assessing the need for humanitarian interventions. Deference to the opinions of others requires consultation and real deliberation. The actual structure of existing international institutions, such as the United Nations and the International Court of Justice, gives undue weight to the views of repressive governments, including many human rights violators and non-democracies. Consultation and deliberation become difficult and less reliable when governments shut their peoples out from the discussion. Non-democratic governments have no way of judging or constraining their own judgments of illegality, and therefore no valid basis for engaging in humanitarian intervention, except in cooperation with democratic states. Democratic states should seek the views of other democracies, and above all the perceptions of those on whose behalf they seek to intervene, before taking action.

The actual views of those oppressed carry particular weight in contemplating the method of enforcement, whether by arms, economic sanctions, or simple criticism of the oppressive regime. The enforcement of human rights law protects the interest in human dignity that all states owe to all others, but also shields particular individuals against particular harms. Humility requires not only that states should question their own judgments of harm, but also that they should measure their own interest in human dignity against the more direct sufferings of individual persons. When humanitarian intervention will harm its supposed beneficiaries too much, or against their wishes, it may no longer be justified.

8. Protecting universal human rights

States will act to prevent human rights violations for the same reasons that people have always acted against injustice. These include sympathy for the victims, fear of the perpetrators, and the general desire to establish just legal principles by enforcing them against violators. Legal action against human rights violations may be as trivial as verbal criticism, or as serious as armed intervention. The appropriate level of response depends on the circumstances. Nations deserve a zone of sovereignty or "domestic jurisdiction" within which to develop their own histories and cultures, but governments should never have and do not deserve a license to oppress or to exploit the peoples subject to their power. The sovereign rights of states derive from the human rights of individuals. Governments that deny human rights are violating international law.

The principle of non-intervention in the internal affairs of states does not extend to protect human rights violators because human rights violations concern all human beings. To forbid humanitarian intervention would discredit international law, by denying the fundamental justice on which all law must rest. This does not mean that enforcement should be indiscriminate or disproportionate, but rather that transgressions should be punished as fairly and objectively as possible. Sometimes the use of force will be justified to put an end to serious breaches of human rights obligations, when gross and systematic violations such as slavery or genocide cannot be prevented in any other way, but all interference or intervention to enforce human rights should reflect international consensus after democratic deliberation, and due concern for the rights of others.

Humanitarian intervention is legitimate under international law whenever serious human rights violations can be prevented in no other way, so long as the states enforcing international law respect the territorial integrity and political independence of the peoples that they protect. All nations have the equal right to self-determination, so that the people themselves may decide who their rulers shall be. Governments that deny their peoples human rights and fundamental freedoms forfeit their right to rule. The limits of humanitarian intervention depend on the value of human dignity, the welfare of those oppressed, the objectivity of the enforcers, and their humility in the face of public opinion. As the framers of the United Nations Charter recognized: states must conform to the principles of justice and international law, or there will be no peace.[34]

17
The Authority of the International Court of Justice

Recently some lawyers and statesmen have begun to cite judgments of the International Court of Justice as if they were decisive evidence of the content of international law. This trend, if it continues, will tend to diminish the influence of international law on the actions of states and others, by arrogating the authoritative determination of the content of international law to a tribunal that was never intended to generate rules of universal application, is ill-equipped to do so, and ought not usually to be viewed as having done so, except in very exceptional circumstances.

1. Why people exaggerate the Court's authority

The tendency to view the judgments of the International Court of Justice as if they were decisive evidence of the content of international law arises by analogy with the role of courts in certain Western liberal democracies, and particularly with that of the Supreme Court of the United States of America, which gives final and decisive interpretations of the constitution and laws of the United States, including international law and treaties.[1] Collectively these constitute the "supreme law of the land," and are binding throughout the Union.[2] As Chief Justice John Marshall explained on behalf of a unanimous court in *Marbury v. Madison* in 1803, although "the people collectively have the right to establish for their future government, such principles as, in their opinion, shall most conduce to their own happiness" as "supreme and paramount law," it is "emphatically the province and duty of the judicial department to say what the law is" and therefore to "expound and interpret" the law of the land.[3]

The doctrine of the separation of powers, as embodied in the many written constitutions that have developed in the two-hundred years since Marshall wrote his famous opinion, have confirmed the judiciary in most such regimes as the ultimate arbiter of the content of law. Legislatures draft statutes, according to this theory, but the judiciary says what the law is. So long as the executive power in the state remains willing to enforce and to respect the courts' decisions, then law will be whatever the courts say it is. Oliver Wendell Holmes expressed the view of many advocates litigating under separation-of-powers constitutionalist regimes when he said that the business of lawyers is "the prediction of the incidence of the public force through the instrumentality of the courts." Since "in societies like ours" the "whole power of the state will be put forth to carry out their judgment and decrees." A strictly practical man, a "bad man" as Justice Holmes put it, living under the rule of law and the separation of powers of a modern constitutional state, will pay attention to what courts say, and treat this as "law," or suffer the consequences.[4]

The United Nations Charter was drafted in the same style and structure as the Constitution of the United States of America, using much of the same vocabulary. "We the Peoples of the United Nations"[5] echoed "We the People of the United States"[6] in seeking to establish conditions under which justice and respect for the obligations arising from treaties and other sources of international law can be maintained."[7] Both establish a "House of Representatives" (United States)[8] or "General Assembly" (United Nations).[9] Both establish a "Senate" (United States)[10] or "Security Council" (United Nations).[11] Both establish an "executive" (United States)[12] or "secretariat" (United Nations).[13] And both establish a "Supreme Court" (United States)[14] or "International Court of Justice" (United Nations).[15] The United States Supreme Court holds the ultimate "judicial power of the United States"[16] and the International Court of Justice is "the principal judicial organ of the United Nations."[17] This is not to say that the United Nations enjoys an independent power or internal checks and balances that in any way resemble those of the United States, but rather that these superficial similarities can mislead the unwary.

2. The International Court of Justice was never intended to determine the law

Notwithstanding its rhetorical parallels with ordinary democratic constitutions, the Charter of the United Nations did not create new system of laws, and was not intended to do so. The primary purpose of the

United Nations Charter was to "save succeeding generations from the scourge of war"[18] by "maintaining international peace and security"[19] based on the "sovereign equality of all its members."[20] While the United Nations will "adjust" or "settle" those international disputes which might lead to a breach of the peace "in conformity with the principles of justice and international law,"[21] the Organization does not exist for the purpose of enforcing international law, and will not always do so. The General Assembly and Security Council are not the world's legislature, the Secretary-General is not the world's president, and the International Court of Justice is not the world's court, or the ultimate arbiter of international law, even under the terms of its own statute.

The Statute of the International Court of Justice creates a body of fifteen judges,[22] elected by majority vote in the United Nations General Assembly and Security Council,[23] for nine year terms, and eligible for re-election.[24] In this the International Court of Justice differs from the supreme courts of modern constitutional democracies such as the United States, where Justices are selected by democratically elected officials[25] and hold their seats *quam diu se bene gesserint*, which is to say, for life.[26] The judges of the International Court of Justice are selected with the significant participation of the many non-liberal, non-democratic governments that hold seats in the United Nations General Assembly and Security Council, and inasmuch as the judges are eligible for periodic re-election, they remain subject to the continuing influence of non-democratic and illiberal regimes. This deprives the International Court of Justice of the democratic legitimacy and independence necessary before any court can deserve the deference of its subjects. The International Court of Justice lacks the basis in the people collectively that gave John Marshall's court its decisive authority.

The Court's own Statute recognizes this shortcoming, by extending the jurisdiction of the International Court of Justice only to those cases "which the parties refer to it," either directly, or by treaty.[27] Many cases are not heard by the full court, but rather by smaller chambers of judges approved by the parties to a particular dispute.[28] In any case, the International Court of Justice Statute makes it clear that the decisions of the court have "no binding force except between the parties and in respect of that particular case."[29] According to the terms of its own statute, the International Court of Justice will refer to judicial decisions (including its own) only as "a subsidiary means for the determination of the rules of law," on the same level of authority as the teachings of publicists, and inferior to international conventions, custom, and the general principles of law accepted by civilized nations.[30]

3. The International Court of Justice is ill-equipped to determine the content of international law

The International Court of Justice is ill-equipped to determine the content of international law for precisely the same reasons that it is so well-designed to "adjust" or to "settle" international disputes, which is to say, because it is subject to the political control and oversight of interested states. As part of the United Nations System, the Court's primary emphasis is on the peaceful settlement of disputes, and not on the enforcement of justice. Cases come before the Court only when parties to a dispute have agreed that they should do so. This implies a general willingness in advance to abide by its decisions, but creates no actual mechanism for imposing unwelcome decisions of the International Court of Justice on recalcitrant parties, unless the Security Council makes an independent decision to do so, in response to a threat to the peace.

The International Court of Justice is subservient in the first instance to the Security Council[31] and in the second instance to those states which use it to resolve their disputes. While the Court should arbitrate such disputes "on the basis of international law," it may also decide them *ex aequo et bono*, or on the basis of other stipulations made by the parties.[32] The settlement of disputes within the United Nations System seeks solutions "by peaceful means in such a manner that international peace and security ... are not endangered."[33] This requires the International Court of Justice to consider the particular situation and relative power of the parties, rendering all decisions of the Court too idiosyncratic to be decisive "except between the parties and in respect of that particular case."[34]

Determining the content of law requires procedures designed to elicit the objective requirements of justice with greater accuracy and stability than would be possible through the separate and independent judgment of the law's own subjects, acting without legal control. Domestic legal systems within states claim this authority, which they actually deserve only to the extent that states maintain the liberal and democratic institutions that justify political power. The International Court of Justice makes no claim to decisive authority to determine the content of international law, because it lacks the republican foundations that would support such a claim. Instead the International Court offers a useful forum for the peaceful settlement of disputes between consenting states. Extending this authority to restrict the independent legal judgments of democratic and liberal republican states would undermine international law by separating the law from its ultimate foundation in justice.

4. The authority of the International Court of Justice

The authority of the International Court of Justice has a limited scope, which does not extend beyond settling the disputes that states decide to set before it. These settlements have no precedential value, and should play no more than a subsidiary role even in the court's own subsequent judgments, let alone anyone else's. The International Court of Justice exists to settle disputes, not to declare or to create international law. Capacious claims for the court's decisive authority undermine this useful function, by giving the court's settlements an imperial power, which would dissuade many just and law-abiding states from bringing their disputes before it.

18
Borders and Democracy in International Law

With the collapse of the Soviet Union, and the emergence of democracies or quasi-democracies in Russia, South Africa, and throughout South America, the most powerful and persistent opponents of popular sovereignty have receded, or admitted their mistakes, and a sort of democratic triumphalism has entered the legal literature. Where Hugo Grotius once boldly rejected the idea that supreme power necessarily resides in the people, frankly viewing certain peoples (he mentioned Cappadocians) as fit to be slaves,[1] some scholars now assert an "emerging right of democratic governance" such that no government should be considered legitimate without free, fair and frequent elections.[2]

At the same time, and in some of the same places, new states have emerged from the ruins of the Soviet Union and former Yugoslavia. Czechs, Slovaks, Scots, Québecois, and many others in the provinces or former provinces of larger states have asserted their separate national identities, seeking plebiscites, and claiming democratic support. If democracy is the measure of legitimacy, then such votes should be decisive, and the subjects of non-democratic states should have the right to secede, or to rebel.

Yet proponents of the right to democracy remain extraordinarily vague about which groups should vote and be free. The peoples of non-self-governing colonial territories enjoy the most widely recognized right to secession, but beyond that democrats often equivocate.[3] If democracy through general votes of the population is the ultimate source of governmental legitimacy, then there can be no principled basis for dividing the world into groups for voting. The larger the group, the greater the legitimacy, one might suppose. If so, a consolidated universal world democracy would be the most just form of government.

Democrats do not always seem to want this. To the extent that they do not, democracy is not their fundamental value. Something else must explain the persisting separation between peoples of the world, and justify democrats in accepting such divisions.[4] But any rule that justifies separation faces the opposite problem – of escalating fragmentation. If minorities can separate from larger groups too easily, then they will do so, and each minority will find minorities of its own, until each state is a state of one citizen, alone and unloved. So separatists must have regulating values too, like democrats, to draw the line between isolation and oppression.

1. The republican perspective

Finding the limits of separatism and the democratic entitlement requires a republican perspective, which is to say, the perspective that views laws and legal systems as justified, if at all, by service to the common good of the people.[5] In fact, nearly all legal systems purport to take this perspective, and so to serve "justice." This assertion of justice is the essence of law, without which impositions of power lose the normative element that gives them validity in any legal system.[6] Republicans equate justice with the common good[7] and find the purposes of government and society in promoting a harmony of interests, so that the good of each individual contributes to the benefit of all.[8]

Republican doctrine developed primarily to serve the common good *within* states, such as the Roman republic, Florence, England and the United States of America.[9] Republican authors agreed that popular sovereignty, the rule of law, the separation of powers, checks and balances, representation, and elections would all be necessary to prevent any individual or group of individuals from seizing control of the government, and running the state to serve private or factional interests.[10] Republican conceptions such as the *populus* (the people), *libertas* (liberty), and *jus gentium* (the law of nations) developed to serve this conception of separate peoples, each united around its own sense of justice and agreement about the common good.[11]

When republicans contemplated international relations they did not seek a world republic, despite their belief in universal human community.[12] Usually they proposed an overarching federation of republics, to coordinate their mutual relations.[13] For example, the United States Constitution self-consciously established a federal system, guaranteeing separate republican governments to each of the 13 states.[14] The problem for republicans over the centuries has been the question now faced for the first time by democrats, as they assert their new right to plebiscites and voting. Who are the people? The boundaries between peoples determine the jurisdiction of each republic, and the province of international law.

2. Democracy

"Democracy" in its strictest sense means "rule by the people," which is to say direct participation in all decisions by every citizen, or at least by some large group of citizens chosen, as in Athens, by lot. The excesses and ultimate failures of the Athenian demagogues made the Greek term "democracy" an epithet of abuse for two millennia, until the "Democratic Republican" and later "Democratic" parties in the United States embraced certain aspects of the Athenian model, to differentiate themselves from their "Federalist Republican" and later "National Republican" rivals. Alexis de Tocqueville's famous description of "democracy" in America used the word in a new sense, to describe a state in which the people really did seem to rule, albeit indirectly, through their elected representatives.[15] When contemporary lawyers write of the "right to democracy" they probably mean to require "periodic and genuine elections which shall be by universal and equal suffrage and shall be held by secret vote or by equivalent free voting procedures," as suggested in the Universal Declaration of Human Rights at Article 21.[16]

Proponents of the democratic entitlement assume its value as a source of legitimacy in international law.[17] Republicans value democracy too, but not as the ultimate value. Republican popular sovereignty depends on the perception that unelected or unremovable governments will always subvert the common interest to serve their own ends. Republican doctrine requires democracy, not for its own sake, but because democracy facilitates the finding (or creation) of a common good for all citizens. Democracy is valued because it serves republican ends, by keeping rulers focused on the common good. The underlying purpose of representative democracy in a just state is not to decide every issue by popular vote but rather to secure good government through periodic elections.

This instrumental value of democracy is important, because it explains the limits of voting, and offers criteria for drawing boundaries between districts. The rule of law and balance of powers play at least as large a role in republican government as does democracy, by preventing majority tyranny, or thoughtless populism.[18] Republicans such as James Madison[19] and Immanual Kant[20] made a point of distinguishing republicanism from democracy precisely because democracy often imposes injustices, while republics should not. Kant followed Livy in believing that peoples must be made ready for democracy, and prepared for republican structures of government, before they can safely assume their freedom and independent sovereignty.[21]

3. International law

The democratic entitlement first entered international law as part of the republican complex of ideas that revived the *jus gentium* through Grotius and Vattel after the Protestant reformation in Europe.[22] Grotius believed that sovereignty ("*imperium*") over peoples ("*populi*") passed only by inheritance, lawful war,[23] or consent,[24] because peoples should never be understood to yield their "liberty" involuntarily.[25] Rulers who violate the laws and the "*res publica*" may be resisted by force, Grotius suggested,[26] as may those who prove themselves to be enemies of the people as a whole.[27] Vattel confirmed that all sovereignty originates with the people, who may (if they so choose) confer it on a senate or a monarch,[28] but only for the purpose of serving the common good of all citizens.[29] When a tyrant arises, such as Philip II of Spain, his subjects may properly take up arms to protect their liberty, as did the inhabitants of the Netherlands, and create a new republic that serves their common good.[30]

This underlying conception of justice through popular sovereignty provides the law of nations with its most important and enduring claim to obedience and to respect. As Vattel explained it, nations or states are political bodies or societies united to obtain their citizens' common good and security.[31] This political union creates a new moral person, with obligations and rights of its own.[32] The law of nations governs relationships between such states.[33] Vattel suggested that since nations are composed of individuals who are by nature free and independent, then nations must be free and independent too,[34] subject only to the law of nature and to their own commitments, freely made.[35] Without this principle – that states in some sense speak for the peoples that they represent – international law would lose its moral authority. The United Nations Charter recognizes the importance of this claim in its preamble, purporting to derive constitutional authority from a mandate provided by "We the people of the United Nations."[36]

Contemporary international law endorses popular sovereignty through several other Charter provisions, and related resolutions and conventions of various international bodies. The United Nations Charter seeks as one of its fundamental purposes "to develop friendly relations among nations based on respect for the principle of equal rights and self-determination of peoples."[37] This includes the peoples of non-self-governing territories, whose metropolitan powers must help to develop each territory's "free political institutions,"[38] with a view toward their eventual "self-government" or "independence."[39] The Universal Declaration of Human Rights provides that "everyone has the right to take part in the government of his country, directly or through freely chosen representatives,"[40] as selected in "periodic and genuine elections which shall be by universal and equal suffrage."[41] This right reappears in the International Covenant on Civil and Political Rights, which reaffirms that "the inherent dignity" and the "equal and inalienable rights of all members of the human family is the foundation of freedom, justice and peace in the world"[42] so that "all peoples have the right of self-determination," by virtue of which "they freely determine their political status"[43] though "genuine periodic elections which shall be by universal and equal suffrage."[44]

4. Peoples

The validity of international law rests on the self-determination of peoples in the same way that the legitimacy of the world's separate states rests on the ultimate sovereignty of their various populations. From Cicero to Vattel to the United Nations Charter, the law of nations has claimed binding force because states speak for the peoples that they represent. Even non-democracies have endorsed democratic principles in international relations, because these give each state protection and an independent voice. Republican principles would insist that every people deserves a voice in international affairs, because without it, as in domestic politics, the common good will not be found, or realized. This makes the actual identity of "peoples" a very important question. If every people, including subject peoples, enjoys the right of self-determination, then what counts as a "people" will have significant legal implications.

The use of the word "people" or "*populus*" in international law derives from the republican tradition in Rome ("*res publica res est populi*"),[45] according to which ultimate sovereignty ("*imperium*") belonged to the "people" or ordinary citizens in Rome, whose state existed to serve their common good.[46] As Rome gradually conquered its neighbors in Italy and around the Mediterranean basin (always, the Romans insisted, after "just" wars), the Romans either incorporated the conquered populations into the Roman people, or made their polities into provinces, as subject peoples. Both Grotius and Vattel gave the example of Capua to illustrate national servitude, since Capua lost every vestige of republican government, after its total submission to Rome.[47] The underlying assumption supporting the traditional sense of the word "people" or *populus* was that individuals coalesce as a people by forming a state, which derives its sovereignty from their consent. This sovereignty can be transferred by consent to others, but doing so undermines the integrity of the people, by ceding their "liberty" to someone else.

The historical use of the word "people" to signify the citizens of a state, or residents of a non-self-governing territory or province, was perpetuated by the United Nations, through which existing states, including many multi-ethnic states, spoke as "peoples" to ratify the Charter,[48] forbidding interference with the territorial integrity or political independence of states,[49] and equating "peaceful and friendly relations among nations" with the "equal rights and self-determination of peoples."[50] "Peoples" were described as the "inhabitants" of specific territories, and as such considered deserving of "free political institutions."[51] This usage should be familiar to citizens of the United States, whose own constitution rests on the consent of the "people of the United States" as a whole,[52] confirmed by the peoples of its territorially distinct sub-states, meeting in their own local conventions.[53] Ethnic affinities do not create a people without political and territorial independence, and many ethically diverse "peoples" have expressed their right to self-determination through decolonization, despite extreme ethnic, religious and cultural differences, as in Africa and South America.[54]

5. Secession

The republican origin and proper understanding of "peoples" in international law as essentially territorial and political constructs suggests the missing criteria for evaluating claims to separatism and popular sovereignty that simple assertions of a "democratic entitlement" cannot supply. Each republican "people" shares a homeland, political institutions, and a strong claim to collective sovereignty. Subject peoples, whose sovereignty has been denied, deserve their "liberty," according to republican doctrine, which is to say, they deserve to enjoy those institutions of government best designed to serve the common good, including popular elections, the rule of law, the separation of powers, and governmental checks and balances.[55] The first test of what constitutes a "people" is existing political boundaries. Every sovereign state has a "people" in its territory – the people of Britain, the people of Canada, the people of the United States of America, and so forth, in every state.

As these examples should illustrate, some states also contain subordinate or component peoples, such as the peoples of Scotland, England, Maryland, Pennsylvania, or Québec. All these peoples enjoy stable borders and a measure of self-determination or popular sovereignty in that they elect their own rulers, both at the provincial and the federal levels. Republican principles would deny such "peoples" the right to secession, unless the federal government abuses its power and violates the common good, by discriminating against some particular minority or province. Purposely to exclude some minority or subgroup of the population from the common good of the citizens as a whole expresses the government's view that the group in question does not in fact belong to the "people" that the state must serve and protect. Denying elections, the separation of powers, independent judges, or any of the other basic attributes of republican government to any portion of the population expresses their non-membership in the body politic, and therefore their right to secede.

This right to separation may have a strong ethnic component, when states discriminate by ethnicity, but ethnicity itself does not justify separation without a clear expression of exclusion by the existing authorities. Even a showing of exclusion may not justify separation, without geographic realities to support it. Secession necessarily follows the territorial principle, while ethnicity does not. Finding a new and geographically distinct homeland for oppressed minority populations may often be so impractical (or unwelcome to its supposed beneficiaries) that such solutions should not be pursued. In these situations the proper remedy for violations of the republican principle would be reform or revolution, to prevent ethnic discrimination in the future.

6. Borders and democracy

Republican principles reconcile separatism and the democratic entitlement in international law by explaining how both relate to the common good of particular states, and to that of the international community as a whole. Human nature naturally seeks community. Many human goods would be impossible without cooperation between neighbors, including large-scale cooperation in states. Cultures develop through proximity, which suggests certain limitations on the optimum size of each political community. History has produced states that avoid the natural limits of imperial consolidation. When states get too large they need provinces, to bring government closer to the people.

The optimum size of such republics will vary according to circumstances, reflecting ordinary happenstance, including historical, cultural, linguistic, religious, ethnic, and geographical realities. The dominant project of international law has been to stabilize the boundaries between states, and to bring their peoples into harmony for the common good of all, in the same way that states should do for individuals. Just as states should be republics, to serve the good of their citizens, so the world community should respect republican principles, to serve the common good of all peoples. These principles include popular sovereignty (applied through the democratic principle of election), but also the separation of powers, checks and balances, independent judges, and other fundamental human rights.[56] Denying these rights may justify revolution, or the creation of new and smaller separatist republics.

Democracy is a fundamental entitlement of human community, but it is not the only entitlement of human community, and may be pernicious without other protections of minority rights. Separation is the ultimate refuge of oppressed minorities, subject provinces, and non-self-governing territories, but not the usual, the ordinary, and very seldom the best solution to majority or factional domination. Both democracy and separatism derive their legitimacy, when they have it, from the same source that legitimates all of international law, and any legal system, which is service to the common good of the people. Finding peoples of the world distributed in their respective states, justice requires that they should enjoy their fundamental rights, including democratic governance, and warrants various remedies, including separation, when these rights are denied. Without this basic regard for justice, international law has no authority, and there can be no peace.

19
The Right to Secede

Which groups enjoy the right to secede in international law, under what circumstances, and why? The "right to secede" in this context signifies the right of a group of the citizens or subjects of an existing state to remove themselves from its political jurisdiction, taking with them some portion of their former state's territory, to form a new political entity. Secession diminishes existing states by narrowing their territorial jurisdiction. The right to secede assumes the previous existence of states and depends for its own justification on the antecedent justifications for statehood. When the reasons for secession outweigh the reasons that justify statehood, or serve those ends better than would the continued existence of states within their historical boundaries, then secession will be justified, and citizens will have the right to secede.

1. The common good

States properly exist to serve the common good of the people who are subject to their rule. This "republican"[1] purpose of government provides the basis for all legitimate political and legal authority, including the authority of international law.[2] The following analysis of the right to secede begins with the republican assumption that like all other political structures, states and their national territories deserve respect and stability only to the extent that they serve the common good of their citizens better than other available arrangements.[3] Secession will be justified only when the collective good of all citizens benefits from the change.

This assumes, of course, that separate states should exist at all. Universal empire under a single authority might serve the common good of humanity better than the separate sovereignties of geographically distributed states. If this were true, then independent states should not exist. The argument for states depends on the belief that humans thrive better when divided into politically and geographically separate and largely autonomous units. A single centralized universal government would be too far removed from the differing circumstances in different regions to serve their culture and circumstances properly. This justifies the separate existence of national republics.[4]

Regional diversity justifies a separation of authority between different national republics, but only so long as they remain republics. Governments that do not serve the common good of the people subject to their power do not deserve political authority any more than one world empire would. States' authority can be a matter of degree. Some governments are more justifiable than others, without being fully just. In some cases a local despot would be preferable to a distant ruler. In other circumstances distant tyrants might be easier to evade, and therefore better for the people than local ones. Republican principles stipulate that neither distant nor local governments can ever enjoy legitimate authority without serving the common interests of the people that they rule. Stable national boundaries between the different political states help to develop local solidarity and deeper regional cultures, from which all citizens benefit, when states are properly constructed.

2. States

Separate states are preferable to universal empire because states maintain the local structures of culture, legal rules, and personal security within which citizens develop worthwhile lives. States are also preferable to anarchy, for much the same reasons. "State" signifies here a defined independent territory, with its own separate people and government. States can and have ceded elements of their independence or "sovereignty" to multinational structures such as the United Nations Organization, the European Union, or the United States of America. They retain their "statehood," according to this definition, so long as they retain their independence, territory, people and governments. At some point in the continuum of subordination or consolidation, independence may become so compromised that statehood ceases, as in Brittany or Wales. Secession occurs when some portion of the state obtains its independence, territory, people, and a government, separate from the whole.

States are preferable to anarchy because well- (or even quite badly) structured governments usually serve the common interests of the people of any given territory better than the unregulated interactions of ordinary human nature would, without guidance. One could imagine a territory with independence and a people, but no government. The inhabitants of such a territory would each depend on her or his own strength against the excesses of the others. Coordination in the common interest would depend on good faith and ad hoc cooperation. This absence of institutions would lead to conflict and disaster, not only through natural human selfishness, but also due to simple mistakes, since no objective standpoint or procedure would exist through which to discover or to implement the common good.

The proper purpose of states is to discover, to facilitate and to implement the common good of the people subject to their rule, through whatever procedures will do this best. Those students of statecraft from Cicero to Madison who have accepted this premiss have recognized several elements as essential to "republican" constitutions that serve the common good of all citizens. Government for the common good requires democracy, the rule of law, and checks and balances in government, including an independent judiciary, and certain fundamental human rights that protect the dignity of all individuals and the deliberative capacity of all citizens.[5] Democracy secures government that understands the situation of all citizens, by connecting governments and legislators to their subjects. The rule of law protects particular citizens from their rulers' transient impulses and emotions. Checks and balances in government control corruption and the self-importance of public officials. Independent judges check the executive, and protect the rule of law. Fundamental human rights secure independent citizens who will deliberate freely in pursuit of the common good.[6]

3. Boundaries

Secession concerns boundaries between states and the lines between republics. Since the separation of peoples into distinct and independent states is justified (if at all) by local geographical and cultural differences, to facilitate the development of the public good through national institutions, it follows that these boundaries should be as stable as possible over time. Changing boundaries disrupts the development of community, both directly, by destroying shared institutions, and indirectly, by removing the expectation of permanence that encourages long-term cooperation and mutual compromises for the common good. The common good is partly discovered and partly created from a given set of people, history and circumstances. Changing borders severs this line of development.

The republican requirements of democracy, the rule of law, checks and balances, and fundamental human rights do not provide any obvious rules for drawing the initial borders between states. Pursuit of the common good implies the existence (or the development) of a sense of community, without specifying which community to develop. Borders should be geographically sensible, culturally unified and above all territorially stable to support the development of common interests and public institutions over time. The cardinal rule of republican borders should be that they do not change.[7]

The question of secession arises when states already exist, within established borders. The question presented by the right to secede does not concern the initial allocation of territory, but rather its possible reallocation, to serve the common good. Given the general agnosticism of republican principles of justice about state borders – beyond the fundamental observation that they should not be too large – national boundaries should not be disturbed without some good reason for doing so. This reason should arise from the common good of all citizens, which means in practice from the purpose of advancing those fundamental civil and constitutional procedures that serve the common good best, including democracy, the rule of law, checks and balances, and fundamental human rights.

4. Citizens and *civitates*

The common good for which all states should exist, is the good of their citizens, which is to say of all persons permanently resident within a given state's boundaries. This "common good," as explained by republican authors such as Marcus Tullius Cicero[8] and John Adams[9] was the common good of all citizens, secured by molding government and the laws to create a harmony of all citizens' capacities and desires. States should develop a civic harmony among their citizens so that each citizen's realization of her or his own productive and rewarding life is made as compatible as possible with equally rewarding lives for all other citizens of the state.

This common good should extend at the first and most fundamental level of inquiry to all humanity. Republicans begin with the assumption that all human beings deserve equal concern and respect. Political institutions should serve the common good of all persons. Separate states and nations have emerged and properly exist because humans realize their capabilities and common interests best in somewhat smaller units, adapted to the history, to the geography, and to the culture of particular places and groups of individuals. States do not exist to serve the common good of their peoples at the expense of others, but in concert with other peoples, as part of a "*civitas maxima*" or natural republic that includes all human beings.[10]

This *civitas maxima* is separated into numerous smaller states or *civitates* so that each can serve the common good of its own residents or "people" better. States have a duty to serve all their citizens with equal concern and respect as part of one *populus*, attached to a particular location, so that each *populus* will become over time one "nation," developing a culture and institutions of its own. The common good of the people for which all states exist should not exclude or disregard any citizen, because each citizen constitutes an equal part of the state's essential mission: to construct political institutions through which all citizens can realize their own capacities, and live together in peace.

5. Empires

States as we know them began with a series of secessions from larger empires. "Empire" in this context signifies a larger political unit ruling several different subject nations. Empires are states with more than one *populus*, ruled by a single central political power, which exercises ultimate sovereignty or "*imperium*" over the whole. States emerged in Europe when various nations, with different cultural traditions, separated themselves and their territories from the domination of the Holy Roman emperor and the lingering ideal of imperial Rome. States emerged in America, Africa and Asia as various territories separated themselves from the European empires that had emulated Rome in developing subject colonies overseas.

Empires rest, as the concept of *imperium* implies, on the power of the metropolis to command. The center rules the provinces according to its own judgment. Empires naturally divide themselves into provinces to facilitate this structure of command. The distance from the emperor to the subjects becomes too great for direct supervision. Intermediaries must adapt the metropolitan will to local circumstances, and monitor compliance. Governors, viceroys, satraps and proconsuls emerge to represent the center to the periphery, and to impose the sovereign will. Their separate jurisdictions become provinces, reflecting cultural and geographical differences within the empire.

Empires differ from republics and the usual conception of unitary states in their poly-cultural and multinational character. Republics develop a common civil culture in pursuit of a common good, taking all citizens' interests into account as free and equal members of a single society. Empires rule several distinct societies in the interests of the dominant power. This power may in some circumstances claim to rule for the common good, but does so according to the judgment and perspective of the metropolis. Empires are to international relations as despotisms are to the national government of states. The absence of republican balance blinds imperial governments to the common good of their various subject nations. Empires fail to serve the purposes for which states ought to exist, because they do not understand the needs or interests of their several constituent nations.

6. Nations

Nations are the collective expression of the regional cultural variations that naturally emerge within humanity through proximity and social interaction over time. People born and raised in the same region tend to adapt themselves to their neighbors over generations and to develop parallel or compatible patterns of behavior and beliefs. Stable populations that live together over long periods of time develop a common language, usually develop a common religion, share common customs, common *mores*, and various other similarities. Invasions, immigration, slavery and oppression can and frequently do disrupt and redistribute nations, but nations originate in shared territory and a common birth, influenced by geography, history and events.

Humanity is divided into nations, or divides itself into nations over time. These are contingent and variable, but also often very tenacious. Nations are desirable, because national variations embody the accommodations through which social interactions have built harmonies between disparate interests and individuals. Nationalism and the common cultures and ideals that nations foster make it easier for co-nationals to live together in concord and to share common projects. People need cultures and society to facilitate their interactions, but also (more dangerously) to facilitate the search for advantage against other groups. People naturally unite into groups within which to accommodate and respect each other's interests and welfare, while also often acting, selfishly, irrationally, intolerantly and frequently aggressively toward outsiders.

Large empires founder on these differences of nationality. Fostering national fraternal feeling on a universal scale, embracing all of humanity without mediation, remains an unattainable ideal. Continental empires as attempted by the Romans and their imitators give way to more authentic local national feelings. Regions have different geographies, histories, and cultures, and the region, the culture or the faction that controls the government of the empire will inevitably oppress and exploit the others. National feeling is a powerful force for concord and consensus, but also for conquest and oppression, when co-nationals unite against the rest. Empires universally fail to meet the basic standard of legitimate government, because they inevitably fail to serve the common good of all the people that they rule. National differences make it impossible for imperial masters to understand their subjects.

7. Peoples

Peoples differ from nations in their purely jurisdictional basis. Co-nationals may travel or become dispersed, but the people or *populus* embraces all the citizens of a given territorial state. States are, or should be small enough actually to respond to the political needs of their people, to foster concord among their people, and to develop harmony among their people. Each state has its own "people," which is to say, those persons under its political control on whose behalf and for whose common good the state ought to act. The "people" of any given state properly embraces all the permanent inhabitants of its territory.[11]

The peoples of states within stable borders will gradually become nations as their interests and cultures converge over time. This gradual coordination of habits and aims makes it possible for all citizens to live full lives in pursuit of their interests and capabilities, which otherwise might have clashed, without institutional coordination to bring them into harmony. States properly promote national unity and culture, but must do so in ways that include and respect all the citizens of the state. The good of the people or citizens of a given state being the proper purpose for which all states exist, all states must serve the common good of their people, or forfeit the right to rule.

All good government is republican government, by which I mean government for the common good of the people, citizens or "*populus*" of a given territory. All legitimate states are republican states, by which I mean states that serve the common good of their people. The boundaries between states and peoples should be drawn to serve this purpose. Usually the common good requires stable borders, within which peoples can develop the regional cultures and shared practices as "nations" that constitute and protect the common good. But sometimes stable borders will threaten the common good of the people. These circumstances (and these alone) justify secession, when creating a second state and recognizing a new people will serve the common good of the whole.

8. Diversity

Large empires are simply too big and too diverse to serve the common good of their citizens. States that embrace too many different territorial nations will include persons in so many different geographical, historical and cultural circumstances that finding or constructing a common good becomes almost impossible. As citizens become more and more distant from their rulers, their needs and their insights will be increasingly overlooked. Such states or empires slip into oppression, perhaps inadvertently, when they become too big to understand the people that they rule. Schemes of representation and elections to legislative and executive offices can expand the sphere within which states successfully maintain republican (and therefore legitimate) governments and institutions, but at some point the state becomes too large and geographically or culturally too diverse to serve its citizens well.

Nationalism has often been the standard around which citizens in tyrannical and illegitimate states and empires have gathered to resist oppression. A common language or religion or cultural tradition in a given region or territory provides a focus around which some segment of the people can organize their claim to better treatment. Neighbors may feel that, all other things being equal, government by rulers who understand local circumstances will be better than government by those who do not. This gives nationalism frequent prominence in disputes about secession, which sometimes rest on the assertion that every nation deserves its own state, or that every group that develops its own national identity should have its own territory too. This reverses the proper relationship between nations, peoples, and states.

Diversity will always exist, not only between but within nations. States exist to reconcile diversity, not to abolish it. National differences are simply too malleable, manipulable, and inexact to justify redrawing state boundaries whenever separatists assert divisive new "nations" against the existing state. The peoples of stable states will gradually become nations through the passage of time, but not all nations should become peoples with their own separate states. Boundaries drawn to end anarchy or after the collapse of old empires should follow existing geographical, historical, and national lines to the greatest extent possible. Sometimes such lines do not exist. Many individuals have overlapping identities. Many nations share overlapping territories. Migration, conquest and happenstance muddle national boundaries. Political boundaries, being more certain, provide the natural basis for any democratic reform.

9. Democracy

Democracy is a good first measure of any government's legitimacy. Some might offer it as the only measure, but that does not solve the boundary problems raised by secessionist claims. Democracy provides a useful test of government legitimacy, because without democracy states mistake the basic nature of the public interest and needs. No non-democracy is fully legitimate, because undemocratic states cannot find or understand the common good that would justify their existence.[12] Democracy is necessary, but it is not sufficient. Plebiscites offered to justify secession take this democratic measure of legitimacy to unwarranted extremes. The assumption would seem to be that ambiguous national boundaries can be clarified, and transformed into the borders of states, by allowing peoples to define their national identities through majority vote. This raises certain obvious difficulties.

The most fundamental difficulty with democracy as a measure of legitimate secession arises in identifying the people whose majority will govern the vote. Different boundaries drawn in constructing votes for secession will yield a variety of results. The entire people of the existing state, voting collectively, might prefer to maintain the status quo, while the "people" of a smaller territory that proposes to secede might obtain a majority for secession within their own regional borders. Existing administrative boundaries within the larger state might yield one result, while new boundaries drawn to maximize one particular point of view might yield another. Nothing about the democratic principle itself explains which set of boundaries should prevail. Even where administrative boundaries are settled and respected, democracy alone would not justify regional secession, because it disregards the interests of other members of the former political community.

Every new boundary that creates a new majority out of an old minority, also creates new minorities, trapped within new borders. Democracy's justification as a measure of legitimacy depends on its value in finding and constructing a common good for all the citizens of the state. Secession denies this common good by dividing the old state and people in two. Democracy's value remains as a basis for public deliberation, but not as the sole measure of secession. The proper response to non-democracy within a state should be to implement democracy for all its citizens, within existing boundaries. Regional plebiscites alone cannot justify creating new states.

10. Renunciation

The denial of democracy, the rule of law, checks and balances, fundamental human rights or any other of the basic procedural requirements for finding the common good of the people delegitimizes the state, and justifies revolution, without necessarily legitimizing secession, which would divide the people against themselves. So long as there is one people within a unitary state, that people should seek its common good collectively, through democracy, checks and balances, the rule of law, and fundamental human rights. Secession becomes justified only at the point where the ruling government recognizes the existence within the state of two separate peoples or communities, where each have a separate political identity and will. Secession is justified when the existing government renounces its unity with some segment of the population, and recognizes them as a separate people, divisible from the whole.

Renunciation takes place when the government recognizes the existence of separate peoples among its subjects, with different rights and duties. Renunciations can happen explicitly, when governments declare that two peoples exist, and peacefully relinquish control over some segment of their previous territorial jurisdiction. Renunciation also happens by implication, when the government treats some subgroup of citizens as a separate people, usually by singling them out for oppression or disrespect. Governments without democracy, human rights, checks and balances or the rule of law often impliedly renounce their sovereignty and national unity with some segment of the population through ignorance, exploitation, or both.

Secession after renunciation is only one of several possible remedies to be applied when governments become tyrannical or illegitimate. Secession is neither the only nor the most obvious remedy, nor can it be offered as a remedy at all, unless the existing government has violated one of the cardinal principles of legitimacy, by persecuting one segment of the population more egregiously than the rest. The greater the solidarity between the government and the balance of the people in oppressing the subordinate and downtrodden group, the greater the renunciation of sovereignty, and more justified the secession. Universal oppression, which does not distinguish between persons, should lead to universal rebellion (not secession) and solidarity among the oppressed.

11. Solidarity

Solidarity is the virtue that states best support, and citizens owe each other a duty of solidarity that secession would transgress. Secession without provocation, in pursuit of advantage, is not justified, unless preceded by genuine oppression or comprehensive disrespect.[13] All states have "minorities" in the form of various idiosyncratic self-identified subgroups within the population. So long as the government respects and weighs their views and interests along with the rest, these minorities are being treated as part of the people, and owe a duty of solidarity to the whole.

When a state oppresses its minorities, or denies minorities rights that other citizens enjoy, or systematically disrespects them, then the state is denying that minority group's membership in the people, and its status as part of the nation. By its actions the state has identified that minority as a separate people or nation, and it may be that the new group's separate interests and identity will best be protected and served by giving them a state of their own, carved out of the territory of their oppressor. Governments that violate their duty of solidarity towards specific segments of their population absolve the citizens that they oppress from reciprocal duties to serve the welfare of the state as a whole. Ruptured solidarity can justify a new state.

Solidarity ends where differential treatment begins, so that the right of secession may arise when government oppression recognizes (in effect) the existence of a separate people or proto-nationality, which deserves a national territory of its own. Governments that recognize all permanent residents equally as citizens, and take them equally into account in constructing public policy for the common good, have maintained the requisite national solidarity even if they mistreat the people as a whole. In such cases the remedy belongs to the people collectively, and not to separate minorities or would-be nations within the collectivity. Citizens owe a duty of solidarity to each other, in defense of their common civil and political rights against usurping governments or states.

12. Secession

The right to secede will not be absolute, even in the presence of oppression and differential treatment of citizens by the state. Factors to be weighed include the disfavored minority's geographical location, the severity of their oppression, and the actual desires of the individuals that comprise the disfavored group. The greater the oppressed minority's territorial compactness, and the greater its oppression, the greater its right to secede. The future members of the new nation and would-be state must also have the desire to secede, as measured democratically through plebiscites, but only after it has been determined that the right to secede already exists, in response to lapses in solidarity, or oppression.

State boundaries, including new state boundaries following secession, should be natural boundaries to the greatest extent possible, which in today's world would generally mean historic administrative boundaries.[14] A statesman drawing these lines *de novo* would look to rivers, mountain ranges and the lines between languages, customs or religion. In fact, the necessary administrative lines usually exist already. Boundaries such as those between Maryland and Pennsylvania, or between the United States and Canada, which began as entirely artificial straight lines drawn in Europe on a map of America, became significant in time through the long histories of the peoples living out their lives on either side of the border. For the purposes of plebiscites and secession, the existing administrative boundaries should remain the same.

Secession that diminishes national territory should take place along existing administrative boundaries within the old state, dividing the empire into smaller historical units, but respecting established affinities. When oppressed minorities secede with their own provinces from the old national territory, exchanges of population may be necessary to consolidate the new borders. In such cases the oppressor population should bear the brunt of the dislocation, as the Germans did after the Second World War, but such exchanges should be restricted to rare cases of extreme, irreconcilable and deeply ingrained antagonism, when there is a strong consensus in favor of separation. Legitimate secession follows from government crimes against justice, leaving the new state with its own duties to respect the interests of its citizens.

13. Federalism

The model for world justice implicit in the republican model of separate national states would be an international federation of stable and permanent republics, respecting each other's cultures and cooperating to protect human rights.[15] The nationality principle is deeply embedded in human nature, and nations provide the matrix within which humans best fulfill their natural capabilities, while maintaining the greatest harmony among themselves. But nations can also constitute a threat to the human spirit, through their external rivalries and internal oppression of difference and dissent. Overarching federations of nation-states solve these two problems, first by coordinating peaceful relations between states, and second by guaranteeing human rights and republican institutions within them.

Federations can help to protect smaller states from the short-sighted oppressions that grow out of excessive homogeneity. Secession should not be sought for its own sake, but only in response to oppression, on the road toward a stable pacific federation. This ideal endorsed by Immanuel Kant,[16] the baron de Montesquieu,[17] and James Madison[18] offers the promise of perpetual peace, where justice prevents conflict, local governments serve local needs, and larger federations guide international relations, and protect citizens' individual rights within states against the excesses of their own fellow-citizens and governments.

Secession should only be necessary at the beginning, in establishing a just framework of independent national republics, before they associate into a larger international federation of republican states. The right to secede is a by-product of national prejudice and injustice. Republican federalism would introduce a new world order in which secession will no longer be necessary to protect the common good of humanity.

14. The right to secede

The right to secede rests on the same republican purpose (or principle) mandating the collective pursuit of the common good that justifies all states and politics. Separate states are preferable to universal empire because states maintain the local structures of culture, legal rules, and personal security within which citizens can develop worthwhile lives. To do this collectively citizens will require stable boundaries between states, and governments that respect the common good of all those subject to their control. Large empires cannot find this common good, because their governments will be too far removed from the people that they rule, and the people will eventually separate into several cultural nations, responding to local geography and circumstances.

The state's duty to its people or "*populus*" embraces all citizens. The inevitable diversity within and between nations does not in itself justify secession, without some act of oppression. Nor does the democratic expression of a wish to secede, unless the government renounces national unity, by expressly or implicitly declaring its political separation from some group or minority within the existing state's borders. The citizens within states owe each other a duty of solidarity, which only previous injustice can overrule enough to justify separation from fellow-citizens and the state. This lays the foundation for federations of republics, as the ultimate protectors of justice and the common good, within and between states. The right to secede only exists when the government oppresses a discrete group within its own people, that lives in a geographically distinct region, and wants to separate from the dominant nation and state.

20 International Economic Organization

International law developed primarily to serve the needs of the governments of "states," which is to say, to support the rulers of territorially based subject populations, exercising a monopoly within their boundaries of "sovereign" coercive power. Other non-state international organizations have long existed alongside states, such as the Virginia Company, the East India Company, and the Royal African Company, but none of these institutions enjoyed much formal recognition in the development of international legal structures. Now finally these and similar international economic organizations have finally captured the public imagination, and eager academics seek to apply the insights of institutional economics, law and economics, and industrial organization to international law, to demarcate new lines of competence between states and other international organizations.

The basic premiss of most such studies has been the so-called "Coase theorem," which concentrates on "transaction costs" to explain (and to evaluate) most structures in society, on the assumption that social relations should always be organized to minimize the transaction costs of exchanging economic resources. That Coase never said or wrote any such thing does not diminish the influence of this norm, particularly among lawyers. Applied to international law, this becomes an assertion that international institutions exist to maximize net gains from engaging in "transactions in power" minus transaction costs.[1] Any constraint imposed on a state, according to this definition, is a "transaction in power," which states undertake or allow in order to make gains in other areas.

1. Transactions in power

States have power. The government's power or control over people and territory is what gives those in charge the title to statehood. Governments relinquish this power grudgingly, and if they relinquish too much they cease to constitute "states" in the international sense, becoming mere administrative units of larger federations, like the states of the American union. Power can be spent to buy cooperation from other states, and sometimes both parties can realize absolute gains by such transactions. "Markets" in power trade sovereignty for peace or protection as often as for commerce or wealth. Some state governments seek primarily to maximize the wealth of their rulers, but others seek the common good of their citizens, or of a faction, or to promote world justice, or some religious mandate. "Transaction costs" is a very awkward description of what matters in most international transactions.

Most states claim to serve the common good of their citizens. Some claim to serve "justice" or the common good of humanity. In neither case does "gain" provide a very helpful description of what is sought, or "transaction costs" accurately capture the difficulties involved in getting what states want. In a republic, for example (which is to say, in a state actually committed to pursuing the common good), the primary constitutional question in both external and internal affairs will be how best to identify the common good. The constitution established by such states will seek to minimize mistakes. To call these mistakes "transaction costs" would be misleading.

Perhaps one might understand corruption as the primary "transaction cost" of would-be republican governments. Self-dealing (on this theory) will be present in any bureaucratic structure, but those that seek justice should try to minimize its costs. Yet speaking or writing of "transaction costs" in such situations only confuses the discussion. This will be true of most "transactions in power." States relinquish power to serve determinate ends, and the main question to be asked when states cede power to international organizations should be whether these ends will be served by the transaction. Does this international organization serve justice better than the states would have done on their own?

2. Justice

"Justice" and "the common good" have a resonance in relations between states that the vocabulary of economic theory entirely fails to capture. The comparative-transaction-cost methodology facilitates innovation by viewing institutions as contingent. But this benefit palls when it sacrifices the vocabulary of liberty and justice, which delegitimize bad structures of government much better, with more fidelity to ordinary usage and the issues that are really at stake. Economically minded lawyers tend to speak and write of "satisfying" the preferences of all countries (or their citizens), rather than shaping or judging these preferences, which should have been the primary purpose of law, when developed in pursuit of justice.

The "Coase" theorem applied to law implies a faulty theory of human values and motivation that vitiates its usefulness as a heuristic device. All law claims to be just. Systems of power that do not claim to seek justice are not law. Human nature tends to self-justification, and even repressive systems justify themselves to themselves as serving the common good. This makes interest-based conceptions of law inaccurate, unless one defines justice as an "interest" like any other. But in legal systems justice is not an interest like any other. To describe or to think of justice in this way (if it were possible to do so) would be confusing and misleading.

Lawyers apply the theory of the firm to international institutions to promote cooperative solutions to inter-state coordination problems. Creating an international regime that minimizes the friction involved in necessary international transactions would be a valuable achievement. But any such arrangement not founded on justice will be unstable, or undesirable, or both. Some lawyers may feel, with John Rawls, that justice is found best by avoiding substantive morality, which fosters the transaction cost of self-righteousness. But "efficiency" is not a standard to rally around either. Laws in general, and international law in particular, depend on justice for their binding force. Recycling the vocabulary of economic theory will never produce agreement about the issues that really matter in international law.

3. International organization

Perhaps this is all really just an argument about how best to constitute the international system to serve the purposes of international cooperation, whatever they are. Those who like justice, a lawyer–economist might say, can talk about how best to find justice. Those who like trade, can talk about maximizing trade. Those who would like to enjoy their own private unfettered arbitrary dominion can evaluate international organizations according to how such organizations serve that end. All governments (or the individuals who control them) have interests, and international organizations serve those interests, or they would not exist.

Legal theorists, in such a scheme, write either to describe this situation, or at best to point out how it could run more smoothly. The theory of the firm might be useful here to show how two states could coordinate their disparate interests to achieve mutually satisfactory results with a minimum of transaction costs. The trouble is that states do not necessarily aim at such cooperation, nor should they. States often prefer to *impose* their will on others. States do not only *trade* power to serve their own interests. They also *use* power for domination. Force is just or unjust, lawful or unlawful, according to the ends that it serves. International organizations do and should exist, not simply to facilitate the interests of states, but also to promote certain ends over others. Efficiency is usually a secondary interest.

Some states originated as profit-seeking shareholding corporations. Virginia and Massachusetts still retain traces of their earliest corporate charters in institutions that provided a model for many Western democracies. The analogy between states and corporations is not absurd. States that choose to cooperate through the mediation of international organizations may look a bit like corporations that merge into a single holding company. But this does not mean that international institutions should exist only when their agency costs are smaller than the alternative transaction costs of the same allocation through the market, as the followers of Ronald Coase might have it. International organizations sometimes act to prevent power transactions, and to impose goals that frustrate normal "markets," not make them more efficient.

4. The market of power

International organizations supersede states, in pursuit of certain goals. They emerge not from a "market for power" but from a desire for justice. States control each other's excesses by deferring to international institutions. Some international relationships could be described in Coasian vocabulary. War incurs high transaction costs. A just world order would be a valuable transaction gain, possibly outweighed by the transaction costs of imposing or achieving justice. Simply to speak in these terms illustrates the vacuity of doing so.

International organizations concerned with commerce may fit the "Coasian" model better, because they really are economic constructions, and concerned with self-interest in the narrowest, momentarily quantifiable sense that most economic models necessarily assume. International economic integration may follow the theory of the firm in ways that would permit the application (in some narrow circumstances) of economic formulas computing the net gains from transactions, after subtracting the transaction costs.

The market for power is not a market in goods or interests, but a market in moral perceptions, where states must justify their uses of power to themselves, and sometimes to others. Governments that relinquish power, do so either because they are forced to (in which case their power was limited) or because they are convinced that some interest outside the state justifies weakening the state to serve a greater good. Speaking in terms of the market undermines the moral constraints that sometimes lead to the rare abdications of power that make international institutions possible at all.

5. International economic organization

The best laboratories for analyzing legal institutions will always be comparative and historical.[2] Everything else is pure speculation. Those who propose change must look to what has worked before, in comparable situations. The greatest difficulty lies in identifying what is "comparable," and the proper standards of evaluation. The theory of the firm and other "Coasian" constructs mislead as a basis for comparison, because their circumstances are so different from those of states. They also fail as standards of evaluation, because they rest on economic premisses that contravene the basic purposes of law.

Legal studies have seen a great vogue for importing techniques from other social science disciplines. This reflects a widespread loss of faith in the integrity of law as its own discipline, which should be the study of justice. Unfortunately, techniques from other disciplines usually carry their own ethos with them. The values of the business world are overwhelmingly self-interested and generally mercenary. These may be appropriate in the economic sphere, but they are highly pernicious to national unity and justice. The vocabulary that lawyers use colors the results that they can expect to achieve. "Coasian" terms are not appropriate for principled legal discourse.

International law, more than most law, depends on its own moral weight for compliance, particularly when powerful interests are at stake. The language of institutional economics, law and economics and industrial organization, which carry no such weight, provide a feeble basis for demarcating new lines of competence between states and other international organizations. Their use puts off the day when better institutions will facilitate transactions among well-intentioned states.

21
Economic Sanctions

Economic sanctions have become increasingly common since the end of the Second World War and the adoption of the Charter of the United Nations in 1945.[1] The lessons of the Second World War, as expressed in the Charter, reflected a new determination among states to avoid armed conflict at almost any cost,[2] but also to protect the universal human rights of all persons.[3] Signatories to the Charter agreed to settle their disputes by peaceful means,[4] to respect the equal rights and self-determination of peoples,[5] and to promote respect for human rights and fundamental freedoms for all without distinction as to race, sex, language, or religion.[6] The second and third commitments embodied in the Charter reinforce the first, by supplying the necessary conditions for stable peace and security, but the primary commitment to maintain international peace somewhat limits the others by discouraging recourse to military intervention to protect human rights, national self-determination and other international rights and duties. This leaves economic sanctions as one of the few methods available to enforce international law.

The use of economic sanctions against violations of international law can be understood from five perspectives. (1) from the standpoint of those constrained by international law who might be subject to sanctions; (2) from the perspective of states or institutions confronted with the transgressions of others, evaluating their right (or duty) to sanction or to prevent "foreign" violations; (3) from the position of multilateral organizations or alliances, which may supplement or supersede unilateral enforcement measures; (4) in the light of humanitarian concerns, which sometimes limit the legitimate scope of international economic sanctions; (5) and finally, with regard to the appropriateness of economic sanctions against violations of international law, which depends on their human and moral costs and effectiveness. In each instance, the institutional, philosophical, and historical foundations of international law must be applied to the practice of states to illuminate the current status of the law, its binding force, and its likely development in protecting the common good of all members of the world community. The *content* of the law of nations must be identified, but also the *procedures* for determining when international law has been violated, and who has legitimate *power* to sanction violations. These are three very separate questions: the law may be unclear; the law may be clear, but its applications contested; and even unambiguous violations of international law may not have obvious sanctions or authorities empowered to impose them.

1. The unilateral enforcement of international law

One view of the right to enforce international law understands states as standing in essentially the same position with respect to one another under the law of nations that human individuals do in a Lockean "state of nature," before giving up some of their natural independence to civil society.[7] Governments acting through their officers to enforce the law of nations against themselves and others cannot be expected to act any better than Locke supposed that individuals would act without an impartial judge to regulate their disputes.[8] Like all human beings, even the best-intentioned public officials will make mistakes in judging their own cases, or cases involving their own interests, or even unrelated cases that they do not fully understand. This leads to such serious dangers that most governments of weak states easily perceive the value of independent judges in settling their controversies with stronger powers, and even the governments of powerful nations sometimes concede the benefit of permanent tribunals to maintain peaceful relations among themselves. This explains the general cession by states to the United Nations Security Council of authority to take action by air, sea, or land forces to maintain international peace and security,[9] and the creation of the International Court of Justice to settle disputes among those states that wish to grant it jurisdiction.[10]

The international community's intensified post-Second World War commitment to the peaceful settlement of disputes coupled with a general renunciation of the use of force in most circumstances,[11] gave a new prominence to non-military sanctions among states seeking to realize their rights and obligations under international law. The Charter of the United Nations encouraged the Security Council to "call upon" members in some circumstances to apply measures such as the interruption of economic or diplomatic relations, or of rail, sea or air communications against threats to international peace and security,[12] and the nature of the verb used in this clause reflects a general recognition that such measures would in any case have been available to states acting to vindicate their rights and obligations under international law. International lawyers had often insisted that "armed force should not be used, save in the common interest,"[13] but United Nations members reiterated their reluctance to use force in any circumstances "against the territorial integrity or political independence of any state,"[14] except in self-defence,[15] or at the direction of the United Nations Security Council.[16] Economic sanctions became one of the few tools still available to enforce the renewed international post-war commitment to international law.

2. The nature of economic sanctions

Recently some scholars have proposed to restrict the use of the word "sanctions" in international law to sanctions imposed by international organizations under the authority of multilateral treaties.[17] The rationale for developing this new vocabulary depends on an analogy with domestic legal systems, as understood by certain European authors influenced by Hans Kelsen's[18] elaboration of John Austin's theories of legal "positivism."[19] Positivists suppose that only sovereign governments can make law confirming their normative decisions with penalties or "sanctions" imposed upon subjects who violate formal law-creating expressions of the sovereign's will.[20] "Sanctions" (in this sense) reflect a government monopoly on enforcement that gives the legal system binding authority through state-imposed punishments.[21] Proponents of this positivist vocabulary face two insurmountable difficulties in applying their conception of "sanctions" to the law of nations: no determinate penalties exist for many violations of international law and no international sovereign exists to impose them. This discussion will use the word "sanction" in its looser English sense to embrace any economic or military action taken to enforce international law.[22]

John Austin denied the existence or the possibility of international law, without a sovereign to decree and enforce it.[23] This doctrine denigrates international "law" as simply a glorified (extra-legal) form of "morality."[24] One of the ways in which modern positivists attempt to circumvent the problem presented by the absence of an international sovereign is to put international organizations such as the United Nations into the place of the sovereign as a sort of world-government (thus their new sense of "sanction"). This solution overstates the importance of existing international institutions. So long as states remain subject to international law outside the United Nations system, they will properly enforce the law outside the United Nations system. There is no world government yet and the Charter of the United Nations makes no claim to create one, or to enforce international law as such, but only to maintain "international peace and security."

"Sanctions" under the law of nations are legitimate penalties that enforce international law. Economic sanctions under the law of nations are economic penalties that enforce international law. Denying unilateral economic sanctions their identity as "sanctions" would have the pernicious effect of diminishing their impact, by weakening the moral force of the noun used to describe them. Some would offer "countermeasures" as the proper description of unilateral enforcement measures, (reserving the term "sanctions" for measures taken by international organizations acting under multilateral treaties).[25] The natural use of the term "countermeasure" extends to all legitimate responses to violations of international law, including "sanctions," which has a narrower connotation in English. "Sanction" implies a public purpose and motivation that "countermeasure" does not.[26] "Sanction" is best used of countermeasures undertaken primarily to enforce universal or public interests protected by international law, such as fundamental human rights. "Countermeasure" (without further elaboration) indicates a legitimate measure taken under international law to protect one's own particular interests. The difference is a matter of emphasis, but meaningful, and worth preserving.

The much less significant distinction between economic sanctions and economic "rewards" or "incentives" should also be preserved, for reasons of clarity. As will become apparent in reviewing the cases, economic incentives ("carrots," according to the usual analogy) are often more effective than economic sanctions ("sticks") in securing conformity with international law. As with the difference between "countermeasures" and "sanctions," the difference between economic "sanctions" and "incentives" is often a question of degree. Conditional promises of economic benefits can also be understood as coercive threats not to deliver these benefits unless certain specific conditions are met.

Unilateral economic sanctions imposed to enforce international law can take several forms. As imposed by one government against another that has violated the law of nations, sanctions could include the confiscation of public or private financial assets (or both), the "freezing" (temporary confiscation) of public or private assets (or both), the refusal to trade with public or private entities (or both), the prohibition of imports or of exports in specific categories of goods or services, the prohibition of trade with specific individuals or corporations, and secondary prohibitions against other governments, corporations or individuals that circumvent or disregard these sanctions. Secondary prohibitions are particularly appropriate in enforcing economic sanctions against human rights violations because human rights are universal obligations that every state and subject of international law has the fundamental international obligation to respect.

3. The lawfulness of economic sanctions

The question of the lawfulness of unilateral economic sanctions under international law depends primarily on four central doctrines of the law of nations, concerning: (1) the economic liberty of states; (2) the internal affairs of states; (3) the *erga omnes* obligations of states, and (4) the proportionality of measures taken in response to violations of the law. All four derive from persistent conceptions of the juridical equality of states, repeated and perpetuated in the United Nations Charter. The relevant provisions of the Charter include the Preamble (speaking of the "equal rights ... of nations large and small"); the Article 1.2 commitment to "friendly relations among nations based on respect for the principle of equal rights and self-determination of peoples"; the Article 2.1 commitment to "the sovereign equality of all (U.N.) Members"; the Article 2.4 commitment to refrain from "the threat or use of force against the territorial integrity or political independence of any state"; and the Article 2.7 prohibition of United Nations intervention "in matters which are essentially within the domestic jurisdiction of any state."

3.1. The economic liberty of states

The sovereign equality of states under the traditional law of nations includes the national economic liberty to trade (or not to trade) with other nations, corporations or individuals according to each nation's separate determination of its own people's interests and desires.[27] Applied to economic sanctions in the form of refusals to trade, the traditional doctrine of sovereign equality would recognize the legitimacy of trade embargoes or boycotts imposed for any reason whatsoever, including simple economic coercion to advance national political or economic interests against those of other states.[28] If, as Hugo Grotius observed, individuals have no obligation to sell,[29] then neither,

Christian Wolff added, do states have any obligation to buy,[30] and nations may freely decide whether to engage in commerce with others or not, on whatever conditions they please.[31]

Appeals to economic liberty in opposing economic sanctions against violations of the law of nations must rest either on the economic rights of the citizens of the state imposing the sanctions, the economic rights of the citizens of the target state, or the economic rights of the citizens of third states.[32] Humanitarian limitations might also protect individuals in each of these three categories.[33] The Universal Declaration of Human Rights claims rights for all human beings, without distinction based on secondary categories such as race, language or national origin.[34] The Declaration recognizes international responsibility for economic, social and cultural rights that support the free development of every human personality,[35] including the right to a standard of living necessary for individual health and well-being.[36] The International Covenant on Economic, Social, and Cultural Rights reiterates the universal right to an adequate standard of living[37] and at a minimum to be free from hunger.[38] Comprehensive economic sanctions aimed at the government of a particular state that have the effect of denying its subjects their means of subsistence might violate these provisions of international law.[39]

Arguments against sanctions based on the economic liberty of citizens of the state imposing the sanctions would usually fail in the case of democratic republics, whose citizens control their government's decisions.[40] Sanctions imposed by non-democracies face a stricter standard of proportionality between their aims and the "internal" burdens imposed on the sanctioning government's own subjects.[41] Economic boycotts or embargoes against foreign trade always burden the sanctioning state's citizens. This compromises the state's fundamental duty to serve the common good of those subject to its rule, and would have to be balanced against the universal interest in protecting the human rights of others, including the rights of citizens of foreign states.

The traditional standard limiting embargoes or boycotts that harm the economic interests of the citizens of the target state is very permissive because the background doctrine of national independence supports the freedom not to trade. The Covenant on Economic, Social, and Cultural Rights recognizes the right of "[a]ll peoples ... for their own ends, freely [to] dispose of their natural wealth and resources."[42] Refusals to trade in food when faced with actual starvation abroad might rise to the level of a humanitarian violation,[43] but short of starvation, the exercise of economic freedom by peoples refusing to trade, for whatever reason, usually outweighs the economic interest that others might have in receiving their goods.

The economic liberty of peoples, for their own ends, freely to dispose of their own resources also governs international economic relations with third parties affected either directly or indirectly by economic boycotts or embargoes. Direct effects might take the form of "secondary" boycotts or embargoes against states, individuals or corporations that circumvent or subvert a "primary" set of sanctions against human rights violations.[44] Under long-established international law, the absolute right to suspend commerce would support such third-party sanctions as essentially within the domestic jurisdiction of the sanctioning state.[45] Subsequent treaties of friendship or trade might qualify this right.

Some treaties in support of international friendship or trade extend special privileges against the suspension of economic relations. In such cases, the legitimacy of economic sanctions would hinge on the actual terms of the agreement, and the nature of the violation.[46] Lesser violations of international norms might not warrant secondary measures against third-state partners in contravention of treaty-based free trade regimes. Enforcing the obligation to respect and to advance fundamental human rights, which is owed by all states to all others, would justify broader derogations from background treaty commitments.

3.2. The internal affairs of states

The widely accepted doctrine of the sovereign equality of peoples, as reflected in the Charter of the United Nations, carries with it the implication that outside governments have no business interfering in the internal affairs of states.[47] The Charter explicitly prohibits the United Nations from intervening "in matters which are essentially within the domestic jurisdiction of any state," except to enforce the decisions of the Security Council.[48] Some advocates of the progressive development of international law would extend this prohibition to the application of economic and other non-forcible pressures by states to influence other governments' domestic or "internal" policies.[49] The rationale for this new doctrine depends on an analogy with the emerging post-Second World War consensus against the unilateral use of force to influence another state's domestic affairs.[50] In some circumstances, economic power can be almost as coercive as military force. Since state practice has never hesitated to apply economic pressure in international relations,[51] this new prohibition on economic "interference," if it exists, must derive its legal force from treaty commitments or from natural-law arguments concerning the mutual responsibilities, self-determination and sovereign equality of peoples.

The economic self-determination argument against economic sanctions creates a difficult paradox. Peoples have the right, as recognized both in the *International Covenant on Economic, Social, and Cultural Rights* and in the *International Covenant on Civil and Political Rights*, "freely to dispose of their natural wealth and resources."[52] According to the same covenants, states also have a duty to "pursue economic cooperation, based on the principle of mutual benefit."[53] Prohibitions on the application of economic pressure through trade embargoes or boycotts would limit one state's economic freedom not to trade in favor of another state's interest in trading with an unwilling partner. The threshold for enforcing such an obligation to cooperate would have to be very high to overcome the damage to economic liberty and the sovereign equality of peoples that any forced exchanges would entail. Embargoes or boycotts imposed to punish or to deter violations of international law, to protect fundamental freedoms, or to advance the common interests of humanity, will almost always supersede any particular government's separate interest in expanding its trade.[54]

Several international instruments might seem to support a broad prohibition on economic "interference" or "coercion" through trade. Prior to the Second World War, international lawyers spoke of "intervention" only in cases of armed incursions and the actual use of force.[55] After the war, the Charter of the Organization of American States broadly prohibited members from intervening in the "internal or external affairs" of any other state, by armed force, "but also [by] any other form of interference or attempted threat against the personality of the State or against its political, economic, and cultural elements."[56] In the twilight of the Soviet empire, the Helsinki Final Act of the Conference on Security and Co-operation in Europe required the participating states to "refrain from any intervention, direct or indirect, individual or collective, in the internal or external affairs falling within the domestic jurisdiction of another participating State."[57] The communist and Arab states were particularly active in seeking to broaden this formal norm against domestic intervention whenever they could (despite their contradictory state practice).[58]

The United Nations General Assembly has endorsed the non-intervention norm in several declarations, beginning in the mid-1960s with the *Declaration on the Inadmissibility of Intervention in the Domestic Affairs of States and the Protection of Their Independence and Sovereignty*.[59] The 1970 *Declaration on Principles of International Law concerning Friendly*

Relations and Co-operation among States in Accordance with the Charter of the United Nations expressed a clear intent in its title, as reflected in several of its provisions, to codify and progressively to develop existing norms of international law.[60] For example, the *Declaration on Friendly Relations* proclaimed it as a principle of international law that states have a duty "not to intervene in matters within the domestic jurisdiction of any State, in accordance with the Charter," adding by way of elaboration that no state may "use or encourage the use of economic, political or any other type of measures to coerce another State in order to obtain from it the subordination of the exercise of its sovereign rights and to secure from it advantages of any kind."[61] The Declaration adds, however, that states "shall cooperate in the promotion of universal respect for, and observance of, human rights and fundamental freedoms for all" and that every state has a duty to promote through "joint and separate action" the "universal respect for and observance of human rights and fundamental freedoms."[62]

The difficulty here lies in determining the proper relationship between the conceptions of "intervention" and "domestic jurisdiction" as they relate to the shared international duty to take action to protect human rights. The examples given in declaring the principles of friendly relations concern extreme cases such as "subversive, terrorist or armed activities directed towards the violent overthrow of the regime." Economic sanctions imposed against violations of international human rights norms do not amount to "intervention" or "interference" as described in the *Declaration on Friendly Relations*, because they seek neither national "advantage" nor the subordination of any state in the exercise of its sovereign rights. Even if economic sanctions were in some very broad sense "intervention" or "interference," economic sanctions against human rights violations would not invade the exclusively "domestic" jurisdiction of any state, because human rights are a universal, and not a purely domestic or a national concern. Pressure or influence exerted on governments through economic sanctions and similar non-forcible measures are normally legitimate under international law.[63]

3.3. The *Erga Omnes* obligations of states

The universal nature of certain international norms gives rise to a universal interest in compliance that takes (for example) most questions of universal human rights outside the specifically "domestic" jurisdiction of any particular state. A generation of scholarship, and *dicta* in the International Court of Justice have encouraged the recognition of a class of obligations under international law that are *erga omnes*, which is to say connected to the interests of all states so intimately that all states have an international obligation to all other states to respect them.[64] *Erga omnes* violations give all states a cause of action under the law of nations, because *erga omnes* violations harm the universal interest that all peoples share in human dignity and a just world order.[65] The fundamental nature of *erga omnes* obligations restricts their application to the most essential elements of international law, including the three primary objectives at the basis of the post-war legal order, as elaborated in the United Nations Charter: the ban on aggression; the commitment to self-determination; and the protection of human rights.[66]

The dissolution of the Soviet Empire led directly to a new attitude toward the enforcement of *erga omnes* norms. Prior to 1989 the Soviet Union had compelled its "socialist" subject states to endorse an expanded conception of domestic jurisdiction designed to protect their governments' human rights abuses against outside criticism. After the destruction of the Berlin wall, Russia and its former satellite nations formally embraced international human rights norms as the foundation of their new politics.[67] In a series of agreements made through the Conference on Security and Cooperation in Europe, Russia and other former dissenters recognized human rights, democratic pluralism, and the rule of law as necessary preconditions for peace, security, and justice.[68] This change facilitated a new international consensus in favor of enforcement. For example, the Institute of International Law adopted a resolution to clarify the relationship between international principles of non-intervention and universal human rights,[69] which recognized that every state has a legal interest in protecting fundamental human rights everywhere,[70] with full authority to respond individually or collectively to human rights violations with diplomatic, economic and other measures.[71] The Institute concluded that: "these measures cannot be considered an unlawful intervention in the internal affairs of that State."[72]

A series of meetings of the Conference on the Human Dimension of the Conference on Security and Cooperation in Europe have confirmed the strengthened post-Cold-War recognition of international responsibility for the protection of human rights.[73] Affirming human rights and fundamental freedoms as one of the basic purposes of government,[74] the Copenhagen document of the CSCE (1990) clarified the requirement that national laws, regulations and practices must conform with the human rights standards established by international law,[75] as an integral part of maintaining international peace and security.[76] The Moscow meeting of the Conference on the Human Dimension of the CSCE reiterated the interest that all states have in human rights and fundamental freedoms as one of the foundations of the international legal order.[77]

The "categorical" and "irrevocable" declaration by the constituent states of the former Soviet Union and the formerly communist and "socialist" states of Eastern Europe that human rights and fundamental freedoms "do not belong exclusively to the internal affairs of the state concerned" removes the largest single impediment to enforcing the universal interest in protecting human rights.[78] By recognizing other states' "direct" and "legitimate" interest in human rights everywhere,[79] the Moscow Declaration of the Conference on Security and Cooperation in Europe supported the universal jurisdiction to enforce these norms.

If, as the post-Cold-War consensus has confirmed, "human rights and fundamental freedoms are the birthright of all human beings, are inalienable and are guaranteed by law,"[80] then "their protection and promotion is the first responsibility of government"[81] and governments that violate this responsibility should be guided to reform.[82] The fall of totalitarian regimes and the demise of the ideology upon which they based their oppression opened new possibilities for implementation,[83] supported by the nearly universal recognition of universal principles of human dignity in international law.

3.4. The proportionality of unilateral economic sanctions

The proportionality of unilateral economic sanctions to enforce international law has three aspects, all relating to the severity of: (1) the violation, (2) the response, and (3) the impact of the violation on the state or states that act to enforce international law.[84] All three relate more to the right to impose unilateral economic sanctions than they do to the existence or nonexistence of a previous breach. Minor violations of international law (1) may not warrant unilateral enforcement when the risk of mistake or the consequences of punishment outweigh the benefits of enforcing the law; the difficulty of calibrating responses (2) may make unilateral enforcement excessive; and the lack of a direct connection (3) between the primary victims of violations of the law and those who act on their behalf may at times risk turning the unilateral enforcement of universal human rights into little more than a pretext for interventions really undertaken for unrelated reasons. The differing importance of different international norms differentiates the levels of protection they deserve, despite their universal validity.

Most economic sanctions in the form of boycotts or embargoes are retorsion, and would have been permissible by states even in the absence of another state's violation.[85] This puts them beyond the normal constraint of proportionality, which loses its meaning when no violation is necessary to justify action.[86] Perhaps some question of abuse of rights might arise when states take otherwise legal measures with the purpose of subordinating the sovereign rights of others,[87] but this rationale cannot be extended very far, and does not in any case apply to the protection of universal human rights, which all states have an obligation to respect, and no state has the sovereign right to disregard.[88]

Proportionality imposes the greatest constraints on economic sanctions when they take the form of countermeasures that would not have been legitimate under international law were it not for previous violations of law by the target state.[89] This situation might arise under multilateral trade agreements such as NAFTA or GATT, which regulate trade policy, and forbid restraints on trade.[90] When states party to an international agreement on trade impose economic sanctions contrary to the provisions of the agreement, then these economic countermeasures must be proportionate to the harm caused by the violations themselves.[91]

The Institute of International Law's 1989 resolution on "the protection of human rights and the principle of non-intervention in internal affairs of states"[92] summarized the post-Soviet recognition that all states have both an *erga omnes* obligation to respect human rights and a parallel legal interest in protecting universal rights "throughout the world."[93] The resolution confirmed that states acting in breach of their human rights obligations "cannot evade ... international responsibility by claiming that such matters are essentially within ... domestic jurisdiction."[94] Other states, acting individually or collectively, may properly take diplomatic, economic and other measures against any state that has violated human rights, without perpetrating an "unlawful intervention" in the internal affairs of that state.[95] All such measures must, however (according to the Institute's resolution), also take into account the relative gravity of the violations, and "all the relevant circumstances."[96]

The obligation to consider relative gravity and relevant circumstances in enforcing international law against violations of *erga omnes* norms makes measures to correct "especially grave" violations "particularly justified." The Institute of International Law gave "large-scale" or "systematic" violations as examples of grave violations.[97] Measures should be proportionate to the gravity of the violation, and take into account the interests of individuals, of third states, and of the population concerned.[98] The American Law Institute made similar assertions in its *Third Restatement of the Foreign Relations Law of the United States*.[99] The *Restatement* recognizes obligations resting on international agreements, customary international law, and general principles of law,[100] placing particular emphasis on customary law prohibitions against genocide, slavery, state-sponsored murder, torture, arbitrary detention, racial discrimination, and "consistent pattern[s] of gross violations of internationally recognized human rights."[101]

Acts that would otherwise violate international law can become lawful in response to the internationally wrongful acts of others.[102] When all states are injured by violations of the law, all states might potentially respond with countermeasures,[103] subject to a general restriction against adopting reprisals that are "out of proportion" to the gravity of the internationally wrongful act "and the effects thereof on the injured State."[104] This requirement of proportionality may decrease in the case of international "crimes,"[105] but certain countermeasures are almost always inappropriate, such as conduct that derogates from basic human rights,[106] or extreme economic or political coercion designed to endanger the territorial integrity or political independence of the state which has committed the internationally wrongful act.[107]

4. The right to impose unilateral sanctions

The right to impose unilateral economic sanctions against violations of international law follows from the legitimate interest that all states have in maintaining international justice.[108] In the absence of a reliable world government those in a position to enforce the law of nations should take responsibility for doing so[109] whenever the value of intervention outweighs the danger of mistake.[110] This will vary from case to case, based on circumstances and the nature and political structures of the nations involved. The more democratic, balanced, and lawful the internal government of a state becomes, the greater its authority will be to enforce international law against others, and the less subject its own decisions should be to outside scrutiny.[111]

Most economic sanctions against violations of international law take the form of boycotts or embargoes that would have been legitimate in any case, even without a previous transgression.[112] In those few cases where sanctions might violate international law by threatening human rights or the territorial integrity of states, their legitimacy depends on the seriousness of the transgression that they respond to, their effectiveness in correcting it, and the position (and political structure) of the government that imposes the sanctions. The right to impose unilateral economic sanctions as reprisals (which would otherwise violate international law), may not exist when governments lack legitimate legal and political institutions themselves, or sufficient connection with the transgression to understand properly the violation that they propose to correct.

Violations of international law anywhere threaten states and individuals everywhere, by challenging the just world order,[113] but some individuals suffer more directly, as victims (for example) of human rights abuses. States that act to protect their own interest in human dignity by taking measures against human rights violations are also acting in a sense "on behalf of" more directly injured persons and groups.[114] These identifiable victims of human rights violations deserve consideration in determining the enforcement measures taken to protect their rights,[115] and states have broader jurisdiction to enforce international law against human rights violations when they consult with the violation's more direct victims, and take their circumstances into account.[116]

Reprisals constitute actions that would otherwise have violated international law, and as such they are dangerous, even to enforce international law. Since every state has a legal interest in protecting the law,[117] and the right to take measures to enforce it,[118] some states may use international law as a pretext to advance their other interests. This justifies recognizing the distinction between "serious," "gross" or "systematic" breaches of obligations owed to the international community as a whole, and other breaches, less serious in nature, which may not warrant intervention.[119] More serious breaches deserve proportionally more attention than lesser breaches, and warrant more serious countermeasures.[120]

In its *Third Restatement of the Foreign Relations Law of the United States*, the American Law Institute proposed that customary international law should only reach transgressions that form a "consistent pattern of gross violations of internationally recognized human rights."[121] This statement need not disregard the standing rule that all violations of universal human rights affect the legitimate interests of all members of the international community.[122] The "seriousness" of the violation does not change its legality (or illegality), so much as the nature of the remedies available to correct it. The American Law Institute rightly understood that trivial violations do not warrant an international response.[123] The jurisdiction to impose unilateral sanctions as reprisals against violations of international law only extends only to "gross" or "systematic" breaches.

This distinction between the existence of violations of international law and the jurisdiction to enforce the law against others reflects the general standards of proportionality that control all enforcement of international law. Gross and systematic breaches of international human rights law do such serious harm to their direct victims, to other states aware of the violations, and to the international community as a whole, that unilateral reprisals are warranted, despite the dangers of overzealous enforcement and error by the sanctioning state or states. Less severe or systematic violations of international law, despite their illegal character and the harm that they do to other states, may not be susceptible to countermeasures, because the threat to international peace, justice and security from the countermeasures themselves may outweigh the benefits that they offer in discouraging violations of universal human rights. In such cases multilateral sanctions, positive economic "sanctions" (incentives) or criticism may be the only legitimate methods available for enforcing international law.

5. The multilateral enforcement of international law

Multilateral economic sanctions differ from unilateral economic sanctions in two significant ways.[124] First, because they are more likely to be justified, and second, because they are more likely to be effective. These two differences have separate and contradictory implications for international law. On the one hand, because multilateral sanctions are more likely to be justified (in the sense of having been properly and legitimately imposed), they are more likely to be accurate reflections of international law, and should have a broader scope than unilateral sanctions. On the other hand, because multilateral economic sanctions are more likely to be effective (in the sense of having serious economic consequences in the target state), they will do more harm than unilateral sanctions, and should be undertaken with caution.

Multilateral economic sanctions are more likely to be justified than unilateral economic sanctions for the same reason that any collective decision about law is more likely to be accurate than any individual judgment. Collective decisions are more accurate because they are more likely to transcend the particular interests and natural misperceptions of any single state. Students of international law have long understood that groups of states, acting together, will recognize principles of justice that each separately might have disregarded, in pursuit of its own misguided self-interest.[125] States acting together to enforce international law should have a broader jurisdiction to impose economic sanctions than states acting separately, because the risk of error is smaller, and should therefore weigh less heavily in measuring the proportionality or "commensurability" of the sanctions imposed.[126]

Multilateral economic sanctions are more likely to be effective than unilateral economic sanctions because they are harder to circumvent. The greater the number of states that choose to participate in a sanctions regime, the fewer will be the outside resources available to replace the products unavailable through embargo, or to buy the products left unsold due to boycotts. This makes multilateral economic sanctions inherently more coercive than unilateral economic sanctions, and therefore more damaging. In most cases, the effects of unilateral economic sanctions will be primarily expressive. States imposing boycotts or embargoes harm themselves as much or more than they harm their targets, and this expresses the sincerity of their criticisms. When other states join them in sanctions, the balance of suffering changes. Expressive sanctions become effective, and therefore more damaging.

For this reason it is not accurate to suppose that states may do no more or less collectively than they might have done separately in imposing economic sanctions to enforce international law. Sometimes states may legitimately take stronger measures when they act together, and sometimes not. States may sometimes legitimately do more collectively to enforce international law because they can be more confident in their judgment that the law has been violated, which expands the scope of their right to intervene. This is particularly true of obligations owed collectively to all members of the international community as a whole. States have more authority to act against such violations collectively, because their right is held collectively, and solitary enforcement runs greater risks of being mistaken, or insincere.

Yet states acting collectively to enforce international law may sometimes have less justification for imposing economic sanctions together than they would have had separately, because the coercive and humanitarian impact of their sanctions will be greater. The enforcement of international law should sometimes be coercive, but only when judgments of violation and proportionality have been properly made. The greater the effectiveness of the enforcement, the greater the requirement that legal judgments be correct, and the greater the danger that sanctions will do more damage than necessary. The humanitarian impact of effective multilateral sanctions will be proportionally greater than that of partial unilateral measures. Nations acting separately to enforce international law through economic sanctions generally do not have enough economic power to cause serious humanitarian problems in the target state.[127]

The basis of the jurisdiction to impose multilateral economic sanctions to enforce international law rests on the same foundations as the jurisdiction to impose unilateral economic sanctions. Economic sanctions are legitimate: first, because states possess the economic liberty to trade or not to trade with whomever they please; and second, because all states have an interest in international justice. In the absence of the universal compulsory jurisdiction of international courts, states retain their original right separately to judge and to enforce international law, when circumstances warrant intervention. States may (and, to the extent that independent law-respecting institutions exist, should) relinquish their jurisdiction to neutral independent organizations or tribunals. Some such delegations have already taken place, as to the United Nations Organization concerning the use of force, or to the World Trade Organization, to regulate trade.[128]

Multilateral organizations can supplement or replace states as the locus of jurisdiction to judge violations of international law, or to impose enforcement measures. This takes place either by agreement or by deference to obvious superiority in judgment. For example, the United Nations Organization may be so superior to the separate states in judging the appropriateness of using force that even non-members are precluded from using force to settle their disputes.[129] On the other hand, a multilateral organization delegated broad and exclusive powers by treaty, as was the United Nations with regard to the use of force, may become so obviously ineffective, as did the United Nations during the Cold War period, that the delegation of power lapses, and other enforcement mechanisms must take its place.[130] The refusal or failure of the United Nations Security Council to protect international peace and security, due to permanent member vetoes, may negate some Charter restrictions on the use of force, as applied to serious violations of international law.[131]

6. The United Nations Organization

The authority of the United Nations Organization to impose economic sanctions against violations of international law arises primarily from Article 41 of the United Nations Charter, which empowers the Security Council to "decide" which measures not involving the use of armed force "are to be employed" to give effect to its decisions, when the Council "call[s] upon" members of the United Nations to do so. These measures may include the "complete or partial interruption of economic relations" through boycotts or embargoes.[132] The Security Council's authority to impose sanctions rests on its power to "determine" the existence of "any threat to the peace, breach of the peace, or act of aggression."[133]

The terms of the United Nations Charter give economic sanctions adopted by the Security Council under the aegis of Article 41 the ability to supersede other international economic treaties or agreements.[134] Measures decided upon by the Security Council to protect international peace and security against threats to the peace were consented to in advance by the member states of the United Nations Organization, when they approved the Security Council's power to "determine" the existence of threats to the peace and to "decide" upon measures to avert them. This circumvents the requirement of prior illegality normally necessary to justify reprisals under general international law.[135]

The Charter of the United Nations creates a system and mechanisms to maintain international peace and security that do not necessarily claim to embody international law, or always to enforce it. "Threats to the peace" need not necessarily violate international law to justify United Nations sanctions, nor would all violations of international law necessarily constitute threats to the peace. The members of the United Nations Organization commit themselves collectively to the "prevention" and to the "removal" of threats to the peace, to developing "friendly relations among nations," to solving international economic, social, cultural and humanitarian problems, and to promoting "respect for human rights and fundamental freedoms for all."[136] This is not the entirety of international law. The United Nations undertakes to settle disputes as much as possible "in conformity with the principles of justice and international law,"[137] but not to enforce all laws or to do everything necessary to bring about the full realization of justice.

The principles of justice and international law will not always correspond with all decisions made by a Security Council of fifteen not-necessarily democratic states, in which five have the power to veto all action.[138] The supremacy of the Charter of the United Nations (according to its own terms) over all other international agreements [139] does not supersede general international law, which includes some provisions "from which no derogation is permitted" by treaty or agreement.[140] This puts a limit on the legitimacy even of sanctions imposed by the United Nations Security Council, as it does on any other multilateral sanctions imposed by states, whenever Security Council-imposed sanctions violate fundamental human rights, basic humanitarian obligations, or other obligations under peremptory norms of general international law.[141]

The nearly universal agreement of states to ratify the Charter of the United Nations gives Security Council determinations of the existence of a threat to the peace under Article 39 decisive authority in international law. The power to "determine" the answer to a question connotes finality, as the word is usually understood,[142] and the nearly universal agreement of states is very powerful evidence of law.[143] The Security Council's power to "decide" the measures to be employed to give effect to its decisions has similar weight, such that even though Security Council decisions may be in theory capable of violating international law, no other group or institution has sufficient authority to recognize the violation.[144]

The very broad scope of the Security Council's authority to "determine" when a threat to peace exists and to "decide" which measures to take in response limits the value of challenging the Council's determinations. All members of the United Nations have agreed to carry out the Security Council's decisions,[145] and to assist in doing so.[146] Nevertheless, because all economic sanctions imposed by the Security Council formally respond to "threats to the peace" under Article 39, the connection between peace, security, and international law bears examination.[147] Many violations of international law will not rise to the level the warrants Security Council intervention.

The value of enforcing international law may in some cases justify United Nations economic sanctions coordinated outside the Security Council: Article 10 empowers the General Assembly to discuss questions and matters within the scope of the Charter and to make recommendations to the members;[148] Article 13 encourages the General Assembly to "assist" in the realization of human rights and fundamental freedoms;[149] and Article 14 allows the General Assembly to recommend "measures" for the peaceful adjustment of any situation which might otherwise impair the "general welfare" or "friendly relations among nations," contrary to the "purposes and principles" of the United Nations.[150]

Economic sanctions recommended by the General Assembly of the United Nations would not have the same mandatory force as sanctions imposed by the Security Council, but depending on the degree of consensus achieved in the General Assembly's deliberations, might still exercise considerable authority.[151] The Charter of the United Nations restricts the General Assembly's power to make recommendations concerning disputes over which the Security Council is exercising its functions,[152] but in circumstances in which the Security Council has chosen not to exercise its authority, the General Assembly's power of recommendation extends to the full scope of the Charter.[153] General Assembly recommendations differ from Security Council measures in extending beyond peace and security, because (not being mandatory) they are less likely to be effective.[154]

7. Regional organizations

Multilateral economic sanctions need not achieve the global scale of Security Council measures or General Assembly recommendations to advance the enforcement of international law. Regional arrangements are expressly recognized by the United Nations Charter as legitimate vehicles for regional action to prevent threats to international peace and security,[155] including human rights violations. [156] In regions where the democratic self-determination of peoples has been more firmly established, governments as a consequence have been more respectful of human dignity,[157] and concluded various regional agreements to protect their citizens.[158]

The European Convention for the Protection of Human Rights and Fundamental Freedoms[159] provides for a European Commission on Human Rights and a European Court of Human Rights to encourage compliance.[160] The Charter of the Organization of American States established an Inter-American Commission on Human Rights for the same purpose, supplemented by the Inter-American Court of Human Rights, as established under the Inter-American Convention on Human Rights (1969). These conventions and their enforcement mechanisms reinforce universal human rights on the regional level, but also provide the basis for collective action against human rights violations in non-member states.[161] Both the European Union and the Organization of American States have provided vehicles for the imposition of international economic sanctions when larger international organizations such as the United Nations have been unable to act.[162]

8. Ad hoc multilateral measures

The possibility of world-wide United Nations-mandated economic sanctions, or of regionally unified responses to protect universal values, does not preclude the creation of ad hoc coalitions to enforce international law. Just as states may separately enforce international law through economic sanctions according to their own best judgment, so may ad hoc coalitions of states enforce the law collectively, with greater confidence than if they had acted alone.[163] Multilateral sanctions differ from unilateral sanctions in their greater perceived legitimacy, and in their effects. Multilateral sanctions have the appearance of greater legitimacy in the international community, because more states have endorsed them. Multilateral sanctions usually also have more direct material effects, because broader support makes their restrictions harder to avoid.[164]

9. Humanitarian restrictions on economic sanctions

International economic sanctions imposed by states to punish violations of international law usually take the form of retorsion, in the shape of refusals to trade, which states can undertake at will.[165] Even economic countermeasures, that would otherwise have violated the law of nations can become legitimate, when they respect the limits of proportionality[166] and fundamental purposes of international law.[167] These fundamental purposes, as delineated in the Charter of the United Nations, include the maintenance of peace and security, the principle of the self-determination of peoples, and respect for fundamental human rights.[168] These translate in practice into restrictions against the use of force, against the violation of fundamental human rights, against direct reprisals on persons, and against other violations of peremptory norms of general international law.[169]

The limitations placed on economic sanctions by humanitarian obligations to respect the rights of individuals apply with greater force in the case of unilateral state-to-state countermeasures, outside the United Nations system.[170] Violating human rights to protect international law raises difficult judgments of proportionality, that states are ill-equipped to make, when acting alone.[171] Multilateral measures should also avoid collateral damage to human rights as much as possible.[172] Economic sanctions, too carelessly applied, might threaten several human rights listed in the *Universal Declaration* and the international human rights covenants including the right to life,[173] the right to property,[174] and the right to an adequate standard of living,[175] or at least to the basic means of subsistence.[176]

10. The economic liberty of individuals

The economic liberty of individuals to exercise control over their property through free trade and exchanges constitutes an important parallel on the human level of the economic liberty of states.[177] The well-established principle of international law that states should in most cases be free to trade (or not to trade) at their own discretion[178] reflects an underlying human right to property that embraces the individual's ability to exchange or to dispose of whatever she or he owns.[179] Economic sanctions by states restrict their citizens' economic freedom to trade. This violation of the citizen's economic liberty must be weighed against the importance of the laws that sanctions would enforce.

Limitations on individual economic freedom are frequently and properly imposed by domestic legal systems in support of various national purposes, including economic freedom itself.[180] Like all liberties, economic freedom may be violated as well by individuals as by states.[181] Economic sanctions imposed by democracies to enforce international law are more likely to be justified than sanctions imposed by non-democratic governments, because in democracies the citizens harmed by sanctions have the opportunity through voting and public deliberation to express their opposition or consent to restrictions on trade. Sometimes even democracies will burden one section of society unduly for the benefit of others, but non-democracies will almost always do so, because their governments are separated from public opinion.[182]

11. Economic sanctions harm innocents

Economic sanctions also restrict the economic liberty of the citizens of target states, in ways that may at first seem legitimate. States that limit their national trade with other states simply exercise collectively the economic freedom not to trade that their citizens might in any case have exercised separately.[183] But collective refusals to trade made through national sanctions have a much greater economic impact than separate individual refusals to trade because the replacement of trading partners becomes more difficult.[184] The most direct victims of international economic sanctions are often the innocent subjects of law-breaking governments. Economic sanctions imposed upon states that commit violations against their own citizens usually hurt those same citizens as much or more than they hurt the law-breaking government.[185]

Economic sanctions imposed by states to protect the citizens of other states against their own governments should always take those citizens' interests and (as much as possible) also their actual desires into account.[186] For this reason, states usually exempt food and medicines from otherwise general economic embargoes.[187] The difficulties faced by the government of one state in making decisions about balancing the interests of subjects of other states present a severe but unavoidable challenge when the government violating international law does not have balanced democratic institutions through which its people can express themselves. The internal decisions of democracies may usually be presumed to have taken the interests of their own populations into account, but non-democratic governments enjoy no such presumption. Democracies considering economic sanctions to enforce human rights law against non-democratic states should look as much as possible to popular leaders in the target state to gauge the will and needs of the people that they seek to protect.[188]

Democracies may themselves in certain circumstances properly be subject to economic sanctions to enforce international law. This situation arises when democratic majorities unite to oppress minority groups among their own citizens or fellow subjects, as in the American South during the era of racial discrimination and state-supported segregation. Non-democracies or semi-democracies in which the citizens are overwhelmingly united in national acts of ethnic oppression may also legitimately suffer more serious economic and other sanctions, with fewer humanitarian restrictions, than the innocent subjects of other oppressive regimes. Hitler's Germany, Milosević's Serbia, and the American South under Jefferson Davis all present examples of national majorities united in their democratically expressed desire to subjugate or to eliminate minority populations. National or multilateral responses to democratically supported apartheid, genocide and slavery warrant stronger sanctions applied against entire nations than crimes perpetrated by powerful elites against their subject populations without popular support or participation.

12. Preserving the means of subsistence

The International Covenant on Economic, Social and Cultural Rights and the International Covenant on Civil and Political Rights both mandate that "in no case may a people be deprived of its own means of subsistence."[189] Clearly, the threat of widespread starvation is a consequence so serious as almost always to be "disproportionate" to the aims sought to be enforced by economic sanctions.[190] Violations so serious as arguably to warrant the starvation of populations united in their violation of international law would almost always justify or even require the use of force to end the violation more quickly. Attempted genocides, such as those in Kosovo and Rwanda, while justifying serious responses against populations united in murdering minorities, would not have justified starvation of the perpetrators because starvation would not have prevented the genocide. Starvation in such circumstances would amount to an unacceptable counter-genocide, when swift military action to stop the primary genocide would have been the more effective and appropriate response.[191]

Starvation is usually the product more of bad government and unfortunate circumstances, than of economic sanctions. Democracies do not starve, because their governments respect the basic needs of their subjects.[192] Recent famines in North Korea and Ethiopia followed directly from the policies of non-democratic "socialism."[193] Food and medicine shortages in Iraq, despite the United Nations "fuel for food" program illustrate the problems of maldistribution in non-democratic regimes.[194] Yet all three cases also demonstrate serious difficulties in measuring the proportionality and appropriateness of economic sanctions. Citizens of Ethiopia and North Korea were saved from the most serious consequences of their governments' misallocation of resources by massive food aid from Western democracies.[195] Withholding this aid would have led to starvation, as it may have done in Iraq, when Iraq's government refused to facilitate the United Nations' food scheme.

The cases of North Korea, Ethiopia and Iraq illustrate the paradox that the more illegitimate the government, and the greater its contempt for its own citizens, the less legitimate economic sanctions will be as a method of enforcing international law against its human rights violations. Economic sanctions against non-democratic regimes lead to worse consequences for their innocent subjects than do sanctions against more democratic governments, because non-democratic governments magnify the sanctions' negative effects through the maldistribution of national resources. The citizens of more democratic states will also be less "innocent" when their governments violate international law, because the citizens of democracies have a voice in directing what their governments will do.

13. The appropriateness of economic sanctions

Confirming the legality (in certain circumstances) of economic sanctions to enforce international law still leaves open the question of their appropriateness. Legal economic sanctions may not always be appropriate, for moral or prudential reasons. This depends on the ultimate purpose of the sanctions, and the motives behind them. States or groups of states contemplating the imposition of sanctions to enforce international law must decide not only that the sanctions are legal, but also that they serve a useful purpose in advancing the state's own interests, or the interests of international law.

One purpose of economic sanctions to enforce international law could be to change the behavior of the miscreant states directly, by bringing them into compliance with previously disregarded norms. Economic sanctions are "effective" to the extent that they coerce the violator to respect the law. Measured in this way, the paradox of effectiveness closely parallels the paradox of proportionality that restricts the legality of countermeasures against despotic states. Economic sanctions are much less directly effective against tyrannies than they would be against democracies or states maintaining some consideration for the rights of the citizens that they rule.

Economic sanctions are much more directly effective against democracies because economic sanctions usually hurt citizens in general much more than they hurt governing elites. The more unjust the society, the more this will be true. Governments in democracies take their citizens' sufferings into account in deciding their national policies. Non-democracies do not. This makes economic sanctions more effective against democracies, and therefore more appropriate for use against democracies, than they would be against despotisms. Sanctions might in both cases be legal as reprisals, or as measures applied by way of retorsion, but they would not be as appropriate to impose in circumstances where the target state's rulers do not suffer, the target state's policies do not change, and the target state's population suffers, for no useful purpose.

The proper measures to apply against non-democratic despotic elites for the effective prevention or alteration of human rights violations would be measures that actually directly reach or influence the elite's own interests. These might include measures directed against individuals or selected groups of police or government officials, such as bans on personal transactions, [196] seizures of property, [197] or restrictions on the use of overseas funds or financial resources.[198]

14. Uneven enforcement of economic sanctions

All economic sanctions hurt the citizens of the state that imposes them, as well as their nominal targets. This raises questions of economic freedom, but also serious barriers to effectiveness. The consequences of economic sanctions on the state that imposes them may be so great that citizens choose not to respect the sanctions, or governments choose not to impose them. The uneven enforcement of economic sanctions may come about in two ways: sanctions may be enforced unevenly against their targets in that some states engaging in very similar behavior get sanctioned and others do not;[199] or some states may impose sanctions, while others refuse to participate.[200] This unevenness in applying sanctions undermines both their legitimacy and their effectiveness. Sanctions seem less legitimate when they are imposed unevenly on different states. They are less effective, when some states opt out of sanctions regimes.

The realities of international relations in the absence of a world government guarantee that sanctions against violations of international law will always be unevenly imposed and inconsistently enforced, depending on the identity of the victim, the identity of the perpetrator, and their relative power. Powerful states will act with impunity in violating international law, as Russia has in Chechnya, and China in Tibet. Less powerful states may find themselves sanctioned, as the Serbs have been in Kosovo. This might make it appear to those who rely on state practice to determine the content of international law, that one law applies to powerful states and a different law to the weak. Certainly the differences in enforcement are entirely predictable. But law and enforcement are not the same. Powerful states often respect international law, although no one enforces it against them.

To punish proud, powerful and often nuclear-armed governments with military force would be imprudent, even when they have violated international law. Smaller, weaker states offer easier targets for enforcement, through which to reassert fundamental principles that should have applied equally to the strong.[201] Economic sanctions provide better vehicles than military force for expressing disapproval of powerful governments, without provoking dangerous confrontation, but even economic sanctions may be too costly to the states that impose them. International law extends a universal obligation and protection to every human being in all states. The absence of enforcement does not diminish the validity of these norms. The fact that some states are not sanctioned, when they ought to have been, does not mean that rights should not be enforced, when they can be. By asserting the norm, and enforcing it when possible, states and other international actors encourage respect for law to the greatest extent in their power.

Disapproval can be a strong influence on state behavior, and therefore an effective method for enforcing international law, even against powerful states. States, organizations, or individuals that hesitate to impose economic restrictions against the strong may still communicate their disapproval directly, through speech, or indirectly by imposing sanctions against less powerful offenders. The fact that every violation of international law is not directly punished does not require that none should ever be. International law depends for its enforcement on states or coalitions of states. The costs of enforcement are too high to expect any consistent application of sanctions, or universal cooperation in doing so.

Some sanctions will be unevenly applied, ineffective, and perhaps inappropriate, because the target state is too powerful to challenge directly. Other sanctions may be unevenly applied, ineffective, and perhaps inappropriate because too few states impose or respect them. This second form of ineffectiveness, through some states' disregard of sanctions, may tempt other states to tolerate violations of international law. States perceiving (1) that they will hurt their own citizens by imposing economic sanctions; and (2) that they will not hurt their targets; because (3) other states will step in to replace embargoed trade, may decide to suspend sanctions, which only hurt themselves. Sanctions may fail to be effective through a lack of unanimity, through fear of their targets, or both.

15. The expressiveness of economic sanctions

Economic sanctions are seldom directly effective, are frequently unevenly applied, and sometimes hurt the states that impose them far more than their intended targets. Yet economic sanctions still serve a useful purpose, by expressing convictions about the nature and content of international law. Precisely because of the high costs of imposing economic sanctions, sanctions express very strong disapproval of their targets. Since governments, like persons, dislike disapproval, economic sanctions can influence states without being directly effective, or even very harmful. Economic sanctions give states, organizations and individuals a convincing method of expressing their sincere (because it is expensive) disapproval of violations of international law.[202]

Any state that imposes economic sanctions is punishing itself, or its own people, which guarantees its expressive sincerity. This expression becomes weaker when governments are not democratic, but even despotic rulers draw their wealth from the people, and will eventually become impoverished, if their subjects suffer too much. Unilateral sanctions almost always hurt the states that impose them more than their targets, because target populations can usually circumvent sanctions, while states that impose them cannot. So economic sanctions are almost always expressive rather than directly effective. They express one organization's, state's or group of states' disapproval of another state's action, which sanctions publicly identify and condemn as violations of international law.

Expressions through sanctions have greater force than simple declarations because their cost confirms their sincerity. When strengthened by multilateral consensus, by General Assembly Resolutions, [203] or by the decisions of the Security Council,[204] sanctions can confirm the content of international law, whether or not they are effective. Non-state actors can speak through sanctions as well as states can. The economic boycott of South Africa by certain United States corporations was particularly effective as an expression of disapproval, because the corporations acted before the United States government, with measures that were costly to themselves.

The strength of economic sanctions as an expression of law and disapproval may be counterproductive, when disapproval breeds resentment. Disapproval hurts most when expressed too directly, and sanctions make very direct accusations of illegality. Sanctioned governments respond with self-justifications, counter-accusations and excuses, more often than with compliance. Sanctions may harden a law-breaker's self-exculpatory excuses into a definite ideology, and postpone rather than encourage reform.[205] Just as coercive economic sanctions may be more appropriate against democracies, because their citizens are more truly at fault,[206] so may expressive economic sanctions be more effective against democracies, whose governments are open to reason.[207] Yet the governments and peoples even of democratic states may resent direct criticism, however much they are at fault.

16. Economic incentives

Economic incentives, sometimes known as "positive" economic sanctions, will usually be more effective than the "negative" sanctions of boycotts or embargoes in securing conformity with international law. The line between incentives and sanctions can be difficult to maintain, but the general rule is that incentives hold out a promised benefit for respecting the law, while sanctions threaten to punish violations. The promise of increased trade would be an incentive. The threat of restricting trade would be a sanction. To some extent this difference is illusory: the promise of more trade (if the law is respected) is also a threat to trade less (when laws are broken). This may be a distinction without a difference, but governments respond better to what they perceive as peace-offerings, than they do to threats or criticism.

The conditions imposed by the European Union on its would-be members supply a very good illustration of the greater effectiveness of incentives than sanctions in securing compliance with international human rights norms. Eastern European nations expect great economic benefits from integration into the European Union. To secure this membership they must meet certain conditions, including respect for "democracy, the rule of law, human rights and respect for and protection of minorities."[208] The incentive of European Union membership and its associated benefits has encouraged governments to embrace the economic and political conditions required for membership, including accession to the European Convention for the Protection of Human

Rights and Fundamental Freedoms, with recourse to the European Court of Human Rights for enforcement.

The wealth, peace and stability of the rights-respecting democracies provides them with considerable advantages in encouraging other states to conform to international law without recourse to negative sanctions. The obvious benefits of freedom and prosperity encourage all subject peoples to seek the protection of international law against their oppressive governments. When despotisms fall, their subjects take the opportunity to demand universal human rights. Governments will be more likely to support international law when this has obvious economic benefits. The prosperity that follows respect for international law gives law-abiding people an advantage in reaching out to authoritarian governments, and in encouraging their greater respect for law. The most effective "sanctions" in encouraging democracies and less-severe authoritarian governments to respect the law are the economic incentives of membership in a prosperous economic community.

17. The limits of economic sanctions

Not all governments want peace and prosperity. Some prefer the private luxury of elites, maintained on the backs of their suffering subjects. Despotic governments respond poorly to sanctions because they care so little for their citizens' well-being. Dictators resist world opinion more easily than elected leaders, and respond more truculently to criticism. This means that economic sanctions against non-democratic governments will often have little effect, even when narrowly tailored to hurt the ruling elites. Non-democratic rulers continue their violations in the face of harsh economic sanctions, because human rights violations provide the ultimate foundation of their power. They cannot afford to be gentle. When the violations cease, the people will rise up to punish their oppressors.

Sanctions are most effective against democracies and somewhat liberal regimes, that care about their citizens' welfare. Democracies and somewhat liberal regimes are more affected by criticism, and worry more about their populations, than non-democracies do. Less liberal regimes may be gradually encouraged to liberalize, through economic incentives, or coerced by military force to stop their human rights violations, but negative economic sanctions such as embargoes or boycotts have little effect on their policies. The longstanding intransigence of rights-violating governments in Cuba, North Korea and Burma illustrate the ineffectiveness of economic sanctions in enforcing international law against powerful elites in non-democratic states.

The paradox of effectiveness through which unilateral and multilateral economic sanctions directly influence the policies of democracies, but not despotisms, might seem to imply that economic sanctions should never be imposed against non-democracies, whose innocent citizens suffer from sanctions, while government policies remain the same. This judgment applies most to situations in which the humanitarian burdens imposed by sanctions outweigh the benefits of compliance. In such cases armed humanitarian intervention may be the only legitimate option for enforcing human rights law. States must either intervene by force to stop the violation, or do nothing, because less decisive economic intervention that does not change government policy will only hurt innocents, without enforcing the law.

18. Economic sanctions under international law

The greatest value of economic sanctions lies in their expressive power, to reaffirm the content of international law. This function may justify otherwise ineffective sanctions by confirming the legal status and binding nature of universal legal norms. Expressive sanctions communicate legal values not only to their direct targets, but also to other states and persons subject to the same rule of law. The most appropriate sanctions for reaffirming legal values in this way will be narrowly tailored and often somewhat symbolic prohibitions that hurt law-breaking government and commercial elites directly, without reaching ordinary citizens.[209] Such sanctions may not directly change the illegal behavior of the target government any more than broader sanctions would, but they spare innocents while maintaining the principles of international law. Economic sanctions in the form of boycotts or embargoes are almost always lawful, either as retorsion or as simple expressions of the economic self-determination of states. When economic agreements in support of free trade would otherwise make economic sanctions illegal, economic sanctions will still often be justified as countermeasures to enforce international law, subject to the usual humanitarian constraints, and to the limits of reasonable proportionality.

Multilateral enforcement of international law is more accurate, but also more dangerously coercive than unilateral enforcement, because it is less easy to evade. The jurisdiction to enforce international law through economic sanctions follows the ability objectively to judge the violation's existence. This is why democratic governments have greater authority than non-democracies to enforce international law. All "negative" economic sanctions violate human rights to some degree, and should be supported by democratic procedures that weigh their consequences against the probable benefits to those whom that they seek to protect. "Positive" sanctions or incentives are less coercive, and therefore more effective in enforcing international law. The paradox of economic sanctions arises from their relative utility. Sanctions work best against comparatively decent governments, who care about their subjects and world opinion. Negative sanctions are almost always legal, but almost never directly effective in enforcing international law.

22
Republican Manifesto and Summary of Conclusions

This volume has considered 20 important questions in international law from the perspective of the republican principles that support the international legal order. The purpose of this discussion has been neither to engage the numerous authors who have debated these questions in the past, nor to set out a complete elaboration of republican legal theory, but rather to explain in clear terms some basic implications of certain fundamental truths about law and justice that regulate most international legal obligations. States and individuals have a duty to obey and respect proposed international norms only to the extent that proposed norms respect the basic republican principles of international law. These chapters start from first principles to point out some obvious implications of the republican commitment to justice and the common good of all people. International law rests on republican foundations, and would not be just, binding, or interesting if it did not.

International Law, like all law, begins with the assertion of justice. Law deserves to be obeyed when law serves justice, and legal systems are justified only to the extent that they do so. All legal systems claim to be just, or to find just laws better than other available mechanisms. International law seeks justice among nations, but differs from other legal systems in the relative weakness of its legislative, judicial, and executive institutions. The authority to determine, to interpret, and to enforce international law is dispersed and contested among states. This brings fundamental questions of justice closer to the surface in international law that they are in most legal systems. Professors and publicists adjudicate and determine the legal status of disputes among nations as much as courts and armies do. Disputants speak with varying degrees of authority, and in claiming a legitimate voice in determining the requirements of international law, must offer a theory of the underlying nature and sources of international justice to justify their pretensions.

Republican doctrine recognizes justice in the common good of the people. States and governments are just (and justified or "legitimate" in republican terms) only to the extent that they serve the common good of the people that they rule. Modern international law developed most of its fundamental doctrines in the seventeenth and eighteenth centuries, concurrently with the development of republican legal theory, and therefore embodies many of the same fundamental legal principles that govern republics: law should serve the common good of all those subject to its rule; all subjects of the law should be equal; they should have an equal voice; be independent; protected by checks and balances; and free. These republican principles supply international law with both its historical and its moral foundations. They generated international law and they justify it. But although republican principles permeate international law, they have not been as fully realized in international institutions as they have been in the domestic institutions of some republican states. Law does not yet completely control all international relations, and not all states are republics. To the extent that non-republics have a voice in international relations, they undermine the justice and validity of international law.

The republican principle of popular sovereignty is embodied in the widely recognized right to the "self-determination of peoples." This concept of self-determination rests on two related assumptions: first, that all *people* everywhere are free and equal individuals without whose consent no legitimate national legal system can exist; and second that all *peoples* everywhere should constitute free and independent states, without whose consent no legitimate international legal system can exist. International law has always drawn strength and recognition from this powerful analogy between the liberty of individuals and the liberty of states. Republics properly protect the liberty and human rights of other nations whenever they have the power to do so. Thus international law has three main purposes: first, to protect each nation's sovereignty and self-determination against external and internal threats; second, to protect the human rights of all peoples against their own governments; and finally, to advance the common good of all nations, when collective action is necessary.

The republican principle of *imperium populi* requires that all peoples enjoy self-determination and the right to vote and to be elected in genuine periodic elections. Governments that deny their people democratic rights are not republican and have no legitimate claim either to the loyalty of their subjects or to recognition by other states and nations. People subject to such governments are not fully "peoples" until they can express their identity politically, but they may constitute one or more pre-political nations, whose voices would enrich international law, and whose rights are violated by their governing oppressors. The voices of peoples discover the law of nations whether peoples are the citizens of republics, or the suffering subjects of non-republican states.

Republican states and republican statesmen should always apply republican principles in finding and interpreting international law, as should anyone seeking justice in international affairs. This method requires disregarding deliberative processes tainted by the excessive participation of non-republican actors. When federal institutions embrace non-republican states, the federation's separate component republics and nations must deliberate within themselves to determine their proper international responsibilities. Broader international debate will always be desirable, but in the absence of a larger federation of republican states, republics must rely on the largest republican federation or forum that they can find. In the absence of any legitimate international legislature, all peoples and persons must decide for themselves which standards to apply or to enforce as international law. Because they disregard popular sovereignty, the opinions of despots and non-republican governments never legitimately influence the determination of international law. Non-elected governments can provide no privileged insights into justice or the common good of humanity. Republics should defer to non-republican international institutions only when they judge it to be in the best interests of justice and liberty to do so.

The law of nations is the "law of humanity" in that it governs all persons and peoples and should serve their common interests. Determining its content requires the participation of all persons and peoples through just political institutions. Without guarantees of the basic rights to vote, to free speech, and political checks and balances, persons and peoples will not be able fully to take part in the public deliberation that determines the content of international law. Governments that are not republican cannot legitimately speak for the peoples that they presume to represent. International law is properly mediated through nations, because human culture develops best through nations, responding to local needs and circumstances, but states and their government cannot speak for their peoples without the foundation of popular sovereignty, basic human rights, and respect for the rule of law.

The ultimate sources of international law are the needs of international society, as perceived by governments, jurists, and scholars and accepted by the international community as a whole. The primary difficulty in determining the content of international law lies in identifying who can speak with authority in expressing the needs and perceptions of the various peoples of the world. Republican principles deny the public authority of self-appointed rulers in order to favor the democratic expressions of self-determining peoples and nations. The smaller the democratic participation, the weaker the validity of the norm. This is not because democracy creates laws, but because popular sovereignty best confirms their content. The ultimate source of international law has always been the law of nature applied to nations. Conventions, customs, legal principles, and the opinions of publicists all offer resources for determining this common good of humanity. Without its foundation in justice, international law would lose efficacy and moral influence on the conduct of persons and states.

States are bound by customary international law because the customary practices of states and others in their international relations often reflect the perceptions of peoples about justice and the needs of international society better than other methods of expression. The customary law of nations corresponds to the *lex non scripta* of domestic legal systems. Nations develop customs either from the perception of natural principles or from consent. The widely shared view that certain norms are law and therefore binding offers very good evidence that the norms in question are, in fact, binding as law. In the absence of any international legislature, inference from the purposes of international law (justice and the common good) constitutes a much more direct source of law than would be the case in most domestic legal systems. Customary law, discovered in the views and practices of states provides good evidence of law by revealing either (1) what states or others *have* agreed to, or (2) what all international legal actors *should* agree to because it is widely recognized to be just.

The effectiveness of international law depends on the obedience of states. To be effective, international law must be obeyed. States do so at times due to force or coercion, but more often states obey international law because they desire to be just or to be seen (or seem) to be just by others. Governments and individuals crave praise and fear blame. Blame is often the strongest enforcement mechanism in the arsenal of international law. Blameworthiness itself depends on widely shared perceptions of what is "right" and "wrong." Such perceptions arise in public discourse. Republican principles insist that all voices should be heard in this discourse that are willing to debate the creation of a shared or common good for humanity. The effectiveness of international law ultimately depends on blaming what is blameworthy, after the widest possible discussion with the greatest number of sincere participants.

All states have a right to republican government under international law because only republican government can justify the role that states play in international affairs. States exist for the common good of their subjects. Republican government secures the common good through popular sovereignty, the rule of law, and deliberative checks and balances between the various offices of state. States without independent judges, the rule of law, the separation of powers, a mixed and balanced bicameral legislature, and an elected representative assembly will not defend human rights, treat all citizens with equal concern and respect, or show restraint in their international affairs, because they lack the republican defenses that would enable them to do so. Only republican structures of government can legitimately determine the content of international law sufficiently accurately to deserve deference from actors in the international arena. States properly exist only for the separate and collective well-being of those subject to their control. When governments violate this mandate, they forfeit their authority to rule.

International law, as law, has a basis in justice that is not necessarily present in all facets of international relations between states. Students of international relations have found it difficult to quantify the role of norms in state behavior, and the function of international law in regulating the society of nations. This has led to significant gaps in their scholarship. People want to think well of themselves and to be well thought of by others. This means that even pure instrumentalists seeking to manipulate international relations will need to take into account what people believe to be right and wrong. Such beliefs are manipulable, within limits, but determinate. They regulate the nature and the content of international law. International discourse is almost always normative even when it is insincere. Principled beliefs have as much impact on international relations as mere interests because they provide the framework through which interests express themselves. To understand international law one must understand its sources. There can be no cooperation without norms, no laws without a sense of justice.

The international rule of law begins with a claim to codify justice. The absence of a recognized international legislative, judicial or executive power brings this claim closer to the surface than in many legal systems because the mediating institutions that would settle disputes about the content of the law of nations are weak and lack authority. States and scholars should seek to encourage the development of just institutions of international law enforcement and adjudication, without relinquishing their underlying commitment to justice. Until just international institutions exist, states with comparatively just national structures of government and deliberation will have to decide for themselves what international law requires and do their best to enforce it.

Publicists such as Henry Wheaton have done a great deal to clarify the content and requirements of international law over the past four centuries. The fundamental law begins, as Wheaton explained, with the principles of justice that ought to regulate the mutual relations of nations, deduced from the nature of a society of independent states. Publicists may offer an impartiality in their interpretations of these requirements that is often absent in other arbiters of international affairs. The "absolute" rights of states include self-defense, peaceful internal development and all the other ordinary processes of self-realization naturally due to independent moral beings. These include the power of enforcement or reprisals, when others violate the fundamental rules of justice. Henry Wheaton made it clear that there can be no law without justice, no justice without community, and no international community without reflection about the underlying purposes all states exist to serve.

States exist to serve their peoples, developing collectively into nations in pursuit of the common good. The three terms "people," "nation" and "state" developed together to express different facets of the same concept of government, rooted in human nature. "Peoples" are the inhabitants of politically distinct territories. "Nations" are culturally distinct ethnic groups, not always living in the same territory. "States" are politically independent territories with their own governments and peoples. Stable state boundaries and populations can lead peoples to become nations, and most national identities originated in territorial proximity. In a peaceful, stable world, national identities will gradually coalesce around states. Forcing citizens into non-geographic tribal categories by the exclusion or inclusion of some citizens (and not others) in political life constitutes oppression, since it discriminates on non-functional grounds in what should have been a public function of the state.

The distinction between the governments of states and the interests of the peoples that they rule creates a continuing tension in international law. Not all governments have legitimate authority to speak on behalf of their peoples, but some are "decent" or "reasonable" enough to deserve a voice in international affairs, despite their questionable status. Many peoples need protections against their governments but some governments serve their people fairly well. The difference seems to lie mostly in political institutions and partly in respect for fundamental human rights. Republican governments, with popular sovereignty, political checks and balances, an independent judiciary and the rule of law, will be decent and reasonable in their internal and external affairs. Non-republics will not, but become more legitimate as they incorporate more republican institutions into the basic structures of the state.

A world of republics would live in perpetual peace, but not all states have republican governments, or are likely soon to obtain them. The first step toward world peace would be to stabilize the existing political boundaries of states, within and between which to implement justice. Sometimes peace must precede justice, but justice justifies and perpetuates peace, when peace between states facilitates their mutual reform, and more permanent articles of federation. Immanuel Kant properly anticipated the perfection of international law ("*Völkerrecht*" or "*ius gentium*") through the gradual development of national institutions toward a world-wide federation of free republics. This should be a "*Völkerbund*" or "*foedus pacificum,*" not a "*Völkerstaat.*" The difference lies in maintaining each people's separate identity in separate independent republics. Each republic must be an equal member of the international federation of peoples, just as every person must be equally a citizen of her or his own state, within the federation. All states (even non-republics) have a duty of good will and hospitality. This is the *ius cosmopoliticum* that underlies (and in the end, creates) the rest of international law.

Humanitarian intervention has always played an important part in international relations. In this imperfect world of unfree and non-republican states some governments will violate international law and the laws of humanity both in their internal and their external affairs. Humanitarian intervention constitutes one possible response to such violations, when one state acts to enforce justice and human rights against the government of another. Violations of liberty, justice, or other acts of subjugation, domination and exploitation, or the denial of the rule of law or of a people's right to self-government, can all justify transnational intervention to uphold the underlying sovereignty and self-determination of subject peoples. This does not mean that all such violations will warrant intervention. Enforcement measures have their own costs and should always be proportionate to the offense. Some violations should remain uncorrected, if no appropriate remedies can be found. Governments must exercise humility, and seek the benefits of democratic deliberation and international consensus, before acting to enforce international law.

The International Court of Justice offers a forum for correcting violations of international law without recourse to arms, economic sanctions or other methods of bilateral enforcement. The peaceful settlement of disputes by consent in international tribunals can transfer disputes from the realm of power to reason, by securing impartial arbitration. To be impartial in the necessary sense, however, tribunals must either be mutually acceptable to the parties (which is not in itself enough to give their decisions epistemic value) or learned and independent, as legitimated through a democratic selection procedure. As currently constituted, the International Court of Justice does not enjoy this sort of democratic legitimacy, rooted as it is in the power and politics of existing illiberal and undemocratic regimes. The International Court of Justice and similar courts of arbitration serve a useful purpose in settling disputes by consent, but they lack the authority to clarify or to determine the content of international law.

The republican principle of popular sovereignty provides the international legal order with a preliminary test for the legitimacy of all national and international institutions. This democratic test confronts difficulties, however, in resolving boundary disputes between states. The democratic principle yields different results within differently drawn borders. The boundaries between peoples determine the proper jurisdiction of states and the province of international law. The republican origin and proper understanding of peoples in international law as essentially territorial and political constructs suggests that the best resolution of boundary disputes lies less in democracy than in history. The first test of what constitutes a "people" is existing political boundaries. The dominant projects of international law have been to stabilize such boundaries between states and to bring their peoples into harmony for the common good of all.

The right of subjugated minorities to secede with their territories from oppressive states follows from the fundamental obligation of law and government to serve the common good of their subjects. Secession violates the principle of stable borders but may be justified in some circumstances, when governments forfeit their right to rule. When governments deny equal concern and respect to some segment of their population, they violate the principles that justify their power. Secession may become the best remedy when the existing government renounces its unity with some segment of the population, implicitly recognizing the existence of a separate people, divisible from the whole. When a state oppresses regional minorities, denies minorities rights that other citizens enjoy, or systematically disrespects them, then the state is denying that minority group's membership in the people, and its status as part of the nation. By its actions the state has identified the independent existence of a separate people or nation.

International economic organizations and other non-state actors often structure their affairs very much as states do, and economic considerations often have a strong influence on state policy, which has tempted some observers to muddle the distinction between states and other international organizations and to explain both in purely economic vocabulary. Discarding such terms as "liberty" and "justice" in international affairs to focus on "transaction costs" would remove discussion from the realm of law to that of interest or power. Systems of organization that do not claim to seek justice are not law. Some reformers apply the theory of the firm to international institutions to promote cooperative solutions to interstate coordination problems. Creating an international regime that minimizes the friction involved in necessary international transactions would be a valuable achievement. But any such arrangement not founded on justice would be unstable, undesirable, or both. International organizations do and should exist, not simply to facilitate the interest of states, but also to promote certain ends over others. Efficiency has only a secondary importance.

Economic sanctions offer a good illustration of the practical inefficiency, but moral importance, of most enforcement measures under international law. Economic sanctions almost always have a more severe financial impact on the states that impose them than they do on their intended targets. But economic sanctions can serve a valuable expressive purpose in challenging injustice, even when they have very few direct economic effects. Economic sanctions are often most justified when they are least directly effective, precisely because they have less direct impact on the innocent citizens of sanctioned oppressor states. Economic sanctions express disapproval without war and exert influence without power. They illustrate the central role of opinion in enforcing international law.

A review of 20 contested questions in international law and justice reveals how republican principles have shaped international law from the beginning, and will continue to do so, because they provide the obvious basis of just cooperation between states. Immanuel Kant expressed the sanguine belief that even despots will usually settle on republican principles to govern their mutual relations, and that international society will gradually democratize itself. While this may still prove true in the long run, two thousand years of republican influence have not yet fully effectuated the change. Advocates of international law can hasten the transition by recognizing and advancing law's basis in justice and the common good.

Republican principles in international law begin with the common good of the people, but they also incorporate the legal and political requirements that history and experience have proved necessary for fulfilling the public welfare. There will be no justice within or between states without popular sovereignty, the separation of powers, the rule of law, democratic elections, bicameralism, individual human rights, and the other checks and balances of fully functioning republican governments. The only just basis of international law is, has been, and always will be the deliberate perceptions of republican states as developed in the public sphere. The excessive participation of non-republican powers in formulating international law would deprive the entire structure of its legitimacy and binding force. Non-republican governments should surrender rights and power to their peoples. *Sic semper tyrannis*!

Notes

Preface

i. "Nature, which is to say the law of nations, and also the separate laws of those various states in which different peoples pursue their common good (*res publica*), all concur to forbid anyone from serving his or her own interests by harming someone else."
ii. "Now we must view this entire world as commonwealth (*civitas*) of all the gods and all humanity together."

1 Introduction

1. Emmerich de Vattel, *Le Droit des Gens ou principes de la loi Naturelle appliqués à la conduite et aux affaires des Nations et des Souverains*. A. Droz. Neuchâtel and London, 1758.
2. Ibid., p. xxiv.
3. Ibid. p. xxiv, n. 1. Cf. the frontispiece: "Nihil est enim illi principi Deo, qui omnem hunc mundum regit, quod quidem in terris fiat, acceptius, quam concilia coetusque hominum jure sociati, quae Civitates appellantur." See Marcus Tullius Cicero, *de re publica*, VI.xiii.13.
4. Marcus Tullius Cicero, *de officiis*, III.v.23. Cf. Ibid., *de legibus* I.vii.23: "universus hic mundus [est] una civitas communis."
5. Christian Wolff, *Juris Gentium methodo scientifica pertractatum*. Frankfurt and Leipzig, 1764. Prolegomena, §§7–10, pp. 3–4.
6. Immanuel Kant, *Zum ewigen Frieden*. 1795. Reprinted Reclam. Stuttgart, 1993.
7. Henry Wheaton, *Elements of International Law*. Richard Henry Dana, Jr. (ed.) 8th edn, Little Brown. Boston, 1866, p. 23.
8. For a detailed discussion of the republican origins of modern international law, see Nicholas Onuf, *The Republican Legacy in International Thought*. Cambridge University Press. Cambridge, England, 1998.
9. M.N.S. Sellers, *Republican Legal Theory*. Palgrave Macmillan. Basingstoke and New York, 2003.
10. For more details on this conception of republican theory see ibid., ch. 2.
11. Plato, *Politeia*, I. xv. 342E.
12. Aristotle, *Politica*, III. iv.7.
13. See M.N.S. Sellers, "The Roman Republic and the French and American Revolutions" in Harriet I. Flower (ed.) *The Cambridge Companion to the Roman Republic*. Cambridge University Press. Cambridge, England, 2004, pp. 347 ff.
14. See M.N.S. Sellers, *The Sacred Fire of Liberty*. Macmillan. Basingstoke, England, 1998.
15. See for example, Algernon Sidney, *Discourses Concerning Government* (1698), T.G. West (ed.) Liberty Fund. Indianapolis, 1990, at I.5. Cf. Quentin Skinner, *Liberty Before Liberalism*. Cambridge University Press. Cambridge, England, 1998.

16. See J.G.A. Pocock, *The Machiavellian Moment.* Princeton University Press. Princeton, 1975.
17. For an excellent contemporary articulation of republican philosophy, see Philip Pettit, *Republicanism: A Theory of Freedom and Government.* Clarendon Press. Oxford, 1997.
18. See M.N.S. Sellers, *The Sacred Fire of Liberty: Republicanism, Liberalism and the Law.* Palgrave Macmillan. Basingstoke, England, 2003.

2 Republican Principles in International Law

1. Immanuel Kant, *Zum ewigen Frieden.* 1795. Reclam. Reprinted Stuttgart, 1993. at 10: "Die bürgerliche Verfassung in jedem Staate soll republikanisch sein." Id. at 16: "Das Völkerrecht soll auf einen Föderalism freier Staaten gegründet sein."
2. *U.S. Constitution*, Art. IV, § 4.
3. For example, Kant, supra note 1, at 19: "Denn wenn das Glück es so fügt: dass ein mächtiges und aufgeklärtes Volk sich zu einer Republik (die ihrer Natur nach zum ewigen Frieden geneigt sein muss) bilden kann, so gibt diese einen Mittelpunkt der föderativen Vereinigung für andere Staaten ab, um sich an sie anzuschliessen und so den Freiheitszustand der Staaten gemäss der Idee des Völkerrechts zu sichern und sich durch mehrere Verbindungen dieser Art nach und nach immer weiter auszubreiten."
4. Cf. Marcus Tullius Cicero, *De officiis*, II.viii; III.v–vi; III.xvii. 69. See also Nicholas G. Onuf, " 'Civitas Maxima': Wolff, Vattel and the Fate of Republicanism," 88 *American Journal of International Law* 280 (1994).
5. There is a vast recent literature applying Kant's theories to modern international law: writings which usually do not enquire too closely into the meaning of the word "republican." See for example, Cecilia Lynch, "Kant, the Republican Peace, and Moral Guidance in International Law," 8 *Ethics and International Affairs* 39 (1994); Fernando R. Tesón, "The Kantian Theory of International Law," 92 *Columbia Law Review* 53 (1992); Michael Doyle, "Kant, Liberal Legacies and Foreign Affairs," 12 *Philosophy and Public Affairs* 205, 323 (1993). On the "Kantian Tradition" in international law, see David R. Mapel and Terry Nardin, "Convergence and Divergence in International Ethics" in Nardin and Mapel (eds), *Traditions of International Ethics*, Cambridge University Press. Cambridge, 1992, pp. 297–322. For a non-Kantian discussion of republicanism in International Law. See Onuf, supra n. 4.
6. Kant, supra n. 1, at 10–11: "Die erstlich nach Prinzipien der Freiheit der Glieder einer Gesellschaft (als Menschen), zweitens nach Grundsätzen der Abhangigkeit aller von einer einzigen gemeinsamen Gesetzgebung (als Untertanen) und drittens die nach dem Gesetz der Gleichheit derselben (als Staatsbürger) gestiftete Verfassung – die einzige, welche aus der Idee des ursprünglichen Vertrags hervorgeht, auf der alle rechtliche Gesetzebung eines Volks gegründet sein muss – ist die republikanische."
7. Id., at 13.
8. *Id.*, at 15: "Zu jener aber, wenn sie dem Rechts begriffe gemäss sein soll, gehört das repräsentative system, in welchem allein eine republikanische Regierungsart möglich, ohne welches sie (die Verfassung mag sein, welche sie wolle) despotisch und gewalttätig ist."

9. *Id.*, at 14: "Der Republikanism ist das Staatsprinzip der Absonderung der ausführenden Gewalt (der Regierung) von der gesetzgebenden ..."
10. Ibid.
11. Id., at 16.
12. For a broad overview of the republican legal tradition, see M.N.S. Sellers, *The Sacred Fire of Liberty*. Macmillan. Basingstoke, England, 1998. For bibliographies and (somewhat jaundiced) discussions of recent republican scholarship, see Daniel T. Rodgers, "Republicanism: The Career of a Concept," 79 *Journal of American History* 11 (1992); G. Edward White, "Reflections on the 'Republican Revival': Interdisciplinary Scholarship in the Legal Academy," 6 *Yale Journal of Law and the Humanities* 1 (1994).
13. See M.N.S. Sellers, "The Actual Validity of Law," 37 *American Journal of Jurisprudence* 283 (1992).
14. M.N.S. Sellers, "Republican Impartiality," 11 *Oxford Journal of Legal Studies* 273 (1991). For the *imperium and maiestas* of the people, see M. Tullius Cicero, *Philippicae* IV.4.8; T. Livius, *Ab urbe condita*, II.7.7.
15. See, for example, "Publius" [James Madison], *The Federalist* X, at 126 in Isaac Kramnick (ed.), *The Federalist Papers*. Penguin. London, 1987: "A republic ... [is] a government in which a scheme of representation takes place," so that "the public voice, pronounced by the representatives of the people, will be more consonant to the public good than if pronounced by the people themselves." Cf. Montesquieu, who also considered the structure of the suffrage as fundamental in a republic. Charles de Secondat, baron de la Brède et de Montesquieu, *De l'esprit des lois*, bk II, ch. 2 (1748).
16. Most influentially, see John Rawls, "The Law of Peoples" in Stephen Shute and Susan Hurley (eds.), *On Human Rights: The Oxford Amnesty Lectures 1993*, Basic Books. New York, 1993. 41. Cf. John Rawls, *Political Liberalism*. Columbia University Press. New York, 1993.
17. Rawls, for example, now endorses "a common good conception of justice" in "The Law of Peoples," supra n. 16.
18. See, for example, Marcus Tullius Cicero, *De re publica*, I.xxv.39: "res publica res populi, populus autem non omnis hominum coetus quoquo modo congregatus, sed coetus multitudinis iuris consensu et utilitatis communione sociatus." See also ibid. at III.vi.26:. "Ergo unum debet esse omnibus propositum, ut eadem sit utilitas unius cuiusque et universorum; quam si ad se quisque rapiet, dissolvetur omnis humana consortio."
19. This would seem to have been the worry of John Rawls when he refused to speak of "truth" about justice. See, for example, John Rawls, Political Liberalism, supra n. 16. See also John Rawls, "Reply to Habermas," 150 XCII *Journal of Philosophy* 132–180 (1995).
20. See Sellers, supra n. 14. Consensus and compromise will be more easily achieved in search of the common good than in pursuit of even "rational" self-interest.
21. Ibid.
22. John Adams, *A Defence of the Constitutions of Government of the United States of America*, at I.123 (1787).
23. Kant, supra n. 1, at 16–20.
24. For the origins of the concept of self-determination, see Alfred Cobban, *The Nation State and National Self-Determination*. Thomas Y. Crowell.

New York, 1969; Michla Pomerance, *Self-Determination in Law and Practice.* Martinus Nijhoff. The Hague, 1982; Dov Ronen, *The Quest for Self-Determination.* Yale University Press, New Haven, 1979; A. Rigo Sureda, *The Evolution of the Right of Self-Determination.* A.W. Sijthoff. Leiden, 1973.

25. *The Unanimous Declaration of the Thirteen United States of America,* July 4, 1776.
26. Woodrow Wilson, quoted in Michla Pomerance, "The United States and Self-Determination: Perspectives of the Wilsonian Conception," 70 *American Journal of International Law* 1, 2 (1976).
27. "[The Purposes of the United Nations are] to develop friendly relations among nations based on respect for the principle of equal rights and the self-determination of peoples." *U.N. Charter* art. I, para. 2. art. 55 also speaks of "peaceful and friendly relations among nations based on respect for the principle of equal rights and the self-determination of peoples."
28. Emmerich de Vattel, *Le droit des gens ou principes de la loi naturelle appliqués à la conduite et aux affaires des Nations et des Souverains.* A. Droz. Neuchâtel and London, 1758. Preliminaires §4.
29. For a recent example, see Rawls, "The Law of Peoples," supra n. 16.
30. "Die Natur will unwiderstehlich dass das Recht zuletzt die Obergewalt erhalte." Kant, *supra* note 1, at 32. "durch den wechselseitigen Eigennutz ..." Id. at 33.
31. "Universal Monarchie." Id. at 32.
32. "Kein Staat soll sich in die Verfassung und Regierung eines andern Staats gewalttätig einmischen." Id. at 6.
33. "Dahin würde nicht zu ziehen sein, wenn ein Staat sich durch innere Veruneinigung in zwei Teile spaltete, deren jeder für sich einen besondern Staat vorstellt, der auf das Ganze Anspruch macht; wo einem derselben Beistand zu leisten einem aüssern Staat nicht für Einmischung in die Verfassung des andern (denn es ist alsdahn Anarchie) angerechnet werden könnte." Id. at 7.
34. "Das Recht der Menschen muss heilig gehalten werden, der herrschenden Gewalt mag es auch noch so grosse Aufopferung Kosten." Id. at 49. Cf. Eugene Kamenka, "Human Rights, Peoples Rights," in J. Crawford (ed.), in *The Rights of Peoples.* Clarendon Press. Oxford, 1988, at p. 129 for the republican sources of modern rights discourse in Commonwealth England, France, and the United States of America. Kamenka rightly notes that all "liberal democracy" grew out of the republican tradition.
35. *International Covenant on Economic, Social and Cultural Rights,* Dec. 16, 1966, Part I, art. I.1, 993 *U.N.T.S.* 3, 6 *I.L.M.* 360 (1967) [hereinafter "*ICESPR*"].
36. "All peoples have the right of self-determination. By virtue of that right they freely determine their political status and freely pursue their economic, social and cultural development." *International Covenant on Civil and Political Rights,* Dec. 16, 1966, Part I, art. I.1, 999 *U.N.T.S.* 171, 6 *I.L.M.* 368 (1967) [hereinafter "*ICCPR*"].
37. *ICCPR* art. 9, para.1.
38. *Universal Declaration on Human Rights,* G.A. Res. 217A (III), U.N. Doc. A/810 (1948).
39. For discussions of the modern concept of self-determination, see Hurst Hannum, *Autonomy, Sovereignty and Self-Determination: The Accomodation of Conflicting Rights.* University of Pennsylvania Press. Philadelphia, 1990;

Michla Pomerance, *Self-Determination in Law and Practice,* supra n. 24, at I; Thomas M. Franck, "The Emerging Right to Democratic Governance," in 86 *American Journal of International Law* 46 (1992); "Postmodern Tribalism and the Right to Secession" in Broelmann Catherine, Lefeber Rene and Zieck Marjoleine (eds), *Peoples and Minorities in International Law.* Kluwer. Dodrecht, 1992. Lea Brilmayer, "Secession and Self-Determination: A Territorial Interpretation," in 16 *Yale Journal of International Law* 177 (1991); Frederic L. Kirgis, Jr., "The Degrees of Self-Determination in the United Nations Era," in 88 *American Journal of International Law* 304–310 (1994).

40. *U.N. Charter* art. 2, para. 1.
41. *U.N. Charter* art. 2, para. 4.
42. *U.N. Charter* art. 2, para. 7.
43. Vattel, supra n. 28, Preliminaires, § 4.
44. Id., Preliminaires § 18, as translated in the Fourth Edition (London, 1811).
45. Id., at II.vi.54.
46. Id., at I.iv.38.
47. Id., at I.iv.39.
48. Id., at I.iv.51.
49. "But we ought not to abuse this maxim, and make a handle of it to authorize odious machinations against the internal tranquillity of States." Id. at II.iv.56.
50. Jean Bodin, *Six livres de la République,* Paris 1586, I. 8-II.5.
51. "Atque hoc loco primum rejicienda est eorum opinio, qui ubique & sine exceptione summam potestatem esse volunt populi, ita ut ei reges, quoties imperio suo male utuntur, & coercere & punire liceat: quae sententia quot malis causam dederit, & dare etiamnum possit, penitus animis recepta, nemo sapiens non videt. Nos his argumentis eam refutamus. Licet homini cuique se in privatem servitutem cui velit addicere, ut & ex lege Hebraea & Romana apparet. Quidni ergo populo sui juris liceat se uni cuipiam, aut pluribus ita addicere, ut regendi sui jus in eum plane transcribat nulla ejus juris parte retenta?" Hugo Grotius, *De Jure Belli ac Pacis Libri tres.* rev. edn (1625) Johannes Blaevius. Amsterdam, 1688 at I.iii.viii.1.
52. Id., at 53 (citing Aristotle.)
53. Id., at 53.
54. Id., at 55–56.
55. Id., at 56.
56. Id., at 57.
57. *Cf.* M.N.S. Sellers, "Republican Authority," V *The Canadian Journal of Law and Jurisprudence* 257, 259–60 (1992); Thomas Hobbes, *Leviathan.* Andrew Cook. London, 1651, II.18.1: "And therefore, they that are subjects to a Monarch, cannot without his leave cast off Monarchy, and return to the confusion of a disunited Multitude; nor transferre their person from him that beareth it, to another Man, or other Assembly of men."
58. Example, *Declaration on Principles of International Law Concerning Friendly Relations and Cooperation Among States in Accordance with the Charter of The United Nations,* G.A. Res. 2625, U.N.GAOR, 1883rd plenary mtg, U.N. Doc. A/RES/2625 (1970).
59. Example, Ian Brownlie, *Principles of Public International Law.* 3rd edn, Oxford University Press. Oxford, 1979. Ch. 13: "Sovereignty and Equality of States."

60. Bodin, supra n. 50, II.5 at 609.
61. In addition to the passage quoted above, see Grotius, supra n. 51, at 490–494, in which Grotius admits that slavery violates the law of nature, and recognizes the barbarity of inherited servitude.
62. Grotius, supra n. 51, at 54.
63. "[S]umma [potestas] autem illa dicitur, cujus actus alterius juri non subsunt, ita ut alterius voluntatis humanae arbitrio irriti possint reddi." Id. at 52.
64. Example, Algernon Sidney, *Discourses Concerning Government*. J. Toland. London, 1698, I.5: "For as liberty solely consists in an independency upon the will of another, and by the name of slave we understand a man, who can neither dispose of his person nor goods, but enjoys all at the will of his master; there is no such thing in nature as a slave, if those men and nations are not slaves, who have no other title to what they enjoy than the grace of a prince, which he may revoke whensoever he pleaseth." See, also Sellers, *The Sacred Fire of Liberty*, supra n. 12.
65. Henry Wheaton, *Elements of International Law*. Richard Henry Dana, Jr., 8th edn, Little Brown. Boxton, 1866. Part II, §§ 65–66.
66. See, for example President Monroe's message to Congress of December 2, 1823, the so-called "Monroe Doctrine."
67. "Das Völkerrecht soll auf einen Föderalism freier Staaten gegründet sein." Kant, supra n. 1, at 16 (emphasis added).
68. Id., at 32.
69. "Il est de la nature d'une république qu'elle n'ait qu'un petit territoire ... Dans une grande république, le bien commun est sacrifié à mille considérations; il est subordonné à des exceptions; il dépend des accidents. Dans une petite, le bien public est mieux senti, mieux connu, plus près de chaque citoyen ..." Montesquieu, supra n. 15, VIII.16. Cf. Jean-Jacques Rousseau, *Du contrat social*, bk II, ch. 9; Bk III, ch. 6 (1762).
70. "So wie die Natur weislich die Völker trennt, welche der Wille jedes Staats und zwar selbst nach Gründen des Völkerrechts gern unter sich durch List oder Gewalt ..." Kant, supra n. I, at 33.
71. "Publius" [James Madison], *Federalist* LI, *The Federalist Papers*. "Ambition must be made to counteract ambition. And happily for the republican cause, the practicable sphere may be carried to a very great extent by a judicious modification and mixture of the federal principle." Id. at 319, 322. *Cf. The Federalist* X.
72. Adams, supra n. 22, at III.505.
73. Kant, supra n. 1, at 31.
74. "And according to the degree of pleasure and pride we feel in being republicans ought to be our zeal in cherishing the spirit and supporting the character of federalists." "Publius" [James Madison], *Federalist* X, *The Federalist Papers,* at 128.
75. See, for example, F. Von Savigny, *Vom Beruf unserer Zeit für Gesetzgebung und Rechtswissenschaft*. Mohr und Zimmer. Heildelberg, 1814; Richard Rorty, *Contingency, Irony and Solidarity*. Cambridge University Press. Cambridge, 1989.
76. See, for example, Amy Gutmann (ed.), *Multiculturalism*. 2nd edn, Princeton University Press. Princeton, 1994; Will Kymlicka, *Liberalism, Community and Culture*. Clarendon Press. Oxford, 1989.
77. See, for example, Daniel Patrick Moynihan, *Pandaemonium: Ethnicity in International Politics*. Oxford University Press. New York, 1993.

78. See, for example, Jürgen Habermas, "Human Rights and Popular Sovereignty: The Liberal and Republican Versions," 7 *Ratio Juris* (1994); Frank Michelman, "Law's Republic," 97 *Yale Law Journal* 1493 (1988).
79. See M.N.S. Sellers, *American Republicanism*. Macmillan. Basingstoke, England, 1994 for the traditional desiderata of republican government.
80. Republicans have always been very careful to distinguish their constitution from democracy. For example, Cicero, *De re publica*, supra n. 18, at II.xiii.41; Sidney, supra n. 64, at II.16.30; *The Federalist* X and XIV, *The Federalist Papers*; Kant, supra n. I, at 13.
81. Titus Livius, *Ab urbe condita*, II.l; *see* Sellers, *The Sacred Fire of Liberty*, supra n. 12.
82. Benjamin Constant, *De la liberté des anciens comparée à celle des modernes* (1819).
83. Most critics of the nation-state fear its unifying force in the hands of tyrants. Even Jürgen Habermas, who sees the importance of nationalism in Europe's emerging republican sensibility and the value of common identity in protecting universal human rights, does not understand how weak civic bonds will be without a national identity to support them. See Jürgen Habermas, "The European Nation State-its Achievement and its Limits: On the Past and Future of Sovereignty and Citizenship," in *Challenges To Law at the End of the 20th Century. Papers and Abstracts of the 17th IVR World Congress* 27 (1995).
84. "Respublica res est populi. Populus autem non omnis hominum coetus quoquo modo congregatus, sed coetus multitudinis juris consensu, et utilitatis communione sociatus." Cicero, supra n. 18, at I.xxv.39.
85. *United States Constitution*, art. I, § 4.
86. *United States Constitution*, art. I, §10; see also amendment XIV.
87. Kant, supra n. 1, Erster Zusatz: Von der Garantie des ewigen Friedens.
88. "I1 est de la nature d'une république qu'elle n'ait qu'un petit territoire ..." Montesquieu, supra n. 15, at I.viii.16; "plus l'État s'agrandit, plus la liberté diminue." Rousseau, supra n. 69, at II.9; III.1.
89. Charles Taylor, *The Ethics of Authenticity*. Harvard University Press. Cambridge, 1991; Alasdair MacIntyre, *After Virtue: Whose Justice? Which Rationality?* University of Notre Dame Press. Notre Dame, 1988.
90. "The smaller the society, the fewer probably will be the distinct parties and interests, the more frequently will a majority be found of the same party; and the smaller the number of individuals composing a majority, and the smaller the compass within which they are placed, the more easily will they concert and execute their plans of oppression." See "Publius" [James Madison], *The Federalist* X, *The Federalist Papers*.
91. The Preamble to the United Nations Charter states: "... to reaffirm faith in fundamental human rights, in the dignity and worth of the human person, in the equal rights of men and women and of nations large and small."
92. *U.N. Charter*, art. 55(c).
93. *Universal Declaration of Human Rights*, supra n. 38.
94. *See ICESCR, supra* note 35, and ICCPR, supra n. 36.
95. *ICCPR*, supra n. 36.
96. *ICESCR*, Part II, art. 2, para 1.
97. *ICCPR*, art. 4 para 2.
98. *ICCPR*, Part II, art. 2, para 1.
99. *ICCPR*, art. 6.
100. *ICCPR*, arts. 14, 26.

101. *ICCPR*, arts. 14, 26.
102. *ICCPR*, art. 25.
103. Cf. Kamenka, supra n. 34, at 127, 135.
104. The United States signed the *International Covenant on Economic, Social and Cultural Rights* on October 5, 1977. *The International Covenant on Civil and Political Rights* was also signed on October 5, 1977 and ratified on April 2, 1992. CCH Cong. Index vol. 1, Senate 102 Cong., Sess. 1991–1992. France signed both the International Covenant on Economic, Social and Cultural Rights and the International Covenant on Civil and Political Rights on January 29, 1981. *J. Republique Française* 405.
105. See above and the famous quote from Cicero, "Respublica est res populi," quoted in John Adams, supra n. 22, vol. I, xxi.
106. See Cicero, supra n. 14 and accompanying text.
107. For example, *U.N. Charter*, Art. 55 and art. I, para. 2.
108. For example, *ICCPR*, art. 1, para. 1.
109. Deploring this fact, *see* Richard Falk, "The Rights of Peoples (In Particular Indigenous Peoples)" in *The Rights of Peoples* supra n. 34 at p. 26.
110. For example, Ian Brownlie, "The Rights of People in Modern International Law" in *The Rights of Peoples* supra n. 34 at p.11.
111. *U.N. Charter*, Preamble: "WE THE PEOPLES OF THE UNITED NATIONS. ..." The language consciously echoes the Preamble to the Constitution on the United States of America: "We the People of the United States..." and implies all *citizens* of the republic.
112. The *populus*, or population.
113. "Respublica res est populi. Populus autem non omnis hominum coetus quoquo modo congregatus, sed coetus multitudinis juris consensu, et utilitatis communione sociatus." Cicero, *De re publica*, supra n. 18, at I.xxv.39.
114. Charlton T. Lewis and Charles Short, *A Latin Dictionary*, s.v. "*Natio*" 1189 (1879).
115. See Habermas, supra n. 83, at 28.
116. Id.
117. Id., at 31–32.
118. On *uti possidetis juris*, with bibliography, see Brownlie, supra n. 58, at 137–148.
119. See, for example, the *Declaration on the Granting of Independence to Colonial Countries and Peoples*, G.A. Res. 1514 (1960) para. 1: "the subjection of peoples to alien subjugation, domination and exploitation constitutes a denial of fundamental human rights."
120. See *Declaration on the Granting of Independence to Colonial Countries and Peoples*, supra n. 119, para 6.
121. Some claim that there is a logical inconsistency inherent in this behavior. See, for example, David Makinson, "Rights of Peoples: Point of View of a Logician," in *The Rights of Peoples* supra n. 34 at pp. 75–77. This need not be the case if all ethnically or otherwise distinct populations do not rise to the level of "peoples." Everything hinges on how boundaries will be drawn between "peoples."
122. *The African Charter on Human and Peoples Rights*, "Banjul Charter" art. 20, para. 1 (1981).
123. OAU Resolution 16(1) of July, 196 declared that "all member states pledge themselves to respect the frontiers existing on their achievement of national independence."

124. Jürgen Habermas deplores the natural cultural unity of republican peoples in the name of "pluralism" and multicultural diversity. Habermas, supra n. 83, at 31–36. Habermas's view overestimates the tenacity of tribal affinities and the dangers of cultural union. Republics naturally and properly develop a common sense of identity that includes and builds on all the constituent elements of the population. Habermas and many others have been misled by the recent fluidity of European borders. Immigrants naturally assimilate over time to republican cultures, while contributing aspects of their own previous heritage to the common patrimony. Only strong legal encouragement of differences will preserve significant cultural diversity under free and equal republican governments.
125. This principle is reflected in art. I and 25 of the *ICCPR* (1966).
126. This principle is recognized by art. 2, para. 1 of the *ICCPR* (1996).
127. This right has been recognized by art. 27 of the *ICCPR* (1966).
128. See for example, Brownlie, supra n. 110, at 5–6.
129. For an interesting attempt to define the Rights of Peoples, see, *The Universal Declaration of the Rights of Peoples* ("Algiers Declaration") (1976) in International Lelio Basso Foundation for the Rights and Liberties of Peoples, Universal Declaration of the Rights of Peoples. François Maspero (Paris, 1977), art. 5, partially reprinted in J. Crawford, ed. *The Rights Of Peoples* supra n. 34 at pp. 187–189. See also n. 134 below. For documents on autonomy and minority rights, see Hurst Hannum (ed.), *Documents On Autonomy and Minority Rights*. M. Nijhoff. Boston, 1993.
130. The central importance of human rights and fundamental freedoms to the equal rights and self-determination of peoples is reflected in art. 55 of the United Nations Charter.
131. Lee C. Buchheit, *Secession: The Legitimacy of Self-Determination*. Yale University Press. New Haven, 1978.
132. *Universal Declaration of Human Rights*, supra n. 38, art. 21.
133. *ICCPR*, art. 25.
134. Cf. Hannum, supra n. 39, at 116.
135. For a lucid expression of these principles see *The Universal Declaration of the Rights of Peoples* (1976), with text and commentary in Antonio Cassese, "Political Self-Determination-Old Concepts and New Developments," in Antonio Cassese (ed.), *UN Law: Fundamental Rights*. Brill. Leiden, 1979 at p. 137.
136. This was implied by an international tribunal as early as 1920 in the Report of the International Committee of Jurists entrusted by the Council of the League of Nations with the task of giving an advisory opinion on the legal aspects of the Aaland Islands question, *League of Nations O.J. Spec. Supp.* 3 at 5 (1920), when it reserved the question of the rights of people under such circumstances.
137. *The Aaland Islands Question, Report Presented to the Council of the League by the Commission of Rapporteurs*, League of Nations Doc. 8.7.21 (68) 106 (1921).
138. Id.
139. Id. For modern recognition of this fundamental aspect of the Law of Nations see for example, Hannum, supra n. 39 at 470–74; Bucheit, supra n. 131, at 94; Ved P. Nanda "Self- Determination Outside the Colonial Context: The Birth of Bangladesh in Retrospect" in Yonah Alexander and Robert A. Friedlander (eds.), *Self-Determination: National, Regional, and Global Dimensions*. Westview. Boulder, Colarado, 1980 at 204; Cobban supra n. 24, at 140.

140. G.A. Res. 2625 (XXV), 25 U.N., GAOR, Supp. No. 28, 121, U.N. Doc. A/8028 (1971).
141. Id.
142. Id.
143. See Sellers, "Actual Validity of Law," supra n. 13, at 283–290.
144. See Sellers, *American Republicanism*. Macmillan. Basingstoke, England, 1994; Sellers, "Republican Impartiality," supra n. 14, at 273–282.
145. Sellers, "Republican Authority," supra n. 56, at 257.
146. See *United States Constitution* Preamble, art. 1, art IV.4 and amendment XIV.
147. See Neal Wood, *Cicero's Social and Political Thought*. University of California Press. Berkeley, 1988 at 126–127, 137–146, 165–166, 169. *Cf. Broom's Legal Maxims*. T. and J.W. Johnson. Philadelphia, 1845; Maxim I: "*Salus Populi Suprema Lex*," with citations to Grotius, *De Jure Belli ac Pacis*, III.20.7.1 and Montesquieu, *Esprit des lois*, L.xxvii. 23.
148. Cicero, *De legibus*, III.i.3.
149. *U.N. Charter*, Preamble.
150. Ibid., art. 1, para. 1.
151. Ibid., art. 1, para. 3.
152. Ibid., art. 1, para. 2.
153. Ibid., art. 2, para. 7.
154. Ibid., Preamble.
155. See 1945 *Congressional Record*, Senate 8134.
156. "[The President] shall have Power, by and with the Advice and consent of the Senate, to make Treaties, provided two thirds of the Senators present concur," U.S. *Constitution* art. II § 2.
157. *U.S. Constitution*, art. VI: "This Constitution, and the Laws of the United States which shall be made in Pursuance thereof; and all Treaties made, or which shall be made, under the Authority of the United States, shall be the supreme Law of the Land."
158. *U.N. Charter*, art. 7.
159. Ibid., art. 9.
160. Ibid., art. 18, para. 1.
161. Ibid., art. 10.
162. Ibid., art. 18, para. 2.
163. Ibid., art. 18, para. 2.
164. Ibid., art. 27, para. 3.
165. Ibid., art. 25.
166. Ibid., art. 61, para.
167. Ibid., art. 62, para. 1.
168. Ibid., art. 62, para. 3.
169. Ibid., art. 68.
170. Ibid., art. 86.
171. Ibid., art. 92.
172. Ibid., art. 94, para. 1.
173. Ibid., art. 96. para. 1.
174. Ibid., art. 36.
175. Sellers, *American Republicanism*, at 234–235 et passim; Adams, supra n. 22, at I.viii; xxii; I.125–128; III. 159–160.
176. Sellers, *American Republicanism*, supra n. 175, at 234–235 et passim.

177. *Statute of the International Court of Justice*, art. 13.
178. Ibid., art. 4, para.1.
179. Ibid., art. 10.
180. U.N. Charter, art. 101.
181. Ibid., art. 97.
182. Ibid., arts. 100–101.

3 The Law of Humanity and the Law of Nations

1. On the history of International law and the law of nations, see Henry Wheaton. *History of the Law of Nations in Europe and America*. Gould, Banks & Co., New York, 1845. Cf. Martti Koskenniemi, *From Apology to Utopia*. Finnish Lawyers' Publishing Company. Helsinki, 1989.
2. For example, John Austin. *The Province of Jurisprudence Determined*, Wilfrid Rumble (ed.) Cambridge University Press. Cambridge, England, 1995 (first published 1832). Lecture VI, p. 171.
3. See for example, Gaius, *Institutes*, I.1. Marcus Tullius Cicero, *De officiis* III.v.23.
4. See for example, Richard Falk, "The World Order Between Interstate Law and the Law and the Law of Humanity," 1 *International Legal Theory* 14 (1995).
5. Hugo Grotius. *De Jure Belli ac Pacis Libri tres*. Revised edn, Johannes Blaevius. Amsterdam, 1646 (first edn, Paris, 1625).
6. Samuel Pufendorf. *De Jure Naturae et Gentium Libri Octo*. revised edn, Hoogenhuysen. Amsterdam, 1688.
7. Emmerich de Vattel. *Le Droit des Gens ou principes de la Loi Naturelle Appliqués à la conduite et aux affaires des Nations et des Souverains*. A. Droz. Neuchâtel and London, 1758.
8. See for example, Grotius, supra n. 5, at I.12.
9. This use of "civil society" to signify extra-governmental institutions is extremely confusing, since "civil society" most naturally (and ordinarily) implies the political organization of society as a *civitas*.
10. See for example, Richard Falk, "Law of Humanity," supra n. 4 at 17.
11. Ibid., at 15–16.
12. Jeremy Bentham, "Nonsense Upon Stilts" in P. Schofield, C. Pease Watkins and C. Blamires (eds), *Rights, Representation and Reform: Nonsense Upon Stilts and Other Writings on the French Revolution*. Oxford University Press. Oxford, 2002.
13. John Austin, *The Province of Jurisprudence Determined*. John Murray. London, 1832.
14. H.L.A. Hart, *Essays in Jurisprudence and Philosophy*. Oxford University Press. Oxford, 1983.
15. John Austin, *The Province of Jurisprudence Determined*, supra n. 2, pp. 123–124.
16. *United Nations Charter*, Preamble and art. I.
17. *Universal Declaration of Human Rights*, Preamble and *passim*.
18. See, for example Richard Falk, "Law of Humanity," supra n. 4 at 15.
19. Jean Bodin, *Six livres de la République*. Paris. 1583. Livre II. Ch. 5, p. 609.
20. See supra, Ch. 2.
21. Benjamin Constant, *De la liberté des anciens, comparée a celle des modernes*. Paris, 1819.

22. See M.N.S. Sellers, *The Sacred Fire of Liberty*. Palgrave Macmillan. Basingstoke and New York, 1989, pp. 78–80, 112–116. Modern liberals give their doctrine a more elaborate pedigree, but "liberalism" in the strictest sense, under that name, developed after Constant, as a reaction against the democratic element of republicanism.
23. On this new sense of "civil society," see Richard Falk, "The Law of Humanity," in 2 *International Legal Theory* 14 (1995). This is a new usage, at odds with the more accurate sense of "civil society" as expressed for example by John Locke in his *Two Treatises of Government* (1690).
24. Richard Falk, "The Law of Humanity," in 2 *International Legal Theory* (1995).
25. Ibid.
26. See for example, John Locke, *Two Treatises of Government* (1690) at II. 87–90.
27. *International Covenant of Civil and Political Right* at 1.1; *International Covenant on Economic, Social and Cultural Rights* at 1.1.
28. See M.N.S. Sellers, *Republican Legal Theory*. Palgrave Macmillan. Basingstoke, England, 2003.
29. See M.N.S. Sellers "Republicanism" in the *International Encyclopedia of the Social and Behavioral Sciences*. N.J. Smelser and P.B. Baltes (eds). Elsevier. Oxford, 2001 at p. 1320.
30. See supra, Ch. 2.
31. Kant, *Zum ewigen Frieden*. Königsberg. 1796.
32. See M.N.S. Sellers, "Republican Impartiality," in 11 *Oxford Journal of Legal Studies* 273 (1991).
33. Marcus Tullius Cicero. *De republica*. I.xxv.39. See for example, John Adams, *Defence of the Constitutions of Government of the United States of America*. Dilly. London, 1787–1788, at I.xxi..
34. This was recognized by Americans in the Fourteenth Amendment to the Constitution of the United States of America.
35. Supra, Ch. 2.
36. See for example, Antonio Cassese, "Political Self-Determination: Old Concepts and New Developments" in Cassese (ed.), *U.N. Law/Fundamental Rights: Two Topics in International Law*; *Self Determination of Peoples: A Legal Reappraisal*. Oxford University Press. Oxford, 1995, pp. 101ff.
37. See for example, Richard Falk, "The Law of Humanity" in 2 *International Legal Theory* 20 (1995).
38. I should be clear here that by "civil society" I mean any actual universal *civitas*. Usage has been muddied recently by those who use the phrase "civil society" to describe the role of non-governmental organizations.

4 The Sources of International Law

1. Hugo Grotius, *De Jure Belli ac Pacis Libri Tres* 1st edn, Johannes Blaevius. Amsterdam, 1625 at Prolegomena 8.
2. Ibid., at Prolegomena 20.
3. Ibid., at I.xiv.2.
4. Ibid., at Prolegomena 17.
5. Emmerich de Vattel, *Droit des gens on principes de la loi Naturelle appliqués à la conduite et aux affaires des Nations et des, Souverains*. A. Droz. Neuchâtel and London, 1758 at Preliminaires § 11.
6. Ibid., Preliminaires §26.

7. Ibid., Preliminaires §6.
8. Ibid., Preliminaires § 28i and III.xii. §§ 188–189.
9. Christian Wolff, *Jus Gentium methodo scientifica pertractatum*. Frankfurt and Leipzig, 1749.
10. See for example Jonathan Charney, "International Law-Making in a Community Context," in 2 *International Legal Theory* 38 (1997).
11. Vattel, *Droit des gens*, preliminaires §18.
12. Ibid., at II.iv.§54.
13. See H. Morgenthau and H. Thompson. *Politics Among Nations*. 6th edn. Alfred A. Knopf. New York, 1985 (first edn, 1948).
14. John Austin, *The Province of Jurisprudence Determined*. John Murray. London, 1832. Cf. Hans Kelsen, *Pure Theory of Law*. C. Knight trans. University of California Press. Berkeley, California, 1967.
15. *Statute of the International Court of Justice*, art. 38(a).
16. Hugo Grotius, *De jure belli ac pacis*, Prolegomena 15.
17. Ibid., at I.xiv.2.
18. Dio Chrysostom, *Orationes*, Ixxvi (= p.648).
19. *Statute of the International Court of Justice*, art. 38 (b).
20. Grotius, *De jure belli ac pacis*, Prolegomena 12.
21. Vattel, *Droit des gens*, Preliminaires §25.
22. Ibid., Preliminaires §26.
23. Grotius, *De jure belli ac pacis*, Prolegomena 40.
24. Ibid., Prolegomena 8.
25. Ibid., Prolegomena 17.
26. *Statutes of the International Court of Justice*, art. 38 (c).
27. Jonathan Charney, "International Law-Making," supra n. 10.
28. See supra, Ch. 2.
29. *Statute of the International Court of Justice*, art. 38 (d).
30. See supra, Ch. 2.
31. *Vienna Convention on the Law of Treaties*, art. 53.
32. Vattel, *Droit des gens*, Preliminaires § 26.
33. Ian Brownlie, *Principles of Public International Law*. 4th edn. Clarendon Press. Oxford, 1990, p. 513.
34. Vattel, *Droit des gens*, Preliminaires § 11.
35. *Case Concerning the Barcelona Traction, Light and Power Company. Limited* (New Application 1962) (Belgium v. Spain), [1960] *I.C.J. Rep*. 4. paras 33–4.
36. Jean Bodin. *Six Livres de la République*. Du Puys. Paris, 1576, at II.5. 609–610.
37. Vattel, *Droit des gens*, II.iv.56.
38. Jonathan Charney, "International Law-Making in a Community Context," in 2 *International Legal Theory* 38 (1996); Richard Falk "The World Order between Interstate Law and the Law of Humanity," in 1 *International Legal Theory* 14 (1995).

5 Why States Are Bound by Customary International Law

1. *See* M.N.S. Sellers, "The Value of Purpose of Law," 33 *Baltimore Law Journal* 145 (2004).
2. Hans Kelsen, *Principles of International Law*. 2nd edn, R.W. Tucker (ed.) Holt, Rinehart and Winston. New York, 1966, p. 440; Cf. *Das Problem der Souveränität und die Theorie des Völkerrechts*. B. Mohr. Tübingen, 1920.

3. Anthony D'Amato, "Customary International Law: A Reformulation," in 4 *International Legal Theory* 1 (1998).
4. See supra, Ch. 2.
5. *Statute of the International Court of Justice*, art. 38 (b).
6. Ibid., Article 38.
7. Hugo Grotius, *De Jure Belli ac Pacis Libri Tres*. 1st edn, Johannes Blaevius. Amsterdam, 1625, I.xiv.
8. Ibid., Prolegomena 8.
9. Ibid., at II.i.5.
10. Ibid., Prolegomena. 17.
11. Ibid., at I.xiv.2.
12. Emmerich de Vattel, *Droit des gens on principes de la loi Naturelle appliqués à la conduite et aux affaires des Souverains*. A. Droz. Neuchâtel and London, 1758, preface, viii, and note f.
13. Ibid., preface, xviii.
14. Ibid., preface, xxii.
15. Ibid., preface, xx.
16. See for example, John Austin. *The Province of Jurisprudence Determined*, Wilfred Rumble (ed.) Cambridge University Press. Cambridge, England, 1995, p. 21 (first published 1832).
17. Joseph Raz has developed a more nuanced form of this positivist theory. See *The Concept of a Legal System*. 2nd edn. Oxford, 1980; *The Authority of Law*. Oxford University Press. Oxford, 1979. p. 37ff.
18. See for example, Anthony D'Amato, "Customary International Law," in 4 *International Legal Theory* 1 (1998).
19. Ibid.
20. By *The Treaty of Tordesillas*, concluded on June 7, 1694.
21. See D'Amato, "Customary International Law," at 3.
22. See for example, Sir William Blackstone. *Commentaries on the Laws of England*. Clarendon Press. Oxford, 1765. vol. I, p. 70.

6 The Effectiveness of International Law

1. On sincerity, see M.N.S. Sellers, *Republican Legal Theory*. Palgrave. Basingstoke, England, 2003, pp. 65–66.
2. Joaquín Tacsan, "The Effectiveness of International Law: An Alternative Approach," in 2 *International Legal Theory* 3 (1996).
3. See supra, Ch. 5.
4. See below, Ch. 17.

7 The Right to Republican Government Under International Law

1. See for example, Thomas Franck, "The Emerging Right to Democratic Governance," in 86 *American Journal of International Law* 46 (1992).
2. See for example, Document of the Copenhagen Meeting of the Conference on the Human Dimension of the CSCE (1990).

3. For example, Fernando Tesón, "Two Mistakes about Democracy," in 4 *International Legal Theory* 35 (1998).
4. See for example, Hans Kelsen, *General Theory of Law and the State*, trans. A. Wedberg. Harvard University Press. Cambridge, Mass., 1949.
5. See for example, Fernando Tesón, "Two Mistakes about Democracy."
6. See M.N.S. Sellers, *Republican Legal Theory*. Palgrave Macmillan. Basingstoke, England, 2003.
7. Fernando Tesón, "Two Mistakes about Democracy."
8. M.N.S. Sellers, *The Sacred Fire of Liberty*. Palgrave Macmillan. Basingstoke, England, 1998.
9. Cf. M.N.S. Sellers, "Republicanism, Liberalism and the Law," in 86 *Kentucky Law Journal* 1 (1997).

8 International Relations and International Law

1. Robert Keohane, "International Relations and International Law: Two Optics," 3 *International Legal Theory* 38 (1997).
2. Ibid.
3. Thomas Hobbes, *Leviathan*. Andrew Crooke. London, 1651, ch. XIV, p. 66.
4. *Statute of the International Court of Justice*, art. 38.
5. Supra, Ch. 3.
6. For a bibliography on republicanism, see M.N.S. Sellers, "Republicanism: Philosophical Aspects" in N.J. Smelser and P.B. Battes (eds), *The International Encyclopedia of Social and Behavioral Sciences*. Elsevier. Amsterdam, 2001.
7. See supra, Ch. 3.
8. The view, for example, of Robert Keohane, "International Relations and International Law," in 3 *International Legal Theory* 38 (1997).

9 Justice and the Rule of Law in International Relations

1. See M.N.S. Sellers, "The Actual Validity of Law," 37 *American Journal of Jurisprudence* 293 (1992); "The Value and Purpose of Law," 33 *Baltimore Law Journal* 145 (2004).
2. For cites and excerpts see M.N.S. Sellers, "Republicanism: Philosophical Aspects" in N.J. Smelser and P.B. Baltes (eds.), *The International Encyclopedia of the Social and Behavorial Sciences*. Elsevier. Oxford, 2001.
3. Ibid.
4. M.N.S. Sellers, "Republican Authority," 5 *Canadian Journal of Law and Jurisprudence* 257 (1992).
5. Thomas Hobbes, *Leviathan*. Andrew Crooke. London, 1651, ch. XIV, p. 65. Cf. ch. XVII, p. 88.
6. See the discussion in M.N.S. Sellers, *The Sacred Fire of Liberty*. Palgrave Macmillan. Basingstoke, England, 1998, pp. 84–85.
7. M.N.S. Sellers, "The Actual Validity of Law," 37 *American Journal of Jurisprudence* 283 (1992).
8. M.N.S. Sellers, "Republican Authority," 5 *Canadian Journal of Law and Jurisprudence* 257 (1972).
9. See supra, Ch. 2.

10 The Elements of International Law

1. See for example, Alfred P. Rubin, *Ethics and Authority in International Law*. Cambridge University Press. Cambridge, 1997.
2. Henry Wheaton, *Elements of International Law*. Richard Henry Dana, Jr (ed.) 8th edn. Little Brown. Boston, 1866, p. 3, 20.
3. Ibid., at xv.
4. Ibid., at xiv.
5. Ibid., at xvi.
6. Ibid., at xvi–xvii.
7. Ibid., at xix.
8. Ibid., at 3.
9. Ibid., at 20.
10. Ibid., at 20–23.
11. Ibid., at 20.
12. Ibid., at 25.
13. Ibid., at 27, 44.
14. Ibid., at 28.
15. Ibid., at 29.
16. Ibid., at 77.
17. Ibid., at 75.
18. Ibid., at 75.
19. Ibid., at 75–77.
20. Ibid., at 77.
21. Ibid., at 77–78.
22. Ibid., at 79.
23. Ibid., at 80.
24. Ibid., at 81.
25. Ibid., at 95.
26. Ibid., at 98–99.
27. Ibid., at 100.
28. Ibid., at 103.
29. Ibid., at 97.
30. Ibid., at 174.
31. Ibid., at 174, 177.
32. Ibid., at 178–179.
33. Ibid., at 356.
34. Ibid., at 309.
35. Ibid., at 310.
36. Ibid., at 359.
37. Ibid., at 378.
38. Ibid., at 380.
39. Ibid., at 391.
40. Ibid., at 409.
41. Ibid., at 151, 161.
42. Ibid., at 458.
43. Ibid., at 162.
44. Ibid., at 164.
45. Ibid., at 165–167.

46. Ibid., at 173.
47. Ibid., at 179.
48. Ibid., at 195–196.
49. Ibid., at 20.
50. Ibid., at 416.
51. Ibid., at 40–41, 292.
52. Ibid., at 281.
53. Ibid., at 284.
54. Ibid., at 20.
55. *Statute of the International Court of Justice* at art. 38(c).
56. Wheaton, *Elements*, xi (= Preface to the 1848 edition).

11 Universal Human Rights

1. *Universal Declaration of Human Rights*, December 10, 1948, art. 1.
2. Ibid.
3. *Declaration of Independence of the United States of America*, July 4, 1776.
4. *International Covenant on Civil and Political Rights* (December 16, 1966), art. 4, 6, 7, 8, 11, 15, 16 and 18.
5. *Universal Declaration of Human Rights*, art. 3.
6. Ibid., art. 17.
7. Ibid., art. 23.
8. Ibid., art. 24.
9. Ibid., art. 25.
10. *Declaration of Independence of the United States of America*, July 4, 1776.
11. *International Covenant on Civil and Political Rights* (December 16, 1966), art. 4(1).
12. Ibid., art. 4(2).
13. Ibid., art. 6
14. Ibid., art. 7.
15. Ibid., art. 8.
16. Ibid., art. 16.
17. Ibid., art. 18.
18. See also *Vienna Convention on the Law of Treaties* (22 May, 1969), art. 53.
19. Cf. *Declaration of Independence of the United States of America*, July 4, 1776.

12 International Legal Personality

1. *Universal Declaration of Human Rights*, U.N.G.A. Resolution 217A, December 10, 1948, art. 6.
2. On these questions, see *International Legal Personality*, symposium in *Ius Gentium*, volume 11 (2005); James E. Hickey (ed.) *International Legal Personality, The Hofstra Law and Policy Symposium*. volume 2 (1997).
3. See for example, Emmerich de Vattel, *Le Droit des Gens ou Principes de la Loi Naturelle, Appliqués à la conduite et aux affaires des Nations et des Souverains*. A. Droz. Neuchâtel and London, 1758.
4. Hugo Grotius, *De Jure Belli ac Pacis Libri Tres, in quibus ius Naturae et Gentium item Juris Publici praecipua explicantur*. Rev. edn, Johannes Blaevius.

Amsterdam, 1646. Prolegomena: "Sed sicut cuiusque civitatis respiciunt, ita inter civitates aut omnes aut plerasque ex consensu jura quaedam nasci potuerunt, et nata apparet, quae utilitatem respicerent non coetuum singulorum, sed magnae illius universitatis."

5. Christian Wolff, *Jus Gentium methodo scientifica pertractatum*. Frankfurt and Leipzig. 1764. Praefatio.
6. Ibid. "Cum gentes in civitatem ipsa natura coegerit, quemadmodum eidem convenienter in civitates particulares coiverunt singuli."
7. Vattel, *Le Droit des Gens*, preliminaires § 2.
8. Ibid., preliminaires § 4: "Les Nations étant composées d'hommes naturellement libres et independens ... les Nations, ou les Etats souverains, doivent être considérés comme autant de personnes libres, qui vivent entr'elles dans l'etat de nature."
9. Ibid., preliminaires § 5: "la Nation entiére, don't la volonté commune n'est que le résultat des volontés réunies des Citoïens."
10. *Charter of the United Nations* (1945), Preamble.
11. See M.N.S. Sellers, "The Nature and Purpose of Law," 33 *University of Baltimore Law Review* 145 (2004).
12. See for example, W.M. Geldart, *Legal Personality*. Clarendon Press. Oxford. 1924.
13. See for example, N. Sellers, "Criminal Prosecution of Animals," in XXXV *The Shingle* 179 (1972).
14. See for example, Emmerich de Vattel, *Le Droit des Gens*. Preface, pp. v–xv, for the analogy between nations and persons. Vattel cites Christian Wolff for the idea that nations are "personnes morales" (p.xiv).
15. Hugo Grotius, *De Jure Belli ac Pacis Libri Tres: in quibus ius Naturae et Gentium, item Juris Publici praecipua explicantur*. Prolegomena, p. 4: "Haec vero, quam rudi modi iam expressimus, societatis custodia, humano intellectui conveniens, fons est ejus juris, quod proprie tali nomine appellantur."
16. Savigny is the primary author of this unfortunate tendency.
17. Even Jean Bodin, the evangelist of state power, conceded the right of the people to throw off their oppressors. Bodin, *Les six livres de la république*. Paris. 1583.
18. Jeremy Bentham, *Introduction to the Principles of Morals and Legislation*. 2nd edn. E. Wilson and W. Pickering. London, 1823. II.256. See Percy E. Corbett, *The Growth of World Law*. Princeton University Press. Princeton, 1971, p. 34, 177–178.
19. Henry Wheaton, *Elements of International Law*, Dana, Richard Henry Jr. (ed.) Little Brown. Boston, 1866. I.14 [23] p. 20.
20. Cf. Richard Zouche, *Juris et Judicii Fecialis, sive Juris inter Gentes*. London. 1650.
21. See for example, August Wilhelm Heffter, *Das europäische Völkerrecht der Gegenwart*. Berlin. 1844. See Wheaton, *Elements of International Law* I.10 [16] p. 14. "This law is applied, not merely to regulate the mutual relations of states, but also of individuals, so far as concerns their respective rights and duties."
22. *Charter of the United Nations*. (1945) art. 4.
23. Ibid., art. I (2).
24. Ibid., arts. 55 and 56.
25. Reparation for Injuries case, *ICJ Reports* (1949), 179.

26. *Statute of the International Court of Justice*, art. 34(1): "Only states may be parties in cases before the Court."
27. See for example, *The Mavrommattis Palestine Concessions* Permanent Court of International Justice, 1924.
28. For example Ian Brownlie, *Principles of Public International Law*. 6th edn, Clarendon Press. Oxford, 2003. pp. 648–650.

13 What Are Peoples and Nations?

1. In the words of Humpty Dumpty, as reported by Lewis Carroll, *Through the Looking-Glass and What Alice Found there*. Macmillan. London, 1872, ch. 6.
2. Like Humpty Dumpty himself, after the accident.
3. Samuel Johnson, *Dictionary of the English Language*. J. & P. Knapton. London, 1755, Preface.
4. Thomas Hobbes, *Leviathan*. Andrew Crooke. London, 1651 ch. IV, p. 15.
5. Ibid.
6. "Res publica res populi, populus autem non omnis hominum coetus quoquo modo congregatus, sed coetus multitudinis juris consensu et utilitatis communione sociatus." Marcus Tullius Cicero, *De re publica*, I.xxv.39.
7. "Omnes nationes servitutem ferre possunt, nostra civitas non potest." Marcus Tullius Cicero, *Philippicae* X.x.20.
8. "Scipionem rogemus, ut explicet, quem existimet esse optimum statum civitatis." Marcus Tullius Cicero, *De re publica*, I.xx.33.
9. See for example Grimalde, *Cicero's Offices* (1556) at 22: "To be one countrie, of one nation, one language." Quoted in *The Oxford English Dictionary*, s. v. "*country*." Cf. "ager" in Marcus Tullius Cicero, *De officiis* I. vii.21: "Sunt autem privata nulla natura, sed aut vetere occupatione ut qui quondam in vacua venerunt, aut victoria ... ex quo fit, ut ager Arpinas Arpinatium dicatur, Tusculanus Tusculanorum."
10. See for example, art. 1 of the *Montevideo Convention on the Rights and Duties of States*, signed December 26, 1933.
11. Geographical communities require recognition and careful attention because they are inevitable: all humans benefit from peaceful cooperation with their neighbors. Non-geographical communities can enrich life, but are elective and constructed realities.
12. See Cicero's definition of republic, supra n. 6.
13. Ibid.
14. Cf. *United States Constitution*, Amendment XIV, section 1 (1868). Cf. *United Nations Charter* (1945), art. I, section 3.
15. Ibid., art. I.2.
16. Ibid., art. I.3.
17. *International Covenant on Economic, Social and Cultural Rights* (1966) art. I. 1; *International Covenant on Civil and Political Rights* (1966) art. I. 1.
18. Ibid., art. 14.1.
19. Ibid., art. 25(b).
20. *The Unanimous Declaration of the Thirteen United States of America* (1776).
21. *Declaration on the Granting of Independence to Colonial Countries and Peoples* (1960) United Nations General Assembly Resolution 1514.
22. Ibid.

23. Ibid., art. 1.
24. Ibid., art. 2.
25. Ibid., art. 6.
26. *Cases Concerning the Frontier Dispute* (Burkina Faso v. Mali), *ICJ Reports*, 1986, 565 para. 20. See also at 566, para. 23.
27. See "opinion" no. 2 of the Arbitration Committee established by the "Conference on Yugoslavia" in 3 *European Journal of International Law* 183–184 (1992).

14 The Law of Peoples

1. See for example, E. de Vattel, *Le droit des gens, ou principes de la loi naturelle appliqués à la conduite et aux affaires des Nations et des Souverains*. A. Droz. Neuchâtel and London, 1758.
2. John Rawls. *A Theory of Justice*. Harvard University Press. Cambridge, Mass, 1971.
3. John Rawls, *Political Liberalism*. Columbia. New York, 1993.
4. John Rawls, *The Law of Peoples*. Harvard University Press. Cambridge, Mass, 1999, p. vi.
5. Ibid., p. 3.
6. Ibid., p. 4.
7. Ibid., p. 5.
8. Ibid., p. 6.
9. Ibid., p. 7.
10. Jean-Jacques Rousseau. *Du contrat social*. Rey. Amsterdam, 1762.
11. John Rawls. *The Law of Peoples*, p. 8–9.
12. Ibid., p. 10.
13. Ibid., p. 11.
14. Ibid., p. 12.
15. Ibid., p. 14.
16. Ibid., p. 16.
17. Ibid., p. 17.
18. Ibid., p. 18.
19. Ibid., p. 19.
20. Ibid., p. 21.
21. Ibid., p. 25.
22. Ibid., p. 31.
23. Ibid., p. 25.
24. Ibid., pp. 25–26.
25. Ibid., p. 28.
26. Ibid., p. 28.
27. Ibid., p. 33.
28. Ibid., p. 35.
29. Ibid., p. 37.
30. Ibid., pp. 38–39.
31. Ibid., p. 57.
32. Ibid., p. 46.
33. Ibid., p. 55.
34. Ibid., p. 58.
35. Ibid., p. 59.

36. Ibid., p. 60.
37. Ibid., p. 61.
38. Ibid., p. 61.
39. Ibid., p. 62.
40. Ibid., p. 61.
41. Ibid., p. 63.
42. Ibid., p. 64.
43. Ibid., p. 65.
44. Ibid., pp. 66–67.
45. Ibid., p. 66.
46. Ibid., p. 64.
47. Ibid., p. 67.
48. Ibid., p. 64.
49. Cf. Mussolini's system of consultation with the recognized leaders of socially representative "fasces" in Italy.
50. John Rawls, *The Law of Peoples*, p. 67.
51. Ibid., p. 69.
52. Ibid., p. 71.
53. Ibid., p, 72.
54. Ibid., p. 73.
55. Ibid., p. 78.
56. Ibid., p. 79.
57. Ibid., p. 80.
58. Ibid., p. 81.
59. Ibid., p. 87.
60. Ibid., p. 82.
61. Ibid., pp. 61 and 67.
62. Ibid., p. 79.
63. Ibid., p. 83.
64. Ibid., pp. 84 and 85.
65. Ibid., p. 86.
66. Ibid., p. 37.
67. See supra. Ch. 2.
68. John Rawls, *The Law of Peoples*, p. 37.
69. Ibid., p. 79.
70. Ibid., p. 93.
71. Ibid., p. 93.
72. Ibid., pp. 93–94, footnote 6.
73. Ibid., pp. 65 and 71.
74. Ibid., pp. 65 and 80.
75. Ibid., pp. 69, 82–83.
76. Ibid., pp. 122–123, esp. note 1, in which Rawls seems to sympathize with Jefferson Davis against the "expansionist" North.

15 Perpetual Peace

1. Immanuel Kant, *Zum ewigen Frieden*. Nicolorius. Königsburg, 1795, reprinted Reclam. Stuttgart, 1984.
2. Jean-Jacques Rousseau. *Extrait du projet de paix perpetuelle de M. L'Abbé de Saint-Pierre*. Rey. Amsterdam, 1761.

3. Charles Irenée Castel, Abbé de Saint-Pierre. *Projet pour rendre la paix perpetuelle en Europe*. A. Schooten. Utrecht, 1713.
4. William Penn, *An Essay Towards the Present and Future Peace of Europe by the Establishment of a European Dyet, Parliament or Estates*. 1693. Reprinted in *The Political Writings of William Penn*. Liberty Fund. Indianapolis, 2002, pp. 401–419.
5. All translations here and henceforth by H.B. Nisbet in H.S. Reiss (ed.) *Kant Political Writings*, Cambridge University Press. Cambridge, 1970.
6. M.N.S. Sellers, *American Republicanism*. Macmillan. Basingstoke, England, 1994.
7. See appendix.
8. James Harrington, *The Commonwealth of Oceana*. 1656. J.G.A. Pocock (ed.) Cambridge University Press. Cambridge, 1992, pp. 22–25.
9. John Adams, *A Defence of the Constitutions of Government of the United States of America*. Vol. III. 1788. Dilly. London, p. 505.

16 International Humanitarian Intervention

1. Jean Bodin, *Six livres de la République* Paris, 1583 edition Bk. II, ch. 5, p. 609.
2. *Charter of the United Nations*, art. 2.1.
3. Ibid., art. 2.3.
4. Ibid., art. 2.4.
5. Ibid., art. 1.2.
6. Ibid.
7. Ibid., Preamble.
8. United Nations General Assembly, *Declaration on Principles of International Law Concerning Friendly Relations and Cooperation among States* (1970), First "Convinced" clause.
9. Ibid., Third "Recalling" clause.
10. Ibid., "Reaffirming" clause.
11. Ibid., explaining the First Principle.
12. Ibid., Second "Convinced" clause.
13. Ibid., Explaining the Third Principle.
14. Institute of International Law. Resolution on *"la protection des droits de l'homme et le principe de non-intervention dans les affaires des Etats*, adopted on the thirteenth of September, 1989 at Santiago de Compostela, Preamble.
15. Ibid., art. 2.
16. Ibid., art. 1.
17. Ibid., art. 2.
18. *United Nations Charter*, art. 1.
19. Cf. Resolution of Santiago de Compostela, arts. 2 and 4.
20. International Law Commission, *Draft Articles on State Responsibility*, art. 34.
21. Ibid., Draft art. 52.
22. Ibid.
23. On the *erga* omnes nature of human rights violations, see Case *Concerning the Barcelona Traction, Light and Power Company, Limited*. (New Application 1962) (Belgium v. Spain) [1970] I.C.J. Report 4 paras. 33–34.
24. Henry Wheaton, *Elements of International Law*, 8th edn. Richard Henry Dana, Jr. Little Brown. Boston, 1966, I § 14, p. 23.
25. Charter of the United Nations, art. 1.1.

26. Resolution of Santiago de Compostela, art. 2.
27. *Restatement of the Law Third, Restatement of the Foreign Relations Law of the United States.* As adopted and promulgated by the American Law Institute. American Law Institute Publishers. St. Paul, Minnesota. 1987. § 703 (1).
28. Ibid., § 702 (g).
29. *Draft Articles on State Responsibility*, art. 41.
30. Ibid., Draft art. 51(1)(a).
31. *Charter of the United Nations*, art. 39.
32. Ibid., art. 11(1).
33. *Declaration on the Granting of Independence to Colonial Countries and Peoples.* General Assembly Resolution 1514 (XV) of Dec. 14, 1960. U.N. Ass. Off. Rec., 15th Sess., Supp. No. 16 (A/4684), p. 66.
34. *Cf. Charter of the United Nations*, art. 1.1.

17 The Authority of the International Court of Justice

1. *Constitution of the United States of America* (September 17, 1787) art. III.
2. Ibid., art. VI.
3. *Marbury vs. Madison*, 5 U.S. (1 Cranch) 137 (1803).
4. Oliver Wendell Holmes, Jr., "The Path of the Law," 10 *Harvard Law Review* 457 (1897).
5. *Charter of the United Nations* (June 26, 1945), Preamble.
6. *Constitution of the United States*, Preamble.
7. *Charter of the United Nations*, Preamble. Cf. *Constitution of the United States*, Preamble and art. VI.
8. *Constitution of the United States*, art. I.
9. *Charter of the United Nations*, chapter IV.
10. *Constitution of the United States*, art. I.
11. *Charter of the United Nations*, chapter V.
12. *Constitution of the United States*, art. II.
13. *Charter of the United Nations*, chapter XV.
14. *Constitution of the United States*, art. III.
15. *Charter of the United Nations*, chapter XIV.
16. *Constitution of the United States*, art. III.
17. *Charter of the United Nations*, chapter XIV.
18. Ibid., Preamble.
19. Ibid., art. 1.1.
20. Ibid., art. 2.1.
21. Ibid., art. 1.1.
22. *Statute of the International Court of Justice*, art. 33.
23. Ibid., arts. 4; 8; 10.
24. Ibid., art. 13.
25. *United States Constitution*, art. II. 2.
26. Ibid., art. III. 1.
27. *Statute of the International Court of Justice*, art. 36.
28. Ibid., art. 26.2.
29. Ibid., art. 59.
30. Ibid., art. 38.

31. *Charter of the United Nations*, art. 94(2).
32. *Statute of the International Court of Justice*, art. 38.
33. *Charter of the United Nations*, art. 2(3).
34. *Statute of the International Court of Justice*, art. 59.

18 Borders and Democracy in International Law

1. Hugo Grotius, *De Jure Belli ac Pacis Libris tres*. Johannes Blaevius. (First edn Paris, 1625) Amsterdam, 1646, I.iii. 8, pp. 52–53.
2. For example, Thomas M. Franck "The Emerging Right to Democratic Governance," in 86 *American Journal of International Law* 46 (1992); Henry Steiner, "Political Participation as a Human Right," in *Harvard Human Rights Yearbook* 77 (1988).
3. Franck, "Democratic Governance," p. 55.
4. Example, Thomas Franck, "Is Personal Freedom a Western Value," 91 *American Journal of International Law* 593 (1997), where he advocates individual "autonomy."
5. See M.N.S. Sellers, "Republican Impartiality," in 11 *Oxford Journal of Legal Studies* 273 (1991); Philip Pettit, *Republicanism: A Theory of Freedom and Government*. Oxford University Press. Oxford, 1997.
6. M.N.S. Sellers, "The Actual Validity of Law," 37 *American Journal of Jurisprudence* 283 (1992).
7. Example, "Publius" [James Madison] *Federalist LI* (1787) in Issac Kramnick (ed.), *The Federalist Papers*. Penguin. London, 1987, p. 322.
8. Marcus Tullius Cicero, *De officiis* III.vi.26; *De re publica*, xxv. 39.
9. See M.N.S. Sellers, *The Sacred Fire of Liberty: Republicanism, Liberalism and the Law*. Palgrave Macmillan. Basingstoke, England, 1998; J.G.A. Pocock, *The Machiavellian Movement: Florentine Political Thought and the Atlantic Republican Tradition*. Princeton University Press. Princeton, 1975.
10. Example, "Publius" [Alexander Hamilton] *Federalist* IX (1787) in Isaac Kramnick (ed.), *The Federalist Papers*, 1987, p. 119; See M.N.S. Sellers *American Republicanism: Roman Ideology in the United States Constitution*. Macmillan. Basingstoke, 1994.
11. John Adams, *Defence of the Constitutions of Government of the United States of America*. London, 1787–1788 at I.xxi; Cicero, *De re publica*, I.xxv.39.
12. Cicero, *De officiis*, III.xvii.69.
13. Immanuel Kant, *Zum ewigen Frieden*. Reclam. Stuggart, 1795.
14. *United States Constitution* (1787), art. IV, section 4.
15. Alexis de Tocqueville, *De la democratie en Amerique*, 1835, ch. IV: "Du principe de la souveraineté du peuple en Amerique."
16. See for example, Conference on Security and Co-operation in Europe (CSCE), *Document of the Copenhagen Meeting of the Conference on the Human Dimension*, June 29, 1990, reprinted in 29 I.L.M. 1305; Franck, "Democratic Governance," p. 67.
17. See the CSCE Copenhagen document, above: "the will of the people, freely and fairly expressed through periodic and genuine elections, is the basis of the authority and legitimacy of all government."

18. See Philip Pettit, *Republicanism: A Theory of Freedom and Government.* Oxford University Press. New York, 1997. chaps 6 and 7.
19. "Publius" [James Madison], *Federalist* X (1787) in Isaac Kramnick (ed.), pp. 126–127.
20. Kant, *Zum ewigen Frieden*, Erster Definitivartikel zum ewigen Frieden, in the Reclam 1984 edition (Stuttgart) p. 13.
21. Ibid., Zweiter Definitivartikel zum ewigen Frieden, p. 16; Titus Livius, *Ab urbe condita* II.1.
22. M.N.S. Sellers, "Republican Principles in International Law," Ch. 2 above.
23. Grotius, *De Jure Belli ac Pacis, Libri Tres.* Johannes Blaevins. Amsterdam, 1646 (first edn, Paris, 1625) at III.xv.1.
24. Ibid., I.iii.3.
25. Ibid., II.ix.1.
26. Ibid., I.iv.8.
27. Ibid., I.iv.11.
28. Emmerich de Vattel, *Le droit des gens ou principes de la loi naturelle appliqués à la conduite et aux affaires des Nations et des Souverains* A. Droz Neuchâtel and London, 1758.
29. Ibid., I.iv.39.
30. Ibid., I.iv.51.
31. Ibid., preliminaires, 1.
32. Ibid., preliminaires, 2.
33. Ibid., preliminaires, 3,16.
34. Ibid., preliminaires, 4.
35. Ibid., preliminaires, 24–27.
36. *United Nations Charter*, Preamble.
37. *United Nations Charter*, art. I(2). Cf. art. 55.
38. Ibid., art. 73(b).
39. Ibid., art. 76(b).
40. *Universal Declaration of Human Rights*, art. 21(1).
41. Ibid., art. 21(3).
42. *International Covenant on Civil and Political Rights*, Preamble.
43. Ibid., art. 1(1).
44. Ibid., art. 25(b).
45. Cicero, *De re publica*, I.xxv.39.
46. Grotius, *De Jure Belli ac Pacis*, 11.ix.3.
47. Ibid., at 11.ix.6; Vattel, at 1.16.194.
48. *United Nations Charter*, Preamble; art. 110.
49. Ibid., art. 2(4).
50. Ibid., art. 55.
51. Ibid., art. 73 and 73(b).
52. *Constitution of the United States of America*, Preamble.
53. Ibid., art. VII.
54. Under the doctrine *uti possidetis juris*.
55. For the structures of republican government see Philip Petit, *Republicanism: A Theory of Freedom and Government.* Oxford University Press. New York, 1997; M.N.S. Sellers, *Republican Legal Theory*. Palgrave Macmillan. Basingstoke, England, 2003.
56. See supra, Ch. 1.

19 The Right to Secede

1. For "republican" ideals of the state, with a bibliography, see M.N.S. Sellers "Republicanism (Philosophical Aspects)" in N. J. Smelser and P.B. Baltes (eds), The *International Encyclopedia of Social and Behavioral Sciences.* Elsevier. Oxford, 2001 and M.N.S. Sellers "Republican Philosophy of Law" in Christopher B. Gray (ed.), *The Philosophy of Law: An Encyclopedia.* Garland. New York, 1999 vol. 2, p. 740.
2. Ch. 2, above.
3. Cf. Thomas Paine, *The Rights of Man, Part 2* (1792) on the *"res-publica"* in Bruce Kuklick (ed.) *Paine: Political Writings.* Cambridge University Press. Cambridge, 1989, pp. 167–169.
4. Immanuel Kant, *Zum ewigen Frieden.* Nicolorius. Königsburg, 1795.
5. For a history of republican ideas and comparison of leading republican authors See M.N.S. Sellers, *The Sacred Fire of Liberty: Republicanism, Liberalism and the Law.* Macmillan. Basingstoke, England, 1998 and *American Republicanism: Roman Ideology in the United States Constitution.* Macmillan. Basingstoke, England, 1994.
6. See M.N.S. Sellers, "Republicanism: Philosophical Aspects," in *The International Encyclopedia of the Social and Behavorial Sciences,* supra note1.
7. Cf. the now nearly universal commitment through the *Charter of the United Nations* (1945) to respect the "territorial integrity" and "political independence" of states (art. 2(4)).
8. "Respublica res populi [est]. Populus autem non omnis hominum coetus quoquo modo congregatus, sed coetus multitudinis juris consensu, et utilitatis communione sociatus." Marcus Tullius Cicero, *De re publica,* I.xxv. 39.
9. John Adams, *Defence of the Constitutions of Government of the United States of America* 1787–88. Dilly. London, III.159–160.
10. Christian Wolff, *Jus Gentium methodo scientifica pertractatum.* Frankfurt and Leipzig, 1764.
11. Cf. the Fourteenth Amendment (1868) to the *United States Constitution,* which finally established birth as a basis of citizenship throughout the United States.
12. See chapter 2 and M.N.S. Sellers, "Republican Impartiality," in 11 *Oxford Journal of Legal Studies* 273ff (1991).
13. See for example the litany of complaints that Americans felt it necessary to list in their *Declaration of Independence,* (July 4, 1776) before they separated from Britain.
14. Cf. the international law doctrine of *uti possidetis juris* applied to independence in the South American republics and more recently in Africa, Asia and Europe.
15. Cf. Immanuel Kant, *Zum ewigen Frieden,* Nicolorius. Königsburg, 1795.
16. Ibid.
17. Charles de Secondat, baron de la Brède et de Montesquieu, *De l'esprit des lois.* Barillot. Geneva, 17–48. I.ix.1–2.
18. "Publius" [James Madison], *Federalist* XLV (26 January 1788) in Isaac Kramnick (ed.), *The Federalist Papers.* Penguin. London, 1987.

20 International Economic Organization

1. Joel Trachtman, "The Theory of the Firm Applied to International Organization," in 3 *International Legal Theory* 21 (1997).

2. See M.N.S. Sellers, on legal history as comparative law in *Republican Legal Theory*. Chapters 12 and 13. Palgrave Macmillan. Basingstoke, 2003.

21 Economic Sanctions

1. See for example, M. Reuss, *Menschenrechte durch Handelssanktionen*, Nomos. Baden-Baden, 1999; D. Cortright and G.A. Lopez (eds.), *The Sanctions Decade: Assessing U.N. Strategies in the 1990s*. Rienner. Boulder, Colorado, 2000; W.J.M. van Genugten and G.A. de Groot (eds.), *United Nations Sanctions: Effectiveness and Effects, Especially in the Field of Human Rights*. Intersentia. Antwerpen, 1999; G.E. Shambaugh, *States, Firms, and Power: Successful Sanctions in United States Foreign Policy*. State University of New York. New York, 1999; L.F. Damrosch, *Enforcing International Law through Non-forcible Measures*. M. Nijhoff. The Hague, 1998 (= *Recueil des cours de l'Académie de droit International*, vol. 269 (1997)).
2. This attitude was explained and perpetuated by the International Court of Justice in discussing the United States use of force in Nicaragua. See the case concerning *Military and Paramilitary Activities in and Against Nicaragua (Nicaragua v. United States)* in *ICJ Reports*, 1986.
3. See for example, H. Lauterpacht, *The International Protection of Human Rights*. Sirey. Paris, 1948 (= *Recueil des cours de l'Académie de droit internationale*, vol. 70 (1947)).
4. *Charter of the United Nations*, 26 June, 1945, art. 1.1.
5. Ibid., art. 1.2.
6. Ibid., art. 1.3.
7. Cf. J. Locke, "On the State of Nature," ch. II in his *Second Treatise on Civil Government*. Awnsham and Churchill. London, 1690.
8. Locke, "On the State of Nature." ch. II, Sec. 13.
9. *Charter of the United Nations*, art. 41. *Cf.* art. 2.4.
10. *Statute of the International Court of Justice*, art. 36.
11. See the exceptions for self-defense, regional arrangements and "enemy states" under the *Charter of the United Nations*, arts. 51–53.
12. Ibid., art. 41.
13. Ibid., Preamble.
14. Ibid., art. 2.4.
15. Ibid., art. 51.
16. Ibid., arts. 42–44.
17. R. Ago, "Commentaire du projet d'article 30 sur la responsabilité internationale des Etats, par. 21 s.," *Annuaire de l'Institut de Droit International*, 1979, vol. II, Deuxième partie, p.134 *et seq*. "Sanctions" would be "mésures de réaction appliqués en vertu d'une décision prise par une organisation international, a la suite d'une violation d'une obligation ayant des graves conséquences pour l'ensemble de la communauté international."
18. H. Kelsen, *Reine Rechtslehre*. Franz Deuticke. Vienna, 1960 (1st edn, 1934); *The Legal Process and International Order*. New Commonwealth Research Institute. London, 1935; *Law and Peace in International Relations*. Harvard University Press. Cambridge, Mass., 1942; *Principles of International Law*. Rinehart. New York, 1952 (2nd edn, 1966). Cf. Id., "Théorie du droit international public," *Recueil des cours*, vol. 84 (1953 III), pp. 1–203.

19. J. Austin, *The Province of Jurisprudence Determined.* Cambridge University Press. Cambridge, 1995 (1st edn, 1832).
20. Kelsen, "Théorie du droit internationale," supra n. 18, pp. 13–15.
21. Kelsen, *Principles of International Law*, supra n. 18, pp. 11–13.
22. Cf. *Oxford English Dictionary.* 2nd edn, Clarendon Press. Oxford, 1989, vol. XIV, p. 440 s.v. "sanction" (2d): "economic or military action taken by a state or alliance of states against another as a coercive measure, used to enforce a violated law or treaty."
23. Austin, *The Province of Jurisprudence Determined*, pp. 124, 171.
24. Ibid., p. 123.
25. See supra and (e.g.) J. Combacau, "Sanctions," in R. Bernhardt (ed.), *Encyclopedia of Public International Law.* Vol. 9, Elsevier, Amsterdam. 1986, p. 340.
26. *Oxford English Dictionary.*, s.v. "sanction," asserting its derivation from the Latin "*sancire*," "to render sacred." Cf. "*measure*" (vol. IX, p. 528, entry IV.21), from the Latin "*metiri*" which lacks the moral overtones of "sanction."
27. Vattel, *Le Droit des Gens on principles de la Loi Naturelle Appliques a la conduite et aux affairs des Nations et des Souverains.* A. Droz. Neuchâtel and London, 1758. Chapter VIII, "Du Commerce," section 90, p. 84. Cf. Wheaton, *Elements of International Law.* Richard Henry Dana Jr. (ed.) 8th edn. Little Brown. Boston, 1866, pp. 151–152.
28. Id. Section 92, p. 86: "Puis donc qu'une nation ne peut avoir naturellement aucun droit de vendre ses Marchandises à une autre, qui ne veut pas les acheter ... et qu'enfin le Commerce consiste dans la vente et l'achat réciproque de toutes sortes de marchandises; il est évident qu'il dépend de la volonté de chaque Nation, d'exercer le Commerce arec une autre, ou de ne pas l'exercer.
29. Grotius, *De Jure Belli ac Pacis Libri Tres.* Johannes Blaevius, Amsterdam, 1646 (first edn, Paris, 1625) II.xx.
30. Wolff, *Juris Gentium Methodo Scientifica Pertractatum.* Frankfurt and Leipzig, 1764. "Quoniam Genti nulli competit jus sua apud aliam Gentem vendendi sine consensu ipsius; si quo gens nolit res certas peregrinas in regionem suam transportari, Genti, a qua veniunt, injuriam non facit," sec. 59.
31. Ibid., sections 73, 74.
32. For criticisms of economic sanctions on human rights grounds, see for example, P.L. Fitzgerald, "If Property Rights were Treated Like Human Rights they could never get away with this," 51 *Hastings Law Review*, 73–169 (1999); K. Medhi, "Economic Sanctions: a Negation of Human Rights" in W.J.M. van Genugten and G.A. de Groot (eds), *United Nations Sanctions: Effectiveness and Effects, Especially in the Field of Human Rights: a Multi-Disciplinary Approach.* Intersentia, Antwerp. 1999, pp. 49–70.
33. See below, section IV and (e.g.), R. Normand, "A Human Rights Assessment of Sanctions: the Case of Iraq, 1990–1997" in W. J. M van Genugten and G. A. de Groot (eds), *United Nations Sanctions,* pp. 19–33; E.D. Gibbons, *Sanctions in Haiti: Human Rights and Democracy Under Assault.* Westport. Praeger. Connecticut, 1999; E. Hoskins and S. Nutt, *The Humanitarian Impact of Economic Sanctions on Burundi.* Providence, R.I., Watson Institute, 1997.
34. *Universal Declaration of Human Rights*, art. 2.
35. Ibid., art. 22.

36. Ibid., art. 25.
37. *International Covenant on Economic, Social and Cultural Rights*, art. 11.1.
38. Ibid., art. 11.2.
39. See for example, W.T. Milner, S.C. Poe and D. Leblang, "Security Rights, Subsistence Rights and Liberties: a Theoretical Survey of the Empirical Landscape" 21 *Human Rights Quarterly*, 403–443 (1999); H. Shue, *Basic Rights: Subsistence, Affluence and U.S. Foreign Policy*. Princeton University Press. Princeton, 1996.
40. They would have consented to their own inconveniences through a process of democratic deliberation. See G.H. Fox and B.R. Roh (eds.), *Democratic Governance and International Law*, Cambridge, England, Cambridge University Press, 2000.
41. The Charter of the United Nations recognizes that "special economic problems" may sometimes arise in states imposing enforcement measures, and provides for mitigation when Security Council mandated measures give rise to economic problems. *Charter of the United Nations*, art. 50.
42. International Covenant of Economic, Social, and Cultural Rights, art. 1.2.
43. See the Draft Articles on State Responsibility, *infra* note 86. Cf. H. Hazelzet, "Assessing the Suffering from 'Successful' Sanctions: An Ethical Approach" in to J. M. van Genugten and G. A. de Groot (eds), *United Nations Sanctions*, pp. 71–96; P.F. Fitzgerald, "Pierre goes Online: Blacklisting and Secondary Boycotts in U.S. Trade Policy," 31 *Vanderbilt Journal of Transnational Law*, 1–96 (1998) Cf. H. Gherari, S. Szurek *et al.* (eds), *Sanctions unilatérales, mondialisation du commerce et ordre juridique internationale à propos des lois Helms-Burton et d'Amato-Kennedy*. Montchrestien. Paris, 1998.
44. For "secondary" boycotts or embargoes, see for example, J. Delbrück, "International Economic Sanctions and Third States," 30 *Archiv des Völkerrechts*, pp. 86 (1992) *et seq.*; J. van den Brink, "Helms-Burton: Extending the limits of United States Jurisdiction," 44 *Netherlands International Law Review*, pp. 131 (1997) *et seq.*; B.M. Clagett "The Controversy over Title III of the Helms-Burton Act: Who is breaking international law: the United States or the states that made themselves co-conspirators with Cuba in its unlawful confiscations?," 30 *George Washington Journal of International Law and Economics*, pp. 271 (1996–1997) *et seq.*
45. Cf. *Charter of the United Nations*, art. 2.7.
46. The more comprehensive GATT and W.T.O. regimes raise special problems, see for example, A. Giardina, "The Economic Sanctions of the United States against Iran and Libya and the GATT Security Exception" in G. Hafner (ed.), *Liber Amicorum Professor Ignaz Seidl-Hohenveldern, in honour of his 80th birthday*. Kluwer. The Hague, 1998, pp. 863–894.
47. See for example, L.F. Damrosch, "Politics Across Borders: Nonintervention and Nonforcible Influence Over Domestic Affairs," 83 *American Journal of International Law*, pp. 1 (1989), *et seq.*
48. *Charter of the United Nations*, 2.7.
49. See for example, J. Delbrück, "International Economic Sanctions and Third states," 30 *Archiv des Völkerrechts*, 86–100 (1992) and other articles in the same issue of AVR. Cf. J.B. Busby, "Jurisdiction to Limit Third-Country Interaction with Sanctioned States," *Columbia Journal of Transnational Law*, 621–658 (1998).

50. For example, the judgment by the International Court of Justice on the merits of the Nicaragua case characterized United States activities in support of Nicaraguan rebels as violations of a binding international norm against interference in a state's domestic affairs. *Military and Paramilitary Activities in and Against Nicaragua (Nicaragua v. United States)*, Merits, in *I.C.J. Reports* (1986), pp. 14, 123–127, 146 (Judgment of June 27).
51. See L.F. Damrosch, "Politics Across Borders," pp. 2–3.
52. Art. 1.2 in both covenants.
53. Ibid.
54. On the weight of Human Rights norms in international law, see for example, T. Meron, *Human Rights and Humanitarian Norms as Customary Laws*. Clarendon Press. Oxford, 1989.
55. L.F. Damrosch, "Politics Across Borders," p. 3; T. Mitrovic, "Non-intervention in the Internal Affairs of States," in M. Sahovic (ed.), *Principles of International Law Concerning Friendly Relations and Cooperation*, Belgrade. Institute of International Politics and Economics, 1972, p. 219.
56. Charter of the Organization of American States, April 30, 1948, 2 UST 2394, TIAS No. 2361, 119 UNTS 3, Art. 18. For other inter-American documents supporting the non-intervention doctrine, see A. Thomas and A.J. Thomas, Jr., *Non-intervention: The Law and Its Import in the Americas*. S.M.U. Press. Dallas, 1956, pp. 62–64.
57. Conference on Security and Co-operation in Europe, Final Act (Helsinki Accord), Aug. 1, 1975, *Department of State Bulletin*, vol. 73 (1975), p.323 *et seq.*, reprinted in *International Legal Materials*, vol. 14 (1975), pp. 1292 et seq.
58. The Arab states imposed comprehensive economic sanctions against Israel, and states that trade with Israel. R.M. Mersky (ed.), *Conference on Transnational Economic Boycotts and Coercion February 19–20, 1976*, vol. II, *Materials on the Arab Oil-Producing Nations Boycott*, Oceana. Dobbs Ferry, N.Y., 1978.
59. United Nations General Assembly Resolution 2131 (XX) (Dec. 21, 1965); see also G.A.Res. 2225 (XXI) (Dec. 19, 1966). Other General Assembly Resolutions concerning nonintervention include the *Charter of Economic Rights and Duties of States*, G.A.Res. 3281 (XXIX) (Dec. 12, 1974), ch. I(d) and ch. II, art. 1; and the *Declaration on the Establishment of a New Economic Order*, G.A.Res. 3201 (S-VI) (May 1, 1974).
60. G.A.Res. 2625 (XXV) (Oct. 24, 1970).
61. Ibid.
62. Ibid.
63. This has been recognized since Vattel, see supra n. 27.
64. See for example, T. Gazzini, "Il contributo della Corte Internationale di Giustizia al rispetto degli obblighi *erga omnes* in materia di diritti umani," 55 *La Comunità internazionale*, pp. 19–62 (2000); M. Ragazzi, *The Concept of International Obligations "Erga Omnes."* Clarendon Press. Oxford, 1997.
65. See for example, S. Rosenne, "Some Reflections on Erga Omnes" in A. Anghie and G. Sturgess (eds), *Legal Visions of the 21st Century: Essays in Honour of Judge Christopher Weeramantry*. Kluwer. The Hague, 1998, pp. 509–525; J. Delbrück, "Laws in the Public Interest: Some Observations on the Foundations and Identification of Erga Omnes Norms in international law" in V. Goetz, P. Selmer, R. Wolfrum (eds), *Liber Amicorum Guenther Jaenicke, zum 85 Geburtstag*. Springer. Berlin, 1998, pp. 17–36.

66. *Charter of the United Nations*, art. 1.1–3.
67. This evolution began as early as 1975 with the Helsinki Final Act of the Conference on Security and Cooperation in Europe, which recognized the existence and binding force of universal human rights, without yet providing for enforcement. G. Arangio-Ruiz, "Human Rights and Non-Intervention in the Helsinki Final Act," 157 *Recueil des Cours de l'Académie de Droit Internationale*, pp. 175–332 (1977–IV).
68. This language is in the Copenhagen Document of the Conference on the Human Dimension of the CSCE, 29 June, 1990, Preamble. For the Madrid (1983) and Vienna (1989) Conferences see V.-Y. Ghebali, "La question des droits de l'homme a la réunion de Madrid sur les suites de la Conference sur la sécurité et la cooperation en Europe," *Annuaire Français de Droit International*, 1983, pp. 59–80; Id., "Les résultats de la réunion de Vienne sur les suites de la CSCE." *Défense Nationale*, vol. 4, pp. 61–78 (April, 1989).
69. Resolution on "la protection des droits de l'homme et le principe de non-intervention dans les affaires intérieures des Etats," 63-II *Annuaire de l'Institut de Droit International*, 338–345 (1990) G. Sperduti, "La sauvegarde des droits de l'homme et le principe de non-intervention dans les affaires intérieure des Etats," 63–I *Annuaire de l'Institut de Droit International*, pp. 309–351 (1989) (Rapport provisoire), 376–402 (Rapport définitif); "La souveraineté, le droit international et la sauvegarde des droits de l'homme" in Yoram Dinstein and Mala Tabory, eds. *International Law at a Time of Perplexity: Essays in Honour of Shabtai Rosenne*. Nijhoff. Alphen, 1989, pp. 879–885.
70. For an analysis of the resolution *see* C. Rucz, "Les mésures unilaterales de protection des droits de l'homme devant l'Institut de droit international," XXXVIII *Annuaire Français de Droit International*, 579–628 (1992)
71. Résolution sur la protection des droits de l'homme et le principe de non-intervention, *supra*. *See also*, Rucz, "Mésures de protection," p. 580.
72. Ibid.
73. For example, Second Conference on the Human Dimension of the CSCE, Copenhagen, June 5–July 29, 1990. *Document of the Copenhagen Meeting of the Conference on the Human Dimension of the CSCE*.
74. Ibid., clause 1.
75. Ibid., clauses 2; 5.76
76. Ibid., clauses 1; 41.
77. Third Conference on the Human Dimension of the CSCE. Moscow, September 10–October 15, 1991. *Document of the Moscow Meeting of the Conference on the Human Dimension of the CSCE*. Preamble.
78. Ibid.
79. Ibid.
80. Conference for Security and Co-operation in Europe, 1990 Summit – Paris, November 19–21, 1990. *Charter of Paris for a New Europe*, section on "Human Rights, Democracy and Rule of Law."
81. Ibid.
82. Moscow Document of the CSCE (1991) at 27.1.
83. Conference for Security and Co-operation in Europe, 1992 Summit. Helsinki, July 9–10, 1992. *Helsinki Document: The Challenges of Change*.
84. J. Delbrück, "Proportionality" in R. Bernhardt (ed.), *Encyclopedia of Public International Law*, vol. 7. Elsevier, Amsterdam, 1984; Cf. C. Tomuschat,

"Repressalie und Retorsion," 33 *Zeitschrift für ausländisches öffentliches Recht und Völkerrecht*, pp. 179–222 (1973) at 184–188.

85. See for example, O. Schachter, *International Law in Theory and Practice*. Martinus Nijhoff. Dordrecht, 1991, p. 185–186.
86. Ibid., p. 198.
87. Ibid., p. 199. Cf. the *Declaration of Principles of International Law Concerning Friendly Relations and Co-operation Among States in Accordance with the Charter of the United Nations*, adopted by the United Nations General Assembly in 1970, UNGA Resolution 2625 (XXV.).
88. Cf. Résolution adoptée par l'Institut de Droit International, *La protection des droits de l'homme et le principe de non-intervention dans les affaires intérieures des Etats*. Santiago de Compostela, September 5–13, 1989 arts. 1 and 2. See *Annuaire de l'Institut de Droit International: Résolutions 1957–1991*. Pedone. Paris, 1992, pp. 205–213.
89. See for example, O. Schachter, *International Law in Theory and Practice*, Nijhoff. Dordrecht, 1991, p. 185.
90. NAFTA subjects economic policy to an international treaty regime, with the express purpose of controlling the discretion of national governments to regulate trade.
91. See for example, O. Schachter, *International Law in Theory and Practice*. pp. 193–194.
92. *La protection des droits de l'homme et le principe de non-intervention dans les affaires intérieures des Etats*, Session de Saint-Jacques-de-Compostelle, September 5–13 1989, reprinted in *Annuaire de l'Institut de Droit International: Résolutions 1957–1991*. Pedone. Paris, 1992, pp. 205–213.
93. Ibid., art. 1.
94. Ibid., art. 2.
95. Ibid.
96. Ibid.
97. Ibid.
98. Ibid., art. 4.
99. American Law Institute, *Restatement of the Law: The Foreign Relations Law of the United States*, adopted May 14, 1986, 2 vols., American Law Institute Publishers. St. Paul, Minnesota, 1987.
100. Ibid., section 701.
101. Ibid., section 702. Section 703(2) characterized these as *erga omnes* violations.
102. See for example, *Draft Articles on State Responsibility*, art. 30.
103. See for example, Ibid. at 40(2)(ed.)(iii).
104. *Draft Articles of State Responsibility*, art. 49.
105. Ibid., art. 52.
106. Ibid., art. 50(d).
107. Ibid., art. 50(b).
108. See for example, the Resolution of the Institute of International Law on *La protection des droits de l'homme et le principe de non-intervention dans les affaires intérieures des Etats* (September, 1989).
109. Or the law will not be enforced.
110. Sometimes the costs of enforcement will outweigh the value of enforcing the law.

111. See supra, Ch. 2.
112. See above in this chapter, section 3.1.
113. All states benefit from a just world order, just as all individuals have an interest in justice. States differ, however, in that there is no central authority to enforce the law.
114. *Draft Articles on State Responsibility* art. 54.
115. They are the "beneficiaries" of enforcement.
116. Sanctions against South Africa were supported by Bishop D. Tutu. Sanctions against Haiti were called for by Prime Minister Aristide.
117. See the resolution adopted by the Institute of International Law on, *La protection des droits de l'homme et le principe de non-intervention dans les affaires intérieures des Etats*, Santiago de Compostela, September 5–13, 1989, art. 1.
118. Ibid., art. 2.
119. *Draft Articles on State Responsibility* second reading, art. 41.
120. See the consequences proposed in art. 42 of the current Draft Articles on State Responsibility, which amalgamate the first draft's arts. 51 and 53.
121. The American Law Institute, *Restatement of the Law Third, The Foreign Relations Law of the United States*, vol. 2, West Publishing Company St. Paul, Minnesota, 1987, section 702(g).
122. Cf. the resolution adopted by the Institute of International *Law on, La protection des droits de l'homme et le principe de non-intervention dans les affaires intérieures des Etats*, Santiago de Compostela session, September 5–13, 1989, arts. 1 and 2.
123. *Restatement (Third)*, section 703.
124. On multilateral economic sanctions, see L.L. Martin, *Coercive Cooperation: Explaining Multilateral Economic Sanctions*, Princeton, Princeton University Press, 1992.
125. See supra, Ch. 2.
126. This is vitiated, of course, by the illegitimacy of so many state governments, which undermines the integrity of the international consensus.
127. See below in this chapter at section 14.
128. See supra, chapter 2, for Kant's views on the value of a federation of free republics.
129. This is the implication of the suggestion made by the International Court of Justice in the *Case Concerning Military and Paramilitary Activities in and Against Nicaragua*, in discussing the Jurisdiction of the Court and the Admissibility of the Application (November 26, 1984), when the Court held that the provisions of the United Nations Charter relating to the use of force by States are to some extent "now within the realm of general international law." *I.C.J. Reports*, 1984, pp. 423–424.
130. Compare articles 23, 24 (giving the Security Council "primary responsibility for the maintenance of peace and security," 42 (empowering the Security Council to use force) and 2(4) (in which members of the United Nations renounce the threat or use of force).
131. On Humanitarian intervention, see for example, L. Minear, T. van Baarda, M. Sommers, *NATO and Humanitarian Action in the Kosovo Crisis*. Brown University. Providence, 2000; F.K. Abiew, *The Evolution of the Doctrine and Practice of Humanitarian Intervention*. Kluwer. The Hague, 1999; E. Loeffen, "Humanitarian Intervention: An International Customary Rule," in

K. Koufa (ed.), *International Justice*. Sakkoulas. Thessaloniki, 1993, pp. 805–824; "Symposium on Humanitarian Intervention and International Justice" 31 *Texas International Law Journal*, pp. 1–130 (1996); M. Bettati, *Le droit d'ingérence de l'ordre international*, Editions Odile Jacob. Paris, 1996.

132. *Charter of the United Nations*, art. 41.
133. Ibid., art. 39.
134. Ibid., art. 103.
135. See for example, the *Draft Articles on State Responsibility*, provisionally adopted by the Drafting Committee on Second Reading before the International Law Commission, August, 2000, Art. 23 (cf. First Draft Art. 30) on countermeasures and Art. 20 (formerly 29) on consent.
136. *Charter of the United Nations*, art. 1.
137. Ibid., art. 1.1.
138. Ibid., art. 27(3).
139. Ibid., art. 103.
140. See for example, the *Vienna Convention on the Law of Treaties*, art. 53, U.N. Doc. A/CONF. 39/27, (1969), 63 *A.J.I.L.* 875 (1969), 8 *I.L.M.* 679 (1969). Done in Vienna on May 23, 1969; entered into force on January 27, 1980.
141. Cf. *Draft Articles on State Responsibility* (Second Reading) Art. 51 (= First Reading art. 50).
142. See for example, *The Oxford English Dictionary*. 2nd edn, Clarendon Press. Oxford, 1989, vol. IV, pp. 59 et seq.
143. See supra, ch. 4.
144. The International Court of Justice is the "principal" judicial organ of the United Nations under Article 92 of the Charter, but its competence does not extend to the Security Council decisions, unless the Security Council requests an advisory opinion to clarify some legal question. *Charter of the United Nations Art. 96, Cf. Statute of the International Court of Justice*, art. 34. Cf. *Case concerning Questions of Interpretation and Application of the 1971 Montreal Convention Arising from the Aerial Incident at Lockerbie (Libyan Arab Jamatiriya v. United Kingdom)*, Provisional Measures Order of 14 April, 1992, I.C.J. Reports 1992. p. 15.
145. *Charter of the United Nations*, art. 48.
146. Ibid., art. 49.
147. Cf. for example, A. Clapham, "Peace, the Security Council and Human Rights" in Y. Danieli, E. Stamatopoulou, C.J. Dias (eds), *The Universal Declaration of Human Rights: Fifty Years and Beyond*, Amityville. Baywood. New York, 1999, pp. 375–388.
148. *Charter of the United Nations*, art. 10.
149. Ibid., art. 13.
150. Ibid., art. 14 (including respect for human rights). Ibid., art. 1(3).
151. Some have argued that this authority might even extend to the use of force when the Security Council fails to exercise its primary responsibility. See for example, the *United for Peace Resolution*, G.A.Res. 377 (V), Nov. 3, 1950, supp. No. 20, p. 10, which responded to events in Korea.
152. *Charter of the United Nations*, art. 12.
153. The legislative history of the Charter implies that its framers expected the General Assembly to deliberate over economic and social matters, rather than questions of peace and security. See B. Simma (ed.), *The Charter of the United Nations: A Commentary*. Oxford University Press. Oxford, 1994,

p. 232. Economic sanctions against human rights violations fall into both categories, since human rights violations undermine social stability, while at the same time threatening international peace and security.

154. Ibid., pp. 233–234.
155. *Charter of the United Nations*, art. 52.
156. For a good discussion of regional standards for the protection of human rights, see M.N. Shaw, *International Law*. 4th edn, Cambridge University Press. Cambridge, England, 1997, ch. 7, "The Regional Protection of Human Rights," pp. 255–294.
157. On the inescapable connection between democracy, liberty and universal human rights, see A. Sen, *Freedom, Rationality and Social Choice*. Oxford University Press. Oxford, 2000; *Development as Freedom*. Knopf. New York, 1999.
158. The former Soviet Union vigorously resisted the protection of civil and political rights within its domestic empire and subject states. This restricted the development of European human rights protections to Western Europe during the Cold War. *The European Convention on Human Rights*, which was signed on November 4, 1950, and entered into force in September, 1953, represented a measure of the separation of Europe between free and unfree states. After the Fall of the Soviet Union, Russia and its formerly subject states began formally to endorse these universal human rights. See the Copenhagen Declaration., supra n. 73.
159. See 213 *U.N.T.S.* 221, *E.T.S.* 5, signed at Rome on November 4, 1950; entered into force on September 3, 1953.
160. Ibid., art. 17.
161. See M.P. Doxey, *International Sanctions in Contemporary Perspective*. 2nd edn, Macmillan. Basingstoke, Hampshire, 1996, for various collective measures sponsored by the European Council, and the Organization of American States.
162. Examples include sanctions against Cuba (OAS), and South Africa (EC). See Doxey, *International Sanctions in Contemporary Perspective*, pp. 18–26.
163. The greater the international consensus on any particular point of law, the greater the likelihood that the point of law in question has been correctly understood.
164. This will depend, of course, on the size and power of the states that join in taking multilateral action.
165. See this chapter above at section 3.1.
166. Draft Articles on State Responsibility provisionally adopted by the Drafting Committee of the International Law Commission on Second Reading, August 2000, art. 52 (49 on first reading).
167. Ibid., art. 51 (Art. 50 on the first reading).
168. *Charter of the United Nations*, art. 1.1 (Peace and Security); 1.2 (Self-Determination); and 1.3 (Human Rights).
169. *Draft Articles on State Responsibility*, Second Reading, art. 52. (formerly 49).
170. See for example, *Draft Articles on State Responsibility*, Second Reading, art. 51 (formerly 50).
171. See sections of this chapter on the multilateral enforcement of international law.
172. See H.P. Gasser, "Collective Economic Sanctions and International Humanitarian Law," 56 *Zeitschrift für ausländisches öffentliches Recht und*

Völkerrecht, 871 (1996) *et seq*. For an expansive view of this question see K. Mehdi, "Economic Sanctions: A Negation of Human Rights" in W.J.M. van Genugten and G.A. de Groot (eds), *United Nations Sanctions* pp. 49 ff.

173. *Universal Declaration of Human Rights*, art. 2.
174. Ibid., art. 17.
175. Ibid., art. 25, *International Covenant on Economic, Social and Cultural Rights*, art. 11.
176. *International Covenant on Economic, Social and Cultural Rights 1(2) and International Covenant on Civil and Political Rights* 1(2).
177. Cf. *Universal Declaration of Human Rights*, art. 17.
178. Cf. supra at 2.2.1. H.G. Schermers "The International Protection of the Right to Property" in F. Matschere and H. Petzold (eds), *Protecting Human Rights: Studies in Honour of G.J. Wiarda*. 2nd edn, C. Heymanns. Cologne, 1990, pp. 515–580.
179. Cf. Constitution of the United States, Amendment V.
180. See for example, D.K. Tarullo, "Norms and Institutions in Global Competition Policy," 94 *American Journal of International Law*, pp. 478–504 (2000); "The Sherman Acts First Century: A Historical Perspective," 74 *Iowa Law Review*, pp. 987–1217 (1988).
181. See the recent cases in which large corporations such as Microsoft have been checked in exercising economic power against others. R.A. Cass and K.N. Hylton (eds), "Preserving Competition: Economic Analysis, Legal Standards and Microsoft," 8 *George Mason Law Review*, pp. 1–40 (1999).
182. See A. Sen, *Freedom, Rationality and Social Choice*. M.N.S. Sellers, "Republican Impartiality," 11 *Oxford Journal of Legal Studies*, pp. 273 (1991) *et. seq*.
183. Cf. above in this chapter at section 3.1.
184. Cf. above in this chapter at section 5.
185. H. Hazelzet, "Assessing the Suffering from "Successful" Sanctions: an Ethical Approach" in W. J. M. van Genugten and G.A. de Groot (eds), *United Nations Sanctions*, pp. 71–96.
186. Cf. *Draft Articles on State Responsibility*, Second Reading, art. 54.
187. For example, President Clinton of the United States has recently (October 19, 2000) signed a bill exempting food and medicine from U.S. embargoes.
188. Outsiders should look to elected leaders, when democratic elections have been overturned, as in Burma, Haiti and Panama, or to religious leaders, when they become representatives the public will as in Poland during the Soviet era or Nicaragua under Somoza.
189. Art. 1(2) in both covenants.
190. See R. Provost, "Starvation as a Weapon: Legal Implications of the United Nations Food Blockade against Iraq and Kuwait," 30 *Columbia Journal of Transnational Law*, pp. 577–639 (1992)
191. See the *Convention on the Prevention and Punishment of the Crime of Genocide*, signed December 11, 1948, entered into force 12 January, 1951. Article 1 commits the contracting parties "to prevent and to punish" the crime of genocide.
192. A. Sen, *Development as Freedom*. Anchor Books. New York, 1999.
193. The contrast in circumstances between North and South Korea illustrates the shocking disregard by non-democracies of their citizens' right to subsistence.
194. Citizens of the Kurdish regions of Northern Iraq, which are effectively outside government control, suffered no shortages during the same period.

195. This continued at a time when North Korea was developing nuclear weapons, and threatening its neighbors by firing missiles over their territories.
196. See for example, L.F. Damrosch on "Enforcing International Law Through Non-Forcible Measures," 269 *Recueil des Cours de l'Académie de Droit Internationale* (1997). For measures taken by the United States government against persons belonging to the *de facto* regime of Haiti, 31 *CFR*, Part 580, 58 *Fed. Reg.* 40,043 (July 27, 1993).
197. See Exec. Order 12,872 (18 October 1993); see also 59 *Fed. Reg.* 16,548 (April 7, 1994); Exec. Order 12,922 ("Blocking Property of certain Haitian Nationals") (June 21, 1994).
198. See Exec. Order 12,914 (May 7, 1994). The difficulty here would lie in devising sanctions that would seriously affect government officials without unnecessarily hurting the population.
199. Compare the international reaction to Serbian atrocities in Kosovo with the international response to Russian atrocities in Chechnya.
200. The United States often finds itself isolated in imposing economic sanctions against human rights violators, while European or Canadian companies step in to profit from the trade, as in Cuba and Iraq.
201. Military actions against Serbia and Haiti expressed principles that should apply equally to China and Russia, but cannot be militarily enforced for purely prudential reasons.
202. On the importance of cost to oneself in establishing norms see E.A. Posner, *Law and Social Norms*. Harvard University Press. Cambridge, Massachusetts, 2000.
203. See *Charter of the United Nations*, arts. 11, 14.
204. Ibid., art. 41.
205. The application of the theory of "extraterritoritoriality" to protect violators of international human rights law offers one recent example of this phenomenon. See for example, P. Torremans, "Extraterritoriality in Human Rights," in N.A. Neuwahl (ed.), *The European Union and Human Rights*. Nijhoff. The Hague, pp. 281–296.
206. This is because in democracies, citizens have a strong voice in forming government policies. In non-democracies, they do not.
207. See M.N.S. Sellers, "Republican Impartiality," in 11 *Oxford Journal of Legal Studies*, pp. 271 (1993) et seq.
208. "The Copenhagen Criteria" see the *Copenhagen Presidency Conclusions*, Copenhagen European Council, June 21–22, 1993.
209. Examples of such sanctions would be the travel restrictions against the families of high-ranking military officers in Haiti, and the economic liabilities for firms trading in illegally expropriated Cuban property under the Helms-Burton law.

Index